STRIPPERS,
SHOWGIRLS,
AND SHARKS

Peter Filichia

STRIPPERS, SHOWGIRLS, and SHARKS

*

*A **Very** Opinionated History of the Broadway Musicals That **Did Not** Win the Tony Award*

ST. MARTIN'S PRESS ❧ NEW YORK

www.stmartins.com

Library of Congress Cataloging-in-Publication Data

Filichia, Peter.
    Strippers, showgirls, and sharks: a very opinionated history of the Broadway
musicals that did not win the Tony award / Peter Filichia.—First edition.
        pages   cm
    ISBN 978-1-250-01843-4 (hardcover)
    ISBN 978-1-250-01844-1 (e-book)
    1. Musicals—New York (State)–New York—History and criticism.   I. Title.
    ML1711.8.N3F57 2013
    792.609747'1—dc23

                                                            2013004040

St. Martin's Press books may be purchased for educational, business, or promotional
use. For information on bulk purchases, please contact Macmillan Corporate and Premium Sales Department at 1-800-221-7945 extension 5442 or write specialmarkets@
macmillan.com.

First Edition: May 2013

10 9 8 7 6 5 4 3 2 1

To Edith and Phil La Grassa,
whose soundtracks
and original cast albums
changed my life

CONTENTS

*

Contents

ACKNOWLEDGMENTS

*

Thanks to my agent Linda Konner, who's also the love of my life.

Thanks to "Al" Skip Koenig, who's overly generous with information and functions as the best informal editor anyone could ever have.

Thanks, too, to Val Addams, Dale Badway, Aubrey Berg, Ken Bloom, Mary K. Botosan, Wayne Bryan, Jay Clark, Bill Cox, Joshua Ellis, Larry Fineberg, Alan Gomberg, Marc Grossberg, John Harrison, Kenneth Kantor, Richard A. Lidinsky, Jr., Robert LoBiondo, Jon Maas, Kevin McAnarney, Marc Miller, Dick Minogue, Richard C. Norton, Erin Oestreich, Paul Roberts, Justin Squigs Robertson, Howard Rogut, David Schmittou, Jim Seabrough, Bob Sixsmith, Ron Spivak, Robert Viagas, Walter Willison, and the late, great David Wolf.

STRIPPERS,
SHOWGIRLS,
and SHARKS

INTRODUCTION

*

Charlie Chaplin once finished third in a Charlie Chaplin look-alike contest.

Almonds are members of the peach family.

Duck quacks cannot produce an echo.

Life is full of many oddities. So why should the Tony Awards be exempt?

Strange but true: *Gypsy, Follies,* and even *West Side Story* didn't win the Tony Award for Best Musical.

Although all three losses occurred decades ago, some musical theater mavens are still scratching their heads over them. Thousands loudly support the Tony voters' decision to prefer *The Music Man* over *West Side Story* in 1957–1958, but thousands of others don't.

Others can understand that *Gypsy* would lose in 1959–1960 to *The Sound of Music.* But how did *Fiorello!* wind up in a tie with the Rodgers and Hammerstein hit—leaving *Gypsy* to finish third at best?

And don't get anyone started on how the landmark musical *Follies* lost to the far less distinguished *Two Gentlemen of Verona* in 1971–1972. You'll never hear the end of it.

But each season, voters, critics, and audiences have issues with the Tony Awards, the highest theatrical honor in the land for Broadway plays and musicals.

And while all Tonys from Best Sound Design to Best Play are created equal in height, width, and depth, some awards are more equal than others. The universally acknowledged biggest prize is the Best Musical Tony. On the Monday following a Tony Awards broadcast on national TV, the Best Musical winner experiences a significant boost at the box office.

Did the best musical always win Best Musical? Were there other fac-tors that kept more deserving shows from copping the prize?

Don't merely blame the hundreds of voters who cast their ballots every spring. Before they can take action, the Tony nominating committee must fill the categories from which they'll choose. These groups have histori-cally ranged from the first group of seven nominators to the current forty-two.

Each committee has always been the subject of scrutiny and criticism (and some praise) from the voters and the public. The 1974–1975 group smiled on *The Lieutenant*, a barely remembered musical. The 1960–1961 members spurned *Camelot*, which in the ensuing decades has become a production perennial, and the Best Musical nominees for that season were eventual winner *Bye Bye Birdie* as well as *Do Re Mi* and *Irma La Douce*—but nothing else. The nominators left the fourth slot blank.

To be fair, the template of having four nominated musicals—which has happened forty-seven times out of fifty-eight seasons—had not yet been firmly solidified. There were only two Best Musical nominees in 1955–1956, and five in 1957–1958. The latter was the season that even the wan *Oh, Captain!* was inexplicably nominated.

Perhaps the feeling was that the Oscars routinely nominated five Best Pictures, so the Tonys should nominate five Best Musicals, too. But *Camelot* was held in such contempt that it wasn't even allowed to be nom-inee number four. As we'll see, as the years went on, many far less worthy musicals would fill that fourth (or even third) slot. Is there any fact that better proves what a tremendous disappointment *Camelot* was at the time?

Time, distance, and perspective have all helped Lerner and Loewe's *Camelot* to be judged independently of its illustrious predecessor—no less than *My Fair Lady*. In many a season to follow, it certainly would have been nominated—and in some, it would have easily won. (And to think that this musical that featured Merlin the magician was not nominated while *Merlin* (1982–1983) was—a musical so afraid to face critics that it played for a then-unprecedented sixty-nine previews.) But that's all we'll say for *Camelot*, for this book will only deal with some of the musicals that were actually nominated for Best Musical and lost.

For the first seven years of the Tonys' existence—from 1948–1949 through 1954–1955—only the winner was announced in each category. Thus, one could effectively argue that the seventy-five other musicals that opened between April 16, 1948, and April 14, 1955, were de facto Best

Musical Tony losers—including such well-known titles as *Where's Charley?*, *Gentlemen Prefer Blondes*, *Call Me Madam*, *Can-Can*, *The Boy Friend*, *Peter Pan*, *Fanny*, and *Silk Stockings*. Nevertheless, we'll stick to those that were certifiably nominated and lost.

Not all Best Musical nominees, of course, were artistic triumphs. Some of these shows opened to reviews so putrid that the star's dressing room—which had enjoyed the aroma of opening night flowers only twenty-four hours earlier—now suddenly smelled like a funeral home.

Obviously, various Tony nominating committees had different opinions on how much to value commercial success. Some felt that when a season had yielded few musical artistic achievements, they should still fill the slots with something, anything. Others found the lesser shows too far beneath them to reward them.

Thus, all decisions made by nominating committees must be taken with a shakerful of salt. Who knows but the Lord (in the unlikely event He keeps an eye on the Tonys) how many injustices have occurred and why?

Getting down to brass tacks: how many nominators have refused to vote for artists who (1.) have done them dirty, or have alleged to (2.) have achieved "too much" success, or (3.) were hired in jobs that the nominators themselves wanted to get?

There's another power dynamic. Take it from someone who was chairman of the Drama Desk nominating committee in 1995–1996, the season in which *A Funny Thing Happened on the Way to the Forum* was revived. "Hey," said one nominator with a gleeful look on his face. "Let's *not* give Nathan Lane a nomination. Won't that burn his ass?"

The fact that awards are supposed to celebrate achievement was clearly lost on this critic. He saw himself as a latter-day Roman emperor who could thrust thumbs-up or thumbs-down on any potential nominee that stood before him. That's what interested him most.

Employees of theater organizations also stack the deck. Just as Republicans and Democrats vote the party line, those employed by the Shuberts, Nederlanders, or Jujamcyn tend to vote for shows in their theaters—in every category. Never mind what they *really* feel is the best; charity (sweet or otherwise) begins at home.

Similarly, there are Tony voters who represent theaters outside of New York. When this year's Best Musical Tony winner comes to their town *next* year, they'll want their customers to enjoy it and come back for more.

So the most tourable show often wins. Don't underestimate the influence of what will play best in Peoria—be it the Peoria in Illinois, Ohio, or Arizona.

Before we continue, let's set a few ground rules.

Theatrical historians long ago determined that a theater season officially begins on June 1 of each year and ends on May 31 of the next. Thus, both *The Best Plays* and *Theatre World* list *Gypsy*, which opened on May 21, 1959, as a member of the 1958–1959 season. But not the Tonys, which have had cutoff dates that have moved around even more than *Once Upon a Mattress* did. For years, April 15 was used, but dates as early as March and as late as May (which is now the norm) have been employed, too.

As a result, with this book's purview being the Tonys, each musical discussed here will be parenthetically labeled by its Tony season, and not the official season that it opened. The record books have *She Loves Me*, which opened April 23, 1963, as a participant in the 1962–1963 season, but we must put it in 1963–1964, because that April 15 Tony cutoff pushed it into the following semester.

One other note: standard practice in musical theater books has a character name followed by the name of the person who played it in parentheses: Pseudolus (Zero Mostel). *Every* time you see a performer's name in parentheses here, that's your immediate signal that the person won a Tony for his or her performance in the show cited. No other performers, be they nominees or snubbed, will be identified in parentheses.

You may find more than you expect about *The Lieutenant* and less than you envisioned on *Hair*. That was intentional. I endeavored to describe shows in detail that have seldom, if ever, received intense scrutiny, and felt less compelled to meticulously detail others that have been written about in dozens of other musical theater books. Some nominees don't even deserve to get a passing mention. (You know who you are.)

All set? And the Tony for Best Musical did *not* go to . . .

CHAPTER ONE

*

How Did It Happen? The Best Musical Tony Losers That Should Have Won

The ancient Greeks probably didn't have their own version of the Tony Awards. But if they did, one thing is for certain: each year when winners were announced, some Hellenic hell was raised. "What!? *That* won?" "I can't believe it!" and "(S)he was robbed!" must have rung out across the agora.

Whether or not it happened then, it certainly has been occurring for decades. Whenever any award winner is announced from the podium—be it for a Tony or an AriZoni (Phoenix's top theatrical award)—choked outcries of rage are heard. "How could they *not* have chosen [fill in the blank]?"

When one looks at the seven-decade history of the Tony Awards and its annual Best Musical statuette, the results from three years raise the most eyebrows and voices. They involve one show with strippers, one with showgirls, and one with Sharks. But let's go in chronological order.

In *The Apartment*, Billy Wilder's 1960 Oscar winner, executive Jeff Sheldrake had just arranged to borrow his low-level employee's apartment for a tryst. Sheldrake then called his wife and lied that he'd be home late because he had to entertain a client by taking him to a Broadway show.

When Sheldrake's wife asked him what they would see, he answered, "*The Music Man*. What else?"

How about *West Side Story*? There's a good chance the Arthur Laurents–Leonard Bernstein–Stephen Sondheim masterpiece was also running when Sheldrake made his statement. Of the 1,241 straight days that *The Music Man* played Broadway, *West Side Story* was around for 868 of them—640 during its original 1957–1959 run and 228 more in its 1960 return engagement. But *The Music Man* was apparently the only show on this tired businessman's radar.

And on April 13, 1958, it was the Tony voters' choice, too, as Best Musical.

West Side Story didn't win either Best Book (Arthur Laurents) or Score (music: Leonard Bernstein; lyrics: Stephen Sondheim)—but for good reason. Although those categories had been in place during the first years of the Tonys, they were discontinued in the early fifties and weren't reinstated until 1961–1962. So we'll never know if the show would have won in either, neither, or both of those categories.

But if there had been a Best Book prize, would *West Side Story* have won? Would voters have felt that the strangely unbilled William Shakespeare had provided the template with his *Romeo and Juliet*? Weren't Tony and Maria just updates of the Bard's star-crossed lovers, while the Montagues and Capulets were now two street gangs: the "American" Jets and the Puerto Rican Sharks.

Laurents's critics point out that his book too easily suggested that juvenile delinquency was society's fault. Many wondered why the only parent in the show was Maria's father as an offstage voice. Still others didn't believe that Tony's death would indeed make the Jets and Sharks reconcile. And love at first sight? (But that happens in *Romeo and Juliet*, too, and critics don't seem to mind it there.)

Give Laurents credit for considerably upping Shakespeare's stakes. The Bard had Romeo kill Juliet's cousin, which, although tragic, can't compare to Tony's killing Maria's brother Bernardo. And while the plot of *Romeo and Juliet* turned on an undelivered letter, *West Side Story* was more complicated: Maria asked her best friend Anita to deliver information to the Jets, and after they sexually harassed her, she lied, which resulted in greater carnage.

In *The Music Man*'s favor is that it's an original musical, created from scratch by book writer/composer/lyricist Meredith Willson. So-called "Professor" Harold Hill is actually a con man who comes to River City, Iowa, and promises to start a boys' band, although he doesn't know a lick of music. Much of the town is easily seduced by him, but Marian Paroo, a full-time librarian and part-time music teacher, certainly is not.

At one point, she is about to excoriate him. "Mr. Hill," she says sharply, and when he says, "Uh-uh-uh," audiences fully expected to have him say invitingly, "Call me Harold." Instead, he issues a correction: "Professor Hill."

However, Marian had a much younger brother, Winthrop, who'd been terribly depressed since his father had died. That Winthrop had a pronounced lisp hurt the lad's self-esteem.

But when Harold gave Winthrop a shiny new cornet to play in the band, the boy came back to life—which made Marian immediately love Harold. For months, no one had come close to unlocking the boy's heart. Now that someone had, she was grateful as the first-act curtain fell.

(On the other hand, shouldn't Marian have worried about the day of reckoning that would inevitably come? The boy would undoubtedly become *more* distraught when he learned that the "professor" won't be able to start a band.)

So neither *West Side Story* nor *The Music Man* has a perfect book. What musical does? But both have marvelous scores.

While Bernstein and Sondheim would seem to have easily won over Willson, we can't be certain. Two of *The Music Man*'s songs were showing up on many TV variety shows: "Seventy-six Trombones," Harold Hill's first-act rouser, and "Till There Was You," the big second-act ballad that he shared with Marian. Even the Beatles made the latter the only Broadway show song they'd ever sing.

Bernstein and Sondheim's score had two hits, too: "Maria" and "Tonight." But those became popular only years after, when *West Side Story*'s film version became immensely popular. In the late fifties, the only melody that the nation truly knew from *West Side Story* was the music to which the Jets snapped their fingers in the prologue: it had become the background music in a TV commercial for Ban, a deodorant.

Actually, *The Music Man*'s score shouldn't be sold short. Willson didn't merely write a score full of thirty-two-bar songs. His opener, "Rock Island," may have only had the wisp of a melody, but it was innovative: it had a trainful of traveling salesmen matching the rhythm of their parlor car rolling on the tracks.

Harold Hill's introduction to "Seventy-six Trombones," as well as his warning to River City that "Ya Got Trouble," were each soliloquies set to music. Rhyme was rarely used, but rarely missed, too. Willson's turning a piano lesson into a song was unique and unprecedented, too. Add in three numbers for a barbershop quartet—the last of which formed half of a delightful quodlibet—and *The Music Man* had a solid score.

But of course, so did *West Side Story*. What's remarkable about Bernstein's music is that even now, more than fifty years after its debut, it doesn't feel dated.

West Side Story was Sondheim's Broadway debut. He has often criticized his early work, as most artists do. Nevertheless, he provided some wondrous lyrics. We've all had the experience of waiting all day for something which we've been desperately looking forward to. But have we expressed it as well as "Make this endless day endless night?"

In the "Quintet," the Jets snarled, "Well, they began it!" immediately followed by the Sharks insisting, "Well, they began it!" Yes, there are three sides to every story—the Jets', the Sharks', and the true side.

Later, Anita anticipated that Bernardo will "walk in hot and tired" before approving "as long as he's hot." Here were two different meanings—overheated and sexually charged—from one little three-letter word.

"I like the island Manhattan" by itself didn't show much inspiration, but "Smoke on your pipe and put that in" certainly did. (Given that Oscar Hammerstein II was the most profound influence on Sondheim's professional life, he may have got this reverse syntax idea from his mentor, who had had Ado Annie in his *Oklahoma!* express a cliché in similar fashion: "A lot of tempest in a pot of tea.")

The Music Man won three out of the four awards in the acting categories, too: Robert Preston's Harold Hill, Barbara Cook's Marian, and David Burns as the mayor whom they both fooled. Even Iggie Wolfington, who played Harold's longtime friend Marcellus—and who had only one song—snagged a nomination. *The Music Man* garnered nine in all.

West Side Story, meanwhile, managed three fewer nominations. Carol Lawrence's Maria was nominated, but Larry Kert's Tony was not. Mickey Calin and Ken LeRoy, respectively playing rival gang leaders Riff and Bernardo, were also spurned. Even the actress portraying Anita was snubbed, too. It would be the first in a long line of Tony indignities that Chita Rivera would endure.

How could this happen in the acting categories? Virtually all the *West Side Story* cast members had more to do than most everyone in *The Music Man*. Director-choreographer Jerome Robbins had abandoned the Broadway tradition of hiring one chorus to sing and another to dance. Instead, his ten Jets, nine Sharks, and eleven assorted girlfriends performed both duties, and had plenty to act, too. One size had to fit all.

And did they dance. Robbins designed no fewer than a dozen opportunities, everything from mambo to ballet. He had more dances in his musical than his two choreographer Tony competitors, Onna White (*The Music Man*) and Bob Fosse (*New Girl in Town*), had in their shows combined.

However, Chita Rivera said in her 2005 revue, *The Dancer's Life*, that Peter Gennaro, billed as co-choreographer, had staged "America" and the five sections of "Dance at the Gym." Insisted Rivera, "Peter did every one of those dances, and has never been given the proper recognition." The glint in her eye and knowing smile on her face said, "And you'd better believe that I'm telling you the truth."

Still, Robbins's choreography was palpable and was acknowledged by a Tony, as were Oliver Smith's set designs. But Smith's award was listed with five other productions he'd designed that same season. Because his four competitors didn't design as many as he, we'll never know if the Tony voters were choosing quantity over quality—or if his specific designs for *West Side Story* provided the major factor in their selecting Smith.

Some may be looking for Robbins's name as Best Director, but here's a bizarre Tony fact: the category of "Best Director of a Musical" didn't exist until the 1959–1960 season.

One suspects that Robbins probably would have bested Morton DaCosta. But the facts remain that *West Side Story* is the greatest blue-chip musical theater title to win the fewest Tony Awards: a mere two. Ten years down the line, even two now forgotten musicals, *The Happy Time* and *Hallelujah, Baby!* would respectively win three and four.

Perhaps *West Side Story* was just too dark for Tony voters. Three young gang members died—meaning that *West Side Story* had as many deaths as all previous nine Best Musical Tony winners combined: *South Pacific* saw Lieutenant Joseph Cable die in action; *The King and I* had its monarch pass away at the end of the show; *Kismet* had its evil Wazir drowned. While the death of King Monghut was sad, he may have been older than Tony and Riff put together and had certainly lived a full life. The Wazir was evil and corrupt, so Tony voters felt that he was getting his just deserts. Cable, however, was not much older than any Jet or Shark. But he at least died defending his country in "the Good War." The three gang members lost their lives for less lofty reasons. What's more, the havoc that *West Side Story*'s inner-city juvenile delinquents were causing reminded Tony voters of what was actually happening only some blocks uptown.

No one died in *The Music Man*. The teens in River City, Iowa, in 1905 toed the line, aside from Tommy Djilas. He once lit a firecracker and threw it—a far cry from wielding a knife and using it.

In every political election, the number of votes amassed by each candidate is broadcast and published for all to see. Whether the winner enjoys a landslide of millions—or the loser endures a four-digit humiliation— every result becomes common knowledge.

Luckily for the runner-ups in Tony Awards races, the number of votes is not disclosed. As a result, all losers, no matter how dark the horses they've been riding, can convince themselves that they may have lost by a whisker. Despite what the pundits had predicted, any nominee may think, "Hey, there have been plenty of upsets over the years. For all I know, I might have been just one or two votes away from winning and spinning my Tony."

But the authors of the musical that's one of the very best—*Gypsy* (1959–1960)—could never tell themselves that. For book writer Arthur Laurents, composer Jule Styne, lyricist Stephen Sondheim, and director-choreographer Jerome Robbins not only saw *The Sound of Music* win Best Musical, but they also witnessed *Fiorello!* cop the same prize—in the only tie thus far in the Tonys' Best Musical races.

At best, *Gypsy* finished third.

To use an unfortunate phrase, *Gypsy* got gypped. This is especially galling, considering that Laurents's book is one of the best ever written for a musical.

After what is often called the greatest overture ever composed came a most modest opening number: two little girls sang six lines of "May We Entertain You?" at Uncle Jocko's Kiddie Show, circa 1925. Jocko was hardly avuncular, and wasn't impressed with the acts competing for a prize. "That's what's gonna kill vaudeville," he said, letting us know that this art form was already endangered.

One person didn't believe that: Rose Hovick, mother to blond June and brunette Louise. Suddenly came the unmistakable sound of Ethel Merman's voice: "Sing out, Louise!" Once Rose said "Save your strength,

June," and "Stop sucking your thumb, Louise," she informed us which girl was her favorite.

Rose had probably spent little time in classrooms, but she certainly knew the old-school-tie ploy. She tried to get around Uncle Jocko by seeing if he were an Odd Fellow, Knight of Pythias, or an Elk. She had to, because she'd learned the contest was rigged. (Even at this level, show business is corrupt.)

June and Louise came away with ten dollars. "That rotten little Uncle Jocko," said Rose, as she entered her father's house. "He's as cheap as your grandpa." Even before he made his entrance, Tony voters knew that he wasn't on Rose's side.

Say what you will about Rose, she was literally willing to eat dog food to save money that could be applied to the act. She'd had a dream about a new one: Baby June and Her Newsboys. "Louise can be a boy," she decided, unaware of how that might affect the girl's esteem. Ditto her allowing June to sleep with her, but not Louise.

The irony was that Louise would become a star playing anything but a boy. That, however, was far in the future. Neither Rose nor her father could have seen that success. When he accused Rose of "foolin' your kids with those dreams," she cried out "They're real dreams!" which made for a splendid oxymoron.

"Running around the country like a gypsy," he muttered, allowing audiences to assume that this was the genesis of the name Gypsy Rose Lee. Not at all; it was a clever red herring from Laurents.

That Rose would find work for "Baby June and Her Newsboys" seemed unlikely until she found a man: Herbie, once an agent but now a candy salesman. "I was always giving my clients their commission and telling them they got a raise," he said, words that would later be significant. But his attraction to Rose would return Herbie to agenting.

In the act, June said "Everybody has someone to thank for their success. Usually it's their mother." Yes, Rose would include that to remind June (and, oh, Louise) of her importance. As Rose said later while stealing silverware from a restaurant, "Charity begins at home."

Time to applaud director-choreographer Jerome Robbins for his innovative way of transforming the young June, Louise, and the boys into older versions of themselves: by setting up a strobe light that fooled our eyes as the young performers shuffled off and the older ones shuffled on. Four years of time evaporated in forty seconds.

Soon everyone celebrated Louise's birthday—although June got the present of a new act. (Audiences would soon see how "new" it was.) The celebration rankled the hotel manager, and Rose played the rape card to get rid of him. Herbie's response when he heard about it: "Again?"

A nod to Sondheim here: after everyone celebrated, Louise sang to one of her birthday presents—a "Little Lamb." Until now, audiences had only heard her sing in the act; now they'd finally hear what was on her mind: "I wonder how old I am." Kids are always obsessed with their ages and want to be older—Louise and certainly June did—so our learning that Louise didn't know this taken-for-granted fact was powerful.

Laurents didn't make Rose one-dimensional. Although she had a nightly ritual for getting the girls ready for bed, she did tell Herbie, "They can skip the cold cream for one night," so that she could be with him. Did she feel she'd better throw him a bone? Did she love him? Both? Laurents left the answers for the audiences.

And yet, soon Rose was angry with Herbie when he told her that the girls were "almost young women." Rose's ability to deny reached its apotheosis here: "They're not and they never will be," she said—and meant it.

Herbie tried to have her face another reality: "Don't you know there's a Depression?" Rose's response was pure Rose: "Of course I know. I read *Variety*," she said, reminding us of one of journalism's most famous headlines: WALL ST. LAYS AN EGG. (Actually, Rose probably only saw that headline, and did no additional reading. If she did, it was undoubtedly in a store where she'd picked up *Variety* and perused before the proprietor could yell out, "Hey, this ain't a library!")

Herbie stayed disgruntled. "If I ever let loose," he said, "it'll end up with me picking up and walking." Audiences wondered if this was foreshadowing or if Rose was right when she said, "Only around the block."

Audition day came. Herbie said, "It's a privilege to audition for you, Mr. Grantziger." Said Rose, "This is gonna make ya!"

The "new" act, Dainty June and Her Farmboys, had the same six-line introduction as the Newsboys had. June then recited that she was leaving the farm to perform on Broadway—before she decided to stay put, because she couldn't bear to leave her beloved cow Caroline. Interesting, isn't it, that Rose should conjure up an act with this message? It's hardly what she believed.

Mr. Grantziger was impressed enough with June to pay for her acting lessons if Rose didn't interfere. A good mother would have seized the opportunity for her child, but Rose needed June as a meal ticket. ("How are Louise and I supposed to live?") Of course, she loved her, too: "He's trying to take my baby away from me!" she moaned—unaware that soon her "baby" would take herself away from her.

June was furious that Rose wouldn't take the offer. She erupted to Louise, condemning the act—including "wearing those same awful costumes." Then June remembered that Louise made them: "I didn't mean it about the costumes," she said. A lesser writer would have had Louise explode: "Hey, I made those and put a lot of work in them!" Laurents much more wisely had Louise state, "No, you just mean you're too big for them." Now audiences liked Louise even more for not taking the remark personally.

Thus, they were rooting for her when she came upon Tulsa, a Farmboy, who was rehearsing his song-and-dance act. Louise predicted great things for him after reading his palm. (Is that where "gypsy" came from? Another red herring.)

Tulsa returned to practicing, and Louise joined in the joyous "All I Need Is the Girl." He seemed happy to have this impromptu partner, and audiences hoped that this might be Louise's first love.

No. As if being in June's shadow all life long wasn't enough, Louise would now see June, albeit inadvertently, take Tulsa away from her, too. As Rose learned while waiting to take the act on a train, the two had been married three weeks earlier and were now gone to forge their own act.

Audiences' hearts broke for the couple, too. Vaudeville wasn't just dead for Rose; June and Tulsa too would now suffer plenty. So would the other Farmboys who then deserted the act—although Herbie had been paying them on the side, just as he'd done in his previous life as an agent.

With June gone, Herbie told Rose he'd return to sales and would provide a home for "you and me and our daughter." (Nice, wasn't it, that he chose that last word?) Louise said, *"Yes! Momma, say yes!"* (Italics: Laurents.)

Rose was fixated on what June had written in her good-bye note. "She says I can't make her an actress," she muttered. Rose took that as a challenge, and suddenly believed that "Everything's Coming Up Roses" for a new act starring Louise.

So after an intermission in which theatergoers discussed the wonders they'd just seen (which had to be too short an intermission under these circumstances), Rose unveiled her new act. Laurents's stage directions said, "What they lack in talent—everything—they make up for in enthusiasm." Actually, they didn't, and Rose knew it.

She was part of the problem, because it was the same ole act, only set to a Spanish orchestration. "Madame Rose's Toreadorables" was a cute name, but notice for whom it was named. Louise couldn't have been happy that Rose put her in a blond wig that made her look more like June.

Moments later, when Louise was out of earshot, Rose confided in Herbie that "If I was doing it for June, I'd have it all set." Usually when someone walks in at the wrong time in musicals, plays, and movies, audiences roll their eyes at the all-too-convenient device. Laurents did it so quickly here that no one had time to notice, because Louise didn't come in prematurely and watch the scene for some moments while displaying her reaction. She just strolled on and said, "But you're not, and I'm not June." Having no fit, no fight, no feud, and no ego from Louise made the moment more powerful.

Louise came up with a good idea: make the Toreadorables blond. But after she suggested that they be billed "Louise and Her Hollywood Blondes" (show that backbone, Louise!), Rose still wanted top billing: they'd be "Rose Louise and Her Hollywood Blondes."

Yes, it was all too convenient of Laurents to have them enter the rear of Wichita's one and only burlesque theater. Had they entered from the more logical front, they would have seen the marquee and immediately known what it was. But they found out soon enough, and Rose rebelled— only to see Louise take control here. The young woman had been around show business long enough now to be first and foremost pragmatic. Pointing out that they had no money, Louise said, "Even if we wanted to quit and go home, we'd have to take it."

And just when audiences expected to see Rose at her worst—when Herbie arrived and said he hadn't known that this was a burlesque theater—she was understanding. But she was hurting: "They say when a vaudeville act plays in burlesque, it's all washed up."

They made the best of a bad situation. Louise enjoyed chatting with the strippers. "My grandpa says we've covered the country like gypsies," she said, leading a stripper to say, "Well, you may be a gypsy, Rose Louise—say, that ain't a bad name if you ever take up strippin'," in another excellent foreshadowing.

A defeated Rose agreed to marry Herbie, but "not while we're in burlesque . . . the day we close." It arrived quicker than she'd thought. Starting that night, she'd be living life in a living room.

Then came a variation on one of show business's greatest clichés: the understudy to the rescue bit. The star stripper was arrested for prostitution and a replacement was needed. Rose volunteered Louise. While management was wary, it had to concede that Louise did have one asset: "She's young."

"It's the star spot!" Rose excitedly told Louise. "I promised my daughter we'd be a star." (Note the use of "we'd.")

"No rouge. No beauty marks . . . you're a lady." For the first time, Rose rose to the occasion and quickly came up with a unique persona—"You're a lady"—for the newly named Gypsy Rose's Louise. (See how Laurents kept us guessing about that name?)

Herbie was disgusted and made good on his earlier claim of "If I ever let loose it'll end up with me picking up and walking." He did just that, and Rose mourned for a few moments—enough time for Louise to be alone and look in the mirror. She just didn't notice "I'm a pretty girl," but said, "I'm a pretty girl, Momma." She was still filtering her feelings through her mother.

Rose pushed her daughter on stage, where she was mistakenly announced as "Miss Gypsy Rose Lee." You can bet that if the "Rose" had been mangled, Momma would have immediately corrected it. But the metaphor of Louise being replaced by someone else was fitting, too.

A montage took Tony voters from "the lovely newcomer" in Detroit to "the lovely new star" in Philadelphia to "The Queen of the Striptease" in Minsky's, New York. At the last-named venue, a sign said "The mother of Miss Gypsy Rose Lee is not allowed backstage." Easier posted than accomplished. Rose came in, still believing that her daughter desperately needed her. Their showdown resulted in Rose's demanding to know "All the working and pushing and finagling . . . the scheming and scrimping and lying awake nights. How do I make an act out of nothing? What did I do it for?"

To which Gypsy simply said, "I thought you did it for me, Momma."

Checkmate. Yes. Parents *are* supposed to sacrifice for their kids. That's their role. Rose fulfilled it. What else could she want?

"You want to know what I did it for?" Rose asked herself. "Because I was born too soon and started too late," she stated, before launching into one of musical theater's greatest eleven o'clock numbers: "Rose's Turn."

"I had a dream," she once again insisted. "It wasn't for me, Herbie," meaning "I didn't do it for my benefit"—but when she sang the same phrase to Miss Gypsy Rose Lee, "If it wasn't for me," she meant "If I hadn't been there to help you along, you wouldn't have become a success."

Indeed. In the previous scene, Louise had admitted that she "loves" Gypsy Rose Lee. Already she wasn't above referring to herself in the third person. And where *would* you be, Miss Gypsy Rose Lee, if a quick-thinking Rose hadn't seized the opportunity in Wichita as a strange kind of consolation prize for herself—and, yes, you?

Gypsy would now have an exciting and glamorous life because of her mother. If Rose had agreed to *"Yes! Momma, say yes!"* Louise would have wound up in a house with three ducks, five canaries, a mouse, two monkeys, one father, and six turtles. Shouldn't she have been grateful that Rose gave her a different life?

Indeed she was. Mother and daughter reconciled, although Gypsy was glad that her mother could finally admit, "I guess I did do it for me."

And Rose found time to relate one final dream: a magazine spread. It would feature, she said, tracing a name high in the air, "Madame Rose"—before pausing and moving that arm up substantially higher for "and her daughter Gypsy." There was Rose's ultimate compliment: top billing.

There were those who said the final scene was unnecessary, but the reconciliation was important. Many came to this conclusion because "Rose's Turn" was so galvanic. And if we compare it to the eleven o'clock numbers in the two Best Musical Tony winners, we have "Edelweiss," which is appropriately poignant, and "The Very Next Man," which does contain a lovely irony in that Fiorello's secretary says that she'll give up on him and marry anyone who'll ask her. It turns out to be Fiorello.

Both are very nice, but "Rose's Turn" . . .

Jule Styne had more than a dozen musicals reach Broadway, but he'd never compose music as fine as this. He often credited Stephen Sondheim for getting his best work out of him. In "Some People," in which Rose complained of those who "got the dream, yeah, but not the guts," the pulsating melody as much as the lyric told us how no-nonsense Rose was before she slammed the door on the song's last word. ("Rose," of course.)

After she'd met Herbie, she turned on the charm as easily as Styne could turn out a lovely melody. "We have so much in common, it's a phenomen-on" isn't just a terrific rhyme; it also allowed Merman the chance to do her famous scoop on that last "on."

Later, after June had eloped with Tulsa and a Farmboy said, "The act's washed up," certainly Merman's wasn't. "Everything's Coming Up Roses" added extra brass to an orchestra that was already sporting plenty. Theatergoers had to clap twice as hard to acknowledge the two emotions they had surging through them: admiration and hatred for Rose.

So this *is* a great book, and certainly superior to *The Sound of Music* and *Fiorello!* But Laurents is guilty of one lapse in logic. After Rose had an offstage fight with Mr. Grantziger, Herbie returned to June and Louise, still in Grantziger's waiting room. He told them that Rose wasn't feeling well, and that he was bringing her back to the hotel. Why did he leave them there? They literally had no business there.

The reason, of course, was to give the girls a private moment to do "If Momma Was Married"—as good an argument as you can get for the end's justifying the means. These two sisters weren't just complaining about their lot, but they were also truly bonding, perhaps for the first time in their lives.

Would that every musical be as accomplished as *Gypsy*, the most revived of any Tony-losing musical. So why didn't it win?

It opened too early, some said. And true, when the 1959–1960 Tonys were dispensed on April 24, 1960, *Gypsy* had already been running for eleven months. But *South Pacific* won the 1949–1950 Best Musical Tony literally on its first anniversary, and *The King and I* got the 1951–1952 prize a year and a day after opening. *The Pajama Game* and *Damn Yankees* saw nearly eleven months pass from their opening to their Best Musical victories, and *My Fair Lady* was remembered as Best Musical a full thirteen months after it opened. However, all these winners were smash hits that were still selling out when the Tony voters submitted their ballots. *Gypsy* had shown itself to be a moderate seller. *The Sound of Music* and *Fiorello!* had been on Broadway for only five months and were still going clean.

Time to say the sentence that includes the words "nothing," "succeeds," "like," and "success."

What's harder to believe is that in the six-year history of the Tony's announcing nominees, *Gypsy* set the record for the most nominations (eight) without a single win: Merman, Robbins (director), Jack Klugman (Herbie), Sandra Church (Louise), Milton Rosenstock (conductor), sets (Jo Mielziner), and Raoul Pène Du Bois (costumes).

Robbins didn't even get a nod for his choreography; the prize went to Michael Kidd for *Destry Rides Again*. The dancing in *Gypsy* wasn't as extensive or as extraordinary as it was for his previous show—*West Side*

Story—for which he had won the Tony. Perhaps the nominators felt that, despite an exciting dance that Robbins devised for "All I Need Is the Girl," his choreography for Baby June and Her Newsboys, Dainty June and Her Farmboys, and Madame Rose's Toreadorables was, after all, the same set of steps simply done on three different occasions. That was the point of the number, however. Rose Hovick wasn't much of a choreographer and certainly not an adventurous one. But we can't blame Robbins for that.

One 1959–1960 nominee for Best Choreographer was Lee Scott for the five performance flop *Happy Town*, which Walter Kerr said offered "the same dance in three different places. Clap hands horizontally, clap hands vertically, girls swish skirts to right and left, everyone do the gallop that began with 'Rodeo,' then do it backward on one foot." So the one-trick pony got the Tony nomination, while the choreographer whose show demanded repetitions of the same number was denied.

Another irony was that *Happy Town* had actually officially closed in Boston until more money was suddenly raised (and wasted) to brave Broadway. Had it stayed shuttered in the Hub, Robbins would have had his nomination.

And that would have meant that *Gypsy* would have lost all *nine* nominations.

Longtime Broadway observers have alleged that since the Tonys debuted on national television in 1967, voters have made a concerted effort to choose a Best Musical that will appeal to at-home viewers. Promoting feel-good shows with happy endings is good for business. *West Side Story* and *Gypsy*'s losses suggested that that policy might have been in place years earlier when smaller ceremonies were held in hotel ballrooms and broadcast only on local television. So when these future legendary shows lost, a comparatively small number either mouthed or shrieked, "*What?*"

However, on April 23, 1972, The Tonys were in Broadway's biggest theater—the one called the Broadway. In addition to nearly two thousand in attendance there, tens of millions more were watching the national broadcast. (Hard as it may be to believe these days, the Tonys were then getting healthy ratings.)

So when Ingrid Bergman announced that the winner of the 1971–1972 Best Musical was *Two Gentlemen of Verona* and not *Follies*, the mouthings and shrieks of "*What?*" had to be the most pronounced of any that had ever followed a Tony envelope opening. And considering how the ratings have plummeted, the decibel level heard 'round the world will never be eclipsed.

By this point, even Broadway musical aficionados who lived far from New York had had nearly a year to listen to the *Follies* original cast album. Truncated as it was (so that it would fit on one LP record), it showed that Sondheim's fourth Broadway score was his finest. In the twenty-six years of the Tonys, it could boast the best opening number ("Beautiful Girls") and the best song written out-of-town ("I'm Still Here"). Those who'd seen the show knew it also had the best production number ("Who's That Woman?").

(By the way, it also had the best logo ever, with that sculptured haughty face of a *Follies* girl enduring a large divisive crack.)

Eight months later, when the album of *Two Gentlemen of Verona* was released, it didn't have nearly the same impact. And wouldn't you know, *it* got the two-record set?

Follies was the greater achievement. Like Laurents, John Guare and Mel Shapiro had used a Shakespeare play as their template. And while they took a (then) contemporary and freewheeling approach to the material, they even retained a good portion of the Bard's dialogue word for word.

Like Willson, James Goldman was writing an original. He gave life to two showgirl roommates: Phyllis Rogers (Alexis Smith) and Sally Durant. They'd met and worked together in 1941 in *The Weismann Follies*, then respectively married Benjamin Stone and Buddy Plummer, two college chums who'd been their Stage Door Johnnies. How much everyone had grown apart would be shown this night when they reconvened for a *Weismann Follies* reunion in New York. Other showgirls from the past would be there, too.

Needless to say, Sondheim's meticulous lyrics were far superior to Guare's often misaccented ones. ("That's the way he set them," Guare has since explained, citing composer Galt MacDermot.) And while no song from either musical ever showed up on the *Billboard* charts—in the last third of the twentieth century few songs from Broadway did—there have since been many recordings and cabaret performances of "Broadway Baby," "Losing My Mind," and "I'm Still Here." No song of the three dozen from *Two Gentlemen* remotely approached any similar success.

Since their original runs, *Follies* has had two Broadway revivals, while *Two Gentlemen* has had to settle for one summer run in Central Park. Both shows received original and London cast albums, but *Follies* has since enjoyed three subsequent (and sumptuous) recordings, while *Two Gentlemen* has never had any.

So why didn't *Follies* win?

One of the first stage directions that Goldman wrote in his libretto was "At first, we're not sure what we see." In fact, many Tony voters weren't *ever* sure of what they saw during the long intermissionless show.

Some had trouble catching on to one of the show's most dazzling concepts: that most of the characters who were attending the reunion were followed by younger versions of themselves.

Theodore S. Chapin called his making of *Follies* book *Everything Was Possible*, in honor of the first three words of a Sondheim lyric in the song "Waiting for the Girls Upstairs." Many instead judged the show by the last three words of that lyric: "Nothing made sense."

Who *were* these ghosts at "a party on the stage of the Weismann Theatre. Tonight," as the *Playbill* informed? Did former impresario Dimitri Weismann really invite his former cast members to his theater the night before it was to be razed in favor of a parking lot? Was there even a reunion to begin with, or was this just someone's dream or someone else's fantasy?

Goldman, Sondheim, and codirectors Harold Prince and Michael Bennett thought that *Follies* offered a metaphor for the decline of America. Everyone else could be pardoned for taking the story at face value and assuming that they were simply mired in a story about two terrible marriages.

Follies actually made too much sense for some Tony voters. For almost its entire length, Goldman was truthful when dangerously peeling off layer after layer of those awful marriages.

Phyllis admitted that "I wanted something when I came here thirty years ago, but I forgot to write it down." But Ben, like so many husbands, wasn't interested in attending his wife's reunion. If saying to Phyllis "I'm glad you're glad to be here" wasn't direct enough, he added "That makes one of us" to make perfectly clear how displeased he was.

When some long-suffering wives get such an insensitive remark from their husbands, they don't even react or respond; it's just another in the long list of insults they've learned to endure after decades of such nastiness. Others cope by simply pretending that they didn't hear the verbal slam. Already some Tony voters were being reminded of their own marriages, or ones they knew too well.

Phyllis, however, was a tougher-than-average wife: "I love the way you hate it when I'm happy and you're not." And while some appreciated her response, they weren't happy to be in this couple's company.

Of the four, Sally was the most enthusiastic about the reunion. What fervor she showed when given a sash that said "1941." Her plea of "Can I keep it?" showed how she valued her past.

What was startling to learn was that Sally had flown from Phoenix without informing her husband of her plans. Once Buddy had discovered what she'd done, he quickly followed her. His goal was to stress one "fact": "You're my girl, honey. Just remember that."

Buddy had reason to worry. Sally, like so many reunion attendees, was there in hopes of rekindling a long-out romantic fire. That was her folly.

Through the young alter egos, audiences learned that the last time that Sally had seen Ben, she'd been furious with him. She'd believed that they were a serious couple, and now he was telling her that he would marry Phyllis. So Sally married Buddy on the rebound, and for nearly thirty years has wished that she'd played her cards differently. Now, on this night, she reasoned, she might have a second chance if Ben attended. And while Tony voters could certainly relate to that, they didn't necessarily want to.

They learned, too, that the once-strong relationship between Buddy and Ben wasn't what it was. At college, Buddy was more economically secure than the less fortunate Ben. Eventually, however, Ben leapfrogged high over Buddy in both financial success and prestige. Buddy was now a salesman, while Ben had just left an influential political post to head a foundation. That he wrote a bestseller had added to his mystique.

Goldman was reminding Tony voters of their estranged old friends. Some had been in the position where they had endured their colleagues' greater successes. Others were victimized when old friends felt that they'd "outgrown" them.

And yet, after Ben leapfrogged, where did he land? Money can indeed buy happiness, but only to a point. His being married to a woman he no longer loved made his happiness drain quicker than an hourglass with a shattered bottom. Hadn't some Tony voters already reached this conclusion on their own and weren't up to relearning it?

In between our introduction to these two miserable marriages, however, came that great opening number, "Beautiful Girls," the song that had once begun *The Weismann Follies* eight times a week. Back then, the showgirls would descend a staircase while Roscoe, the major domo, sang about their glory: "This is what beauty should be; beauty celestial, the best, you'll agree. . . . This is how Samson was shorn; each in her style a Delilah reborn." (The longest that anyone has ever served as the nation's Secretary of the Interior was thirteen years, during the 1933–1946 reign of Harold L. Ickes. Compare this to Stephen Sondheim's half-century reign as Secretary of the Interior Rhyme.)

"Beautiful Girls" had a glorious melody, too, but it was its pathos that made it extraordinary. The past collided with the present, for the "show-girls" descending the staircase were now middle-aged women in dowdy dresses and orthopedic shoes. Beauty had faded for some and had totally disappeared in others. As Goldman wrote in his stage direction, "We watch the differences great and small that thirty years have made."

This is how *Follies* went all performance long. Sondheim provided thrilling numbers that beautifully evoked the songwriters of yore from Sigmund Romberg ("One More Kiss") to Jerome Kern ("Loveland"). In between these glories, however, Tony voters always had to return to the headache-inducing troubles between Phyllis and Ben and Buddy and Sally.

Phyllis realized the wrong turn she'd taken with Ben, who'd later muse on "The Road You Didn't Take" to Sally. For Sally, that meant the man she didn't get. So now, she'd first try to come across as happily married when she described how well loved she was "In Buddy's Eyes." Later, however, after Ben and Phyllis had had yet another fight—and he was at his most vulnerable—Sally began her quest to get her man. She tried a gingerly approach by speaking about Ben in the third person: "I even think I loved him once." Later, she talked marriage, which was not what Ben had in mind.

Buddy informed Phyllis that Sally still loved Ben. Phyllis muttered "It might have mattered once." Her attitude was the one Irving Berlin had his two spurned women say in *Miss Liberty* in 1949–1950: "You can have him. I don't want him. He's not worth fighting for."

Or so Phyllis believed. Later she realized that even if she didn't want Ben, she didn't want Sally to have him, either. This was raw, real, and human, and Tony voters may well have remembered the times when they were just as petty and irrational over spouses they both wanted and didn't want, too.

Phyllis confronted her rival point-blank: "Buddy thinks you're still in love with him." Sally soft-pedaled with "That man. He gets so jealous some times." And while that statement would have provided Phyllis with an easy out, she instead blatantly and bitterly said, "What of?"

We could have been in for musical theater's biggest catfight, but it was interrupted by that aforementioned greatest production number of the Tony era.

It had to happen. Someone suggested that the ex-showgirls replicate their signature number—the ultimate exercise in nostalgia. Stella Deems was willing, but, as she said, "I'm not making an ass out of myself alone." (Well, if she'd been paying attention, she'd have noticed that Phyllis, Ben, Buddy, and Sally had made asses of themselves in a much different context.)

Soon Stella, Phyllis, Sally, and four others were performing "Who's That Woman?" In it, Stella wondered about the identity of a scorned woman who was having a hard time believing that her "Lothario let her down." But when she looked in the mirror, it didn't lie: "That woman," she had to admit, "is me."

The theme of a mirror was brilliantly upheld by Bennett's choreography, for each ex-showgirl was mirrored by her younger self. By the time Stella concluded the number with "That woman is me," audiences, after cheering wildly, responded, "Well, yes and no"—for Stella and the others no longer resembled the women they once were. As Goldman wrote in his stage direction, "The number ends, the memories disappear, and we are left with seven breathless middle-aged ladies."

We were also left once again with the travails of the Plummers and the Stones. First, however, we got to see another side of Phyllis—one that Goldman might have been well advised not to show. We could understand her fights with Ben and even her criticism of Sally. But then Phyllis had a fierce encounter with former colleague Christine Donovan.

Christine asked Phyllis, "Don't you remember me at all?" to which Phyllis flat-out said, "You never liked me." Give Christine credit: she handled the insult in a classier fashion by remarking with a surprised, "What a thing to say."

Not that that softened Phyllis, who then added, "I never liked you either." Later, when Phyllis angrily described New York as "hostility and filth and rotten manners," she herself had already dispensed the first and third elements. This, for many audiences and Tony voters, was when they officially stopped caring about Phyllis. No wonder that in many subsequent productions this exchange has been dropped. (The first excision happened during the famous 1985 all-star concert at Avery Fisher Hall. One reason, of course, was that the concert greatly pared the book. However, let's not forget that Elaine Stritch, in addition to playing Hattie, was given Christine's lines. One can only shudder when imagining how Stritch would have reacted to such a verbal slap in the face. Lee Remick's Phyllis might soon have been eating through a tube.)

Buddy described his life with Sally: "the mess, the moods, the spells . . . in bed for days without a word . . . (and) the tears." His conclusion was "We're finished." Tony voters couldn't have possibly told him not to despair.

Every bad relationship threatens to reach a point of no return; Sally and Buddy would fly past theirs on this night. Seeing Sally blatantly lie to Buddy—"Ben wants to marry me . . . he's home now packing and we're leaving in the morning"—was particularly pathetic.

Not that Ben wanted to stay with Phyllis. "The only thing I want from you is a divorce," he proclaimed. It's not that many Tony voters couldn't identify with these four; they just preferred not to.

Goldman and Sondheim weren't remotely through. Their next *coup de theatre* allowed Phyllis, Ben, Buddy, and Sally to have a confrontation with, of all people, their four younger selves. Ben roared, "You unfeeling bastard!" Phyllis said, "You threw my life away," while Buddy was less elegant with "You pissed my life away." Sally actually told her younger self, "I could kill you." No one was taking the advice that had just been dispensed by Heidi Schiller that we should "Never look back."

And just as Prince had shown that life was a cabaret five years earlier, now he and his collaborators would stress that we all suffer from our own follies. First up were the youthful ones of Buddy, Sally, Ben, and Phyllis. Young Ben insisted to Young Phyllis that "You're gonna love tomorrow—as long as your tomorrow is spent with me." That reminded many attendees how naïvely if not stupidly they had themselves handled love as twenty-somethings. Whatever was necessary to make love last had turned out to be well beyond their ken.

Young Buddy and Young Sally were at least slightly more realistic. He wanted to "warn you" while she had a "cornucopia of imperfections." (Catch that interior rhyme?) And yet, when she feared that she'd "burn the toast" and he confessed that he would "clutter up the place," each smiled indulgently and forgivingly—because these infractions hadn't yet happened. Neither he nor she was remotely aware of how much frustration and fury that many years' worth of burned toast, cluttered rooms, and other day-by-day so-called trivialities would bring. As murderess Liz in *Chicago* would say a few years later, "You pop that gum one more time . . ."

Tony voters were painfully reminded of the time decades earlier when they too thought that nothing mattered but love. Many had since come to a much different conclusion.

The adult versions of the four principals then came on and performed numbers in the manner of *Follies* entertainers. That Buddy went first might well have flummoxed some Tony voters, for he—and Ben, for that matter—had no connection to the actual *Follies* beyond waiting around for the girls upstairs. Why were *they* performing?

And yet, when Buddy made the observation about "the 'thank-you-for-the-present' 'But-what's-wrong-with-it' stuff?" only the rarest of couples wouldn't have been able to identify. Many husbands and wives could recall words to that effect being said in their households on many birthdays and holidays.

Sally then sang a torch song that showed her regret from the time "the sun comes up" to the "sleepless nights." After a night of alternating between acting brave, smart, irritable, irrational, cute, and coy, Tony voters finally saw her in her most honest and mature guise. How sad, however, that she had to wonder if she were "Losing My Mind."

Phyllis then performed "The Story of Lucy and Jesse" while cautioning that "these are not their real names." No, those would have been Phyllis Rogers, the young woman who once thought herself a parvenu and Phyllis Rogers Stone, who became quite the sophisticate and came to appreciate her younger self. While Ben had earlier wondered about the road he hadn't taken, Phyllis pondered on the persona that she hadn't adopted.

Finally, Ben acknowledged that men have different interests, from collecting stamps to following politics, but as for him, "Me, I like to live. Me, I like to love. Me, I like to laugh." This hadn't remotely been the mantra of the Ben Tony voters had been seeing all night, but soon he revealed what was under the façade when he made an elision: "Me, I like to love *me*."

Actually, Ben eventually decided that he didn't love himself, en route to a nervous breakdown. Although that wasn't what most Tony voters expected from a song, Sondheim then gave them the final nail to slam into *Follies'* Tony-losing coffin: Ben became so rattled that he forgot his lines and had to be cued by the conductor. Yes, it was all part of the act, but many average theatergoers and even seasoned Tony voters came to the understandable conclusion that John McMartin had simply forgotten his lines.

And that, paradoxically, took everyone off the hook in being forced to approve *Follies*. Those ready to spread word of mouth or cast their ballots could snarl, "The guy didn't even know his lines!" All could point to the show's "incompetence" and—speaking of metaphors—use it as Exhibit A that Goldman, Sondheim, Prince, Bennett, and McMartin "just didn't know what they were doing."

And what of that metaphor on how America was breaking down and it all started in the home? As Sondheim would write a decade later in *Merrily We Roll Along*, "Nothing's the way that it was." But average theatergoers and Tony voters were too overwhelmed to think of *Follies*—a word that used to mean happy-go-lucky entertainment—in the word's other context: the illusions we all have about ourselves.

After Ben finished his number, Goldman's stage direction said that "We're back on stage of the Weismann Theatre. Not literally, however. We're inside Ben's mind." It's not where Tony voters expected to be, which is why many never knew they were there. Even if they did understand that they were visiting Ben's brain, they couldn't have been comfortable there because, said Goldman, "we see a kind of madness."

Prince, who had had already won two Tonys for directing, would win for *Follies* too (with codirector Bennett), and would nab five more in the next couple of decades. But even he couldn't be expected to make Tony voters realize where Goldman wanted them to be. And what could anyone do with this stage direction: "as if the night's experiences were being vomited"?

Yes, *Follies* was a work of genius, but such a piece often has trouble reaching nongeniuses—and that would include 1971–1972 Tony voters. One could describe *Follies* as a bitter pill to swallow, but to many it would have been more accurately termed a chugalug of strong medicine that tasted worse than castor oil.

Thank the Lord for the spoonsful of musical sugar from the ole *Weismann Follies'* gang: The Whitmans ("Rain on the Roof"), Solange LaFitte ("Ah, Paree!"), Hattie Walker ("Broadway Baby"), Vincent and Vanessa ("Bolero D'Amour")—and, of course, Stella Deems's "Who's That Woman?" Their numbers were so magnificent that we wished Sondheim had written another musical in which the former showgirls who'd decided *not* to attend the reunion would have been shown in their various living rooms, singing *their* songs from *The Weismann Follies*. Any excuse for more Sondheim pastiche would have been welcome.

Instead, Goldman's stage direction that "the cacophony is terrible" occurred just around the time many in attendance had decided that the show was, too. But what Goldman then wrote may have been, in a strange way, even worse.

It was a new dawn, a new day, and we were asked to believe that it represented a new beginning for both Buddy and Sally's marriage and Phyllis and Ben's. "I'm here, Ben. I'm right here," soothed Phyllis. "I'll help you," Buddy told Sally, who did take time to mention her suicide attempts.

Could we really believe there was any hope for these four after this Walpurgisnacht? Many Tony voters and theatergoers must have felt that Goldman didn't merely cut much too close to the bone, but that he also crushed it and scooped out everything that had been inside. How could they possibly believe now in even one couple's reconciliation, let alone both?

Theater critic Clive Barnes in *The New York Times* would say of the next Sondheim-Prince show, *A Little Night Music* (1972–1973), "Good God! An adult musical!" No argument, but, really, what was *Follies*?

Unless there had been, as Charles Foster Kane proclaimed in *Citizen Kane*, a "fraud at polls," we can at least see why *Follies* could lose when the Tony voters filled out their ballots.

Some may point out that *Two Gentlemen* also had a man cheating on a woman, and, to make matters worse, he was trying to steal the lover of his best friend. But *Two Gents'* characters from Verona were literally foreign to Tony voters. They had such names as Valentine and Proteus and lived in a far-away land and in a time long removed from 1971–1972. Besides, all the cheating was quickly forgiven and everyone was happy at the final curtain. Ben's advice at the end of *Follies*—"Live! Laugh! Love!"—could have served as *Two Gents'* advertising campaign.

At ballot-casting time for *Follies*, Tony voters may also have been thinking about *Company*, the previous Sondheim-Prince-Bennett collaboration that had won Best Musical in 1970–1971. That show at least had had its hero somewhat optimistic about becoming a husband (probably because he'd never been one). The foursome in *Follies* had endured wedlock for decades and had convinced us (if not themselves) that they could no longer feel hopeful staying together and fixing their relationships.

Company, at 705 performances, had had a decent run, but it had never been a big audience favorite or a hot ticket. It had been closed for three months when the 1971–1972 ballots were delivered, so many Tony voters might have felt that if crowds didn't care all that much for *Company*, they would respond even less to *Follies*. The show had already been playing for more than a year and had been steadily waning at the box office. What was the point of giving such an unpopular show a Best Musical Tony and encouraging ticket buyers to see something they wouldn't like?

However, the voters were generous with *Follies*' staff. Sondheim won for Best Score, Smith was named Best Actress in a Musical, Prince and Bennett scored for directing, and Bennett won another for choreographing. Add to these the prizes for sets (Boris Aronson), lights (Tharon Musser), and costumes (Florence Klotz), and *Follies* landed seven Tonys to *Two Gentlemen*'s two: Best Musical and Best Book. The latter may have been the voters' revenge on Goldman for putting them through this harrowing evening.

Follies didn't get the expected box office upswing that most every musical gets when it performs on the Tonys—because it didn't perform. For reasons that may forever remain unclear and certainly will always be unjustified, the nominated *Ain't Supposed to Die a Natural Death* and the non-nominated *Jesus Christ Superstar* were instead featured on the telecast. And why songs from *No, No, Nanette*—the *previous* season's show?

So both *Follies* and *Two Gentlemen* didn't get a platform. How many viewers might have placed ticket orders if they'd seen the glory that was *Follies* on their TV screens? Such Tony night exposure might have extended the show's run, but after the loss and the broadcast snub, *Follies* had only ten more weeks to live.

At least in that original production. But it's still here by virtue of reputation and revivals. When Goldman chose to have the Plummers come from Phoenix, he probably didn't know the irony of that word: his show would rise like one for decades to come.

Notice, by the way, that all three losers have Stephen Sondheim's name attached. Sondheim would eventually win more Tonys than he lost: six wins out of ten nominations. Two of those losses came from shows that were deserving enough to win. But there was good reason why they lost . . .

CHAPTER TWO

*

Find Out What They Like and How They Like It:
The Best Musical Tony Losers That Were Too Good for the Average Man—and Tour

Stephen Sondheim has often criticized lyricist Lorenz Hart for one infraction or another. But there must be one Hart lyric that Sondheim has muttered to himself concerning his own work: "Too good for the average man."

That's what happens when you're the reigning late twentieth-century genius of the Broadway musical—the unquestioned champion in the hall. What you write is lost on the hoi polloi, whose members greatly outnumber appreciative savants.

And so, the 924 performances amassed by his longest-running hit, *A Funny Thing Happened on the Way to the Forum*, is only good enough to get it (as of this writing) to seventy-seventh place on the list of longest running musicals.

In two tries before (in which Sondheim only wrote lyrics) and eleven attempts after (in which he wrote entire scores), he never had a show that outran it.

Sondheim's *Pacific Overtures* (1975–1976) received an outstanding ten Tony nominations. It might have had more had the show been eligible for both of the Best Actress categories. It wasn't, because all the important male and female roles were played by men. There were a few female ensemble members, but many a man played a woman.

Men only was one of the time-honored conventions of Japanese theater that Sondheim and librettist John Weidman were intent on honoring. *Pacific Overtures* was to be a Broadway musical, yes, but it would be as authentically Japanese as possible.

Happily, virtually all were Asians. Fifteen years earlier, *Flower Drum Song* had cast plenty of non-Asians in its cast; fifteen years hence, *Miss Saigon* would notoriously cast an Englishman as a Eurasian. But director Harold Prince also wanted authenticity.

As a result, Prince wouldn't have stars, for America had no Asian stars. Mako had been nominated for a 1966 Best Supporting Actor Oscar for his performance in *The Sand Pebbles*. But he had no name recognition with theatergoers or Tony voters.

He was one of seventeen men who had never appeared on a Broadway stage (and eight of them never would again). The cast member with the most Broadway experience was Sab Shimono, who'd played the houseboy in *Mame*.

Here Mako portrayed the Reciter, a supernarrator who didn't merely set up the action but also occasionally burst in to say what a character was thinking or about to say. This was in keeping with Japanese tradition.

In the seventies, techies clad in black were seen more and more between scenes as they moved sets and props. *Pacific Overtures* wasn't simply getting into the swim; the Japanese theater had been employing this custom for centuries.

Boris Aronson's Tony-winning set design included a *hanamichi*, a runway that bisected the orchestra, going from the Winter Garden stage to the last row—a far greater distance than Gypsy Rose Lee had ever traveled.

That long strip of wood cut down on the potential gross receipts, but *Pacific Overtures* seldom if ever needed those seats. This musical pleased few Tony nominators and presumably not many more Tony voters.

Yes: it was that good. If there was ever a Broadway musical that was sui generis, *Pacific Overtures* was it. As many demands as it made on Tony voters, it made more on the musicians' union. If the show's *shamisen* player was out, Local 802 probably didn't have a replacement. In the union's defense, there isn't much call for people who play either that instrument or the *shakuhachi*.

As the lights came up, Tony voters saw the Reciter on his knees, bent over with his head touching the floor in prayer. (And people once thought that a woman sitting and churning butter was an odd opening for a musical.)

From the way the Reciter was dressed, voters might not have been able to infer that the year was 1853—when Commodore Matthew C. Perry opened Japan to the West.

Not that the Japanese were interested in outside events. "Here we paint screens," the Reciter sang, proud of his culture that made art, not war. Less understandable to Tony voters was that the Japanese were content to have a one-year-old emperor for whom they would calmly wait to grow into manhood.

Leaving the country and returning to it was punishable by death. Manjiro, who'd traveled as far as Massachusetts and had dared to return, was now earmarked to pay the ultimate price. Even more severe was the belief that "no foreigner should ever set a toe, let alone a foot on our sacred soil." (As a man in the lobby of the Shubert Theatre in Boston said during the show's tryout, "So the Jews aren't the only ones who believe that they're the chosen people.")

The Reciter said that this policy had been in place for 250 years. But 1853 would be no time for a sestercentennial celebration. Four warships were spotted in the harbor. Manjiro recognized them as American.

Citizens panicked. A fisherman saw the warships, and said, "I thought it was the end of the world." No: not the end of *the* world—but the end of *a* world.

The authorities quickly promoted Kayama, a minor samurai, to prefect of police. But it was no great honor. He'd bear the responsibility of getting the invaders to leave. His wife sensed that he wouldn't succeed and prepared to commit suicide, an event that didn't often happen in act one, scene two of musicals.

With the warships in the harbor, the Japanese were thinking differently about Manjiro. Perhaps his travel-broadening experience would help him to negotiate with the foreigners and get them to leave without coming ashore.

No. Kayama and Manjiro were told that Commodore Perry would "turn all cannon (sic) on Uraga and blast it off face of earth!!" (Indeed, Weidman's sentence ended with two exclamation points.)

Some decisive action was needed from the Shogun. Unfortunately, his inexperience with conflict made him do nothing. This dismayed his mother, who tried to spur him to action, offering some "Chrysanthemum Tea"— "an herb that's superb for disturb-ances" which will do "while we plan, if we can, what our an-swer ought to be" to those unwelcome Americans. Although she claimed "If the tea the Shogun drank will serve to keep the Shogun tranquil," once this woman saw that her son was incapable of action, she turned out to be a worse mother than Rose Hovick.

She poisoned him.

"When the Shogun is weak," she'd decided, "then the tea must be strong."

At least Kayama had an idea: cover the ground with mats; when the Americans came ashore, they wouldn't touch the ground. Finding this loophole got Kayama promoted to governor. He also got a pardon for his friend Manjiro.

Now he was looking forward to sharing his success with his wife—only to find that she'd killed herself. Hara-kiri wasn't easily understood by Tony voters who believed that a better solution was to learn from your mistakes and get on with your life.

Kayama kept the news from Manjiro, who was predicting that the Americans "coming here is the best thing that ever happened to Japan."

Well, yes and no, as Sondheim and Weidman would show.

The changes were small at first. Kayama indulged himself with imports, starting with "A Bowler Hat." He continued with an umbrella stand, pocket watch, and white wine. A monocle led to glasses, and ceremonial robes to cutaways. Not only did Kayama brag that "I read Spinoza every day," showing the influence from the Dutch, but he also assessed the man's writing as *"Formidable!"*

Less good was hearing the Reciter, playing the role of Emperor, decide that "In the name of progress, we will turn our back on ancient ways. We will open up Formosa, Korea, Manchuria, and China. We will do for the rest of Asia what America has done to us."

More to the point: "We must appease the Westerners until we have learned of their power and success."

That meant Pearl Harbor. But the musical continued to the then-present day by which point the United States and Japan had learned that each country needed the other.

Sondheim's haunting score managed to mix Japanese sounds with Broadway, although Tony voters' ears may have heard more of the former than the latter. And while Sondheim's skill with tricky and intellectual rhymes was second to none, he also knew that at certain times the simplest approach was best. So in "Next," the final song, to mark the many changes that Japan had experienced, he straightforwardly had the chorus sing, "See what's coming!" and immediately follow it with "See what's going."

After musical theater aficionados had seen Sondheim's *Company, Follies,* and *A Little Night Music* in less than a three-year span, they certainly saw *Pacific Overtures* coming, and counted the days to its arrival the way a kid fervently awaits his birthday.

Tony voters saw it going, which it did after 193 performances. Even if it hadn't had the bad luck to do battle with *A Chorus Line*, it would have had a hard time winning the Best Musical Tony in any season.

A musical about a *painting*?

When word got out that *this* would be Sondheim's entry in the 1983–1984 season, Broadway was startled.

Wouldn't it be as exciting as watching paint dry?

But with Sondheim on board, even a musical based on *A Sunday Afternoon on the Island of La Grande Jatte* couldn't be dismissed out of hand.

However, Sondheim's triumphs had mostly come in the seventies from shows produced and directed by Hal Prince. Their first one of the eighties—*Merrily We Roll Along*—would turn out to be their last one of the eighties (and nineties, too). Sondheim received a Best Score nomination, but that was the only Tony nod that the production received.

And now he was doing a musical about a *painting*?

Sondheim took another large chance with James Lapine, a playwright with no Broadway experience. He'd written and staged two of his plays off-Broadway, and had directed *A Midsummer Night's Dream* there, too. But at least his off-Broadway credentials included one impressive musical: *March of the Falsettos*.

The chance paid off. Lapine came through and has since worked on ten Broadway productions, including three more with Sondheim.

How smart they were to concoct a life for each of the characters in *A Sunday Afternoon on the Island of La Grande Jatte*—as well as for the man who created the painting in 1884. Long before there was the term "workaholic," there was Georges Seurat (1859-1891), whom we'd watch start, continue, and complete his masterpiece.

(Note that the writers abridged Seurat's first name to George. Yes, *Sunday in the Park with Georges* would have been too strange.)

They created a fictitious girlfriend for him: Dot, his model for the painting's most prominent woman on its right-hand side.

As with all Sondheim romances, matters did not go smoothly. Once more, two opposites suffered after being attracted to each other. While George was painting Dot, she complained about the bustle she wore, but defended her choice by saying that "Everyone is wearing them!"

Mandy Patinkin's George muttered, "Everyone!" with such sadness. How disappointed he was that Dot continued to follow the crowd—especially when that crowd literally put her in an uncomfortable position.

After a hard day of modeling, Dot wanted a night on the town. George had told her that he'd take her to the Follies (!), but then reneged. In one of their contretemps, she accused him of not caring. When he insisted that "I care about many things," she rebutted, "Not things—people!"

Which nobody can deny. Sondheim didn't make George critical of Dot and all the women who came before her: "They have never understood—and no reason that they should." A lesser writer would have had George staunchly say that he didn't care that he broke his promise to Dot, but Sondheim had George ask himself, "Do I care?" before admitting, "Yes."

George's inevitable conclusion was not that he loved Dot less, but that he loved his art more. His acknowledging that *he* was part of the problem kept us from disliking him.

Dot tried to make George jealous by seeing Louis, the local baker. While Sondheim and Lapine never introduced him to audiences, they could summon up an image of him from Dot's quick description: "Louie drinks a bit; Louie blinks a bit."

Every artist gets discouraged from time to time. At one particular low point, George actually told his troubles to a dog. "Look, I made a hat," he said, in a mocking voice that minimized what he'd done.

The mewing way that Patinkin said it stressed that painting an animal was no particular achievement. George was mocking himself and in essence seeing things from Dot's point of view.

But that moment passed. George immediately got his priorities back in order and had his self-respect return when he said, almost in awe, "Where there never was a hat."

That was the whole show in a couplet.

Other characters got their due. Given that we only saw the Boatman's left profile in the painting, Lapine took the liberty of giving him one working eye and an eyepatch on the other. That also allowed him to be belligerent when insisting that he saw more with his one eye than many others see with two. In rationalization, there was characterization.

Two young women—"the Celestes"—came to the park to both literally and figuratively fish. Catching as much as a minnow would have been nice, but hooking and reeling in a man would have been substantially better. But who today remembers these ladies or the men they made the center of their lives? George made much more of his time in the park by concentrating on art.

The Nurse cared for George's mother, who was simply called the Old Lady. "Tending to his (mother), though, is perfectly fine," sang the Nurse. "It pays for the nurse that is tending to mine." Yes, mothers aren't as demanding of nurses as they are of daughters, so working for someone else is ultimately easier on the nerves.

The Old Lady rued that her view had been spoiled, because of "Trees cut down for a foolish tower!" Ah, but the Eiffel Tower is art, too. Interesting, too, that the tower at first got poor reviews from critics; now, for more than a century, it has been an important and beloved work. Lapine reminded us that some people need time to catch up with great art.

Perhaps Tony voters needed time to catch up with *A Sunday in the Park with George*—or they simply felt that *La Cage aux Folles* would bring more pleasure to more people. It was commercial; *Sunday* had reservations about commercialism.

Hence the more successful Jules. Although he was ostensibly George's friend, he certainly wasn't supportive when the man was out of earshot. As he and his wife Yvonne said of George's paintings, "No life."

When George was around, Jules sharply told him, "Go to some parties. That is where you'll meet prospective buyers"—showing that even in the nineteenth century, networking was deemed important.

He also urged George to take some time off. But was the advice given because he cared about George or because he was frightened that if George continued working, the day would come when he would eclipse him as an artist?

Ironically, when the Nurse spied Jules in the park, she included him when she said, "I can never remember their names." In fact, people would forget Jules as time went on. Seurat, however, would be remembered.

Yvonne too didn't recognize art when she saw it (as so many still haven't after they've encountered the works of Sondheim and Lapine). While Jules was studying what was becoming *Sunday Afternoon on the Island of La Grande Jatte*, Yvonne said, "We must be going." Perhaps if she hadn't insisted that he leave, Jules would have had more time and might have begun to see the wonder of the painting. Now it wasn't Dot but a different woman and her concerns that got in the way of appreciating George's achievement.

As Jules started to leave, George said, "Thank you for coming." How many times have artists had to say that, after critics have expressed little or no enthusiasm for their works? Lapine was acknowledging all those who have been deeply disappointed by adverse criticism but had to show that they were good sports and grateful for at least the chance to be assessed.

Dot had challenged Yvonne that Jules was simply jealous of George. Although audiences might have suspected that Yvonne would deny it, Lapine dared to have her virtually admit it by conceding "Jealousy is a form of flattery."

That brings us to the 1983–1984 Tony Awards. After the Best Score award was given to Jerry Herman for *La Cage aux Folles* and not Sondheim's *Sunday*, Herman said in his acceptance speech that "the simple, hummable tune was still alive on Broadway." While Herman has since repeatedly said that he didn't have Sondheim in mind while stating this, he's probably convinced few. (And does anyone think that if Sondheim had won that he would have bothered to have alluded to Herman in his speech?)

Best Musical winner *La Cage* was as ornate a production as *Sunday*, but it couldn't match the beauty that the latter achieved at the end of act one. George positioned the actors and cutouts to make up *Un dimanche après-midi à l'Ile de la Grande Jatte*.

In act two, Tony voters returned to the painting, which soon disappeared along with 1884. Some needed time to digest that they were being whisked to the present. But if they'd remembered the show's logo, they might have anticipated this. Artist Frank Verlizzo had used the torsos of Seurat's two most prominent subjects, but tore off their bottom halves and replaced them with contemporary clothes.

Hence, a museum and more fictional people: Marie, the now-aged daughter of Dot and Seurat, and her grandson who was also named George. Lapine made act two George thirty-two—already one year older than Seurat had lived. That was a nice metaphor about survival.

Marie remembered that her mother had bragged about the number of times that Seurat had painted her into the portrait. Yes, once the work became celebrated and valued, Dot certainly wanted to stress her part in it. Where was her enthusiasm when George was working hard on it?

Audiences knew that, but Marie didn't. "Mama is everywhere," she said. "He must have loved her so much." As we'd seen, he actually had loved her *only* so much.

Marie dwelled on Seurat and only fleetingly mentioned Louis, her stepfather, although in raising her, he'd in essence become her real father. But Louis was not the father of whom Marie was proud. Louis's art—bread—may not have been "hard to swallow," as Dot had earlier noted, but it was, by its very nature, ephemeral. Seurat's art was longer lasting; the Art Institute of Chicago is counting on *A Sunday Afternoon on the Island of La Grande Jatte* to live forever.

But if George had succumbed to Dot and had taken her to the Follies, he might have wanted to go again and then again. Paris has always offered good times; if Seurat had got off track and availed himself of pleasure, his daughter wouldn't have had, as the cast of *Working* had sung, "Something to Point To."

Lapine's making act two George a divorced man rang true. Although being married can be very difficult (as we all know from either *Company* or real life), a married artist may be in for a harder time. Nine-to-fivers have very specific off-hours and holidays that allow them to spend, as the cliché goes, "more time with my family." Artists, however, are on call to their art 24/7; they never know when inspiration will strike and spur them to finish the hat, novel, play, symphony, or statue. Such bursts of creativity don't bring pleasure to spouses.

Act two George was creating a very different kind of art from Seurat's: an electronic piece that he called a Chromolume. At one point, it blew all the museum's fuses. That made some laugh. Would they have reacted with such derision if someone had stuck a knife in Seurat's canvas?

Probably not. Traditional art somehow seems more precious and implies an involvement of more work than "new" art. Admitted George, "No electricity, no art." Well, that was one advantage of traditional art; the only "electricity" Seurat needed was natural sunlight.

Both Georges had to endure critics. Jules had given way to Blair, who said warningly, "I look forward to see what you'll come up with next." That's how musical theater enthusiasts had felt about Sondheim since *Company* in 1970. The only difference was that Blair said it with an it-had-better-be-good warning, while Sondheim fans had come to believe that if it came from him, it would automatically be startling. The esteemed composer-lyricist always seemed to take the advice he gave George: "Move on." A look at the projects he did reinforced the title of a song Sondheim once wrote for a movie: "I Never Do Anything Twice."

Finally, act two George traveled to the Island of La Grande Jatte and found it looked quite different from the way his great-grandparents saw it. Like it or not, times change. Like it or not, art changes with it.

Some automatically feel that "change is good." Actually, *good* change is good, and *Sunday* qualified. That the Pulitzer Prize committee appreciated it more than the Tony voters righted an important wrong.

After the lights dimmed, an angry-looking man emerged onto a simple but stunning set. He wore an eyepatch on an extremely scarred face. Although he walked with a cane, he barreled his way to extreme stage right. There he turned away from the audience.

And yet, the way he contorted himself made clear what he was doing: shooting a drug into his arm. When he turned around, he looked much happier.

Director-choreographer Tommy Tune wasted no time in letting an audience see that *Grand Hotel* (1989–1990) would be a hard-hitting adult musical.

Book writer Luther Davis and songwriters Robert Wright and George Forrest had first conceived the musical version of the famed 1932 MGM film more than three decades earlier. But *At the Grand* had closed in California. As much as they didn't expect a second chance, they must have been more flabbergasted to have their musical open with this sinister image.

Colonel-Doctor Otternschlag was a much-scarred World War I veteran. Whenever his face showed a smile, it was a most cynical one as he wryly commented on the guests at Berlin's Grand Hotel on this day in 1928.

Many were checking in: Kringelein (Michael Jeter), "a bookkeeper looking for 'Life!'" Otternschlag told us, because the man was dying.

Herman Preysing was Kringelein's boss—"a businessman reporting to his stockholders" not good news, alas, making him increasingly desperate. The fetching and young Frieda Flamm was "a typist—but not for long," Otternschlag said cynically, because she'd use her youth and beauty to get ahead. Finally, there was Grushinskaya, "the fabled ballerina making a farewell tour—her eighth," and Raffaela Ottanio, "her devoted companion."

(Nice play on words for the last one; an actress named Rafaela Ottiano had had a small part in that *Grand Hotel* film.)

One guest had lived here for years: Baron Felix Amadeus Benvenuto von Gaigern, "the famous ladies' man," as Otternschlag told us, "heir to a small title and large debts." He stayed, for if he'd decided to leave, he'd have to settle his bill.

The 1932 film version of the 1930 Broadway play started with Kringelein making a phone call, followed by Preysing doing the same, followed by Raffaela and the Baron phoning, too. It all smacked of exposition.

But Tune improved matters by having the calls made simultaneously in overlapping dialogue. Now an audience was instead challenged to carefully listen in order to glean what was going on.

As nervous as Preysing sounded when he talked with his business associates, he was genuinely panicked when chatting to his wife.

Frieda had to tell her previous beau that she was probably pregnant: "Usually, I'm Miss Swiss Watch." She didn't get the "Darling, I'll come get you and we'll be married" response for which she'd hoped.

Raffaela informed a pawnbroker, "Madame wishes to sell some jewelry she has tired of." We could tell that that was hardly the case. Grushinskaya, despite a long and fruitful career, was now close to penniless.

"So Grushinskaya doesn't sell out anymore," Otternschlag mocked when offered free tickets. No wonder that this former legend had become reclusive. And yet, just as *The Wiz* wisely avoiding having a song in the same spot as "Over the Rainbow," Davis didn't have Grushinskaya say Greta Garbo's famous line, "I vant to be alone."

One would expect to see Grushinskaya dance. Tune instead had audiences see her do monotonous toe exercises. Yes, a good deal of difficult and unglamorous work faces each ballerina.

One subplot included the concierge's frustration at having to work while his wife was giving birth alone in a hospital. Would the baby ever come?

Despite his making a reservation, Kringelein was told there was no room for him. "Is it possible that Grand Hotel does not take Jews?" he challenged. The baron spoke up for him, making both Kringelein and audiences grateful for his intercession. However, when the baron gave Kringelein stock tips, he wasn't doing it first and foremost out of kindness; he needed to convince the bookkeeper that he was in the financial know.

Frieda reinvented herself as the glamorous Flaemmchen.

"I Want to Go to Hollywood," she proclaimed with the confidence that she'd become a star. Then she returned to current reality when she wistfully showed that even a lesser goal would be welcome: "I want to wear nice shoes." Her look of realistic yearning made audiences want her to have them—as well as a different place to live, not a flat where "when things get broken, they stay broken."

She believed her fortunes were changing when she met the baron and he expressed great interest in her. But he again wanted to be nice to Kringelein, and requested that she dance with him. Because Flaemmchen was intent on pleasing a baron, she certainly agreed.

The result was "Who Couldn't Dance with You," an intoxicating fox-trot in which Kringelein reached the apex of his happiness. Tune staged his ensemble around it to make dazzling stage pictures. And yet, as magnificent as it was, it would hardly be the greatest production number in the show.

Audiences rued as Flaemmchen assumed that the baron's interest in her automatically meant that her troubles were over. Just his gleaming silver cigarette case alone was enough to convince her that she was in the world of wealth and royalty. Life with a baron would mean living in a palace with servants attending her every need.

We knew better: that the cigarette case was the last luxury item that the baron hadn't yet been forced to sell. That night, while Grushinskaya was performing, the baron broke into her room to steal her jewelry. What he couldn't anticipate: Grushinskaya would leave her performance when it wasn't going well and return to her room while he was in midtheft.

He pretended that he was an admirer who needed to be close to her, and that's why he was there. She didn't believe him—at first. But as is the case with so many aging one-time beauties, Grushinskaya needed to believe that this younger man could be in love with her.

How young? He admitted to "twenty-nine years" before adding "and twenty-nine months," realizing that he could no longer pass for under thirty. She conceded "forty-nine years," before adding "and forty-nine months."

Actually, the baron *would* come to have much deeper feelings for Grushinskaya than he would have initially imagined. When he told her that he'd meet her at the station and that they'd go away together to Vienna, he genuinely meant it. When he blithely told Flaemmchen, she put on a good front, but was utterly devastated. There went all that money and her lofty title!

The baron was happy, but Kringelein was happier. He'd actually taken that stock tip and in what may have been the first stroke of luck in his entire life, he'd made a fortune overnight. Time for drinks, celebration, and song, which was, to be frank, a paean to money. Jeter threw himself on, above, below, across (and plenty of other prepositions) a horizontal metal bar. That's what getting rich quick does to a man—even a terminally ill one.

"We'll Take a Glass Together" was the unquestioned highlight of the musical, and the second-best production number of the six decades that this book covers. Only "Who's That Woman?" in *Follies* can be deemed stronger.

Otternschlag had said that Grand Hotel was where "People come, people go." It was a case of "easy come, easy go," too. In the midst of the dance, Kringelein dropped his wallet. The baron hated the idea of stealing it, but felt he had no choice.

When Kringelein discovered it was missing, he had a panic attack. "It's everything I own in the world!" he cried. "My savings, my stock winnings, even my burial insurance!"

The baron couldn't go through with the theft, again showing his native nobility. He "reminded" Kringelein that "You gave me your pocketbook to hold."

Kringelein knew he hadn't. And the baron knew he knew. But Kringelein saw that the man needed money and gave him some. The baron in turn gave him his cigarette case "as collateral." It was also a gift of atonement and friendship.

Employee Kringelein was doing substantially better than his boss. Preysing had become involved in a swindle, and needed to leave the country. He'd go to Boston and offered to take Flaemmchen with him. "Is Boston near Hollywood?" she asked.

"Only a train ride away," he said, showing us the type of businessman he was.

But after Preysing took her into his room, Flaemmchen knew she'd made a mistake. A lesser director might have had her strip completely, but Tune knew that having Preysing ask for her panties would cause audiences' skin to crawl at a faster rate. Once the panties were off and on the floor, Flaemmchen longingly looked at them as if she were genuinely seeing her lost virtue before her.

She wanted to leave, but Preysing wasn't going to let his prey escape now that he was so close to conquest. Then the baron entered; this was to be the next room he'd burgle. When he pulled a gun on Preysing, the two fought over it.

Then a shot rang out. Which was the victim? Tune purposely and literally kept his audience in the dark for long, painful, and suspense-building moments.

Actually, both of them would pay a terrible price no matter who "won." The baron died, and Presying was arrested for murder.

Once the baron didn't show at the train station, Grushinskaya would now and forever believe that he had had no intention of meeting her and had always been insincere. Audiences knew that that was not true, and mourned that she would never know that.

This, however, was the moment that Raffaela had been anticipating, as she sang "Twenty-two Years." While Grushinskaya once spent money as if there were no tomorrow, Raffaela had saved hers for this tomorrow. Now she would dare to seize the upper hand. For the first time, she dispensed with the "Madame" and called Grushinskaya "Elizaveta." How pained Liliane Montevecchi's face was when she realized that she would now be conquered both emotionally and sexually. Karen Akers was a gracious winner, however, and showed that her first motivation was genuine love.

When Flaemmchen told Kringelein that she was pregnant, a wonderful moment occurred. Although he was close to death, he was ever the gentleman and concerned for the expectant mother. He took her typewriter out of her hands so that he could carry it for her.

Once the concierge told Kringelein that he'd become a father, the bookeeper gave him the baron's cigarette case as a present. The concierge was overjoyed, but his bliss lasted less than a minute. The chauffeur came in and took it out of his hands with a sense of entitlement. The concierge didn't argue, giving us the impression that he had owed the chauffeur a good deal of money for some time.

Grand Hotel's artistic and commercial success (1,077 performances) was all the more remarkable given that it was cobbled together. After lukewarm reviews in Boston and a less than productive Wright and Forrest, Tune called Maury Yeston, his Tony-winning composer-lyricist from *Nine*, to buttress the score as well as Peter Stone, who'd helped save his *My One and Only*, to do book work.

Stone didn't take official credit, and Davis, perhaps to his dying day, claimed that Stone did nothing. Stone, perhaps to *his* dying day, shrugged and said otherwise: "Those who know about musicals know I did it, so I didn't need the credit. And those who don't know musicals don't know who I am, anyway."

Yeston took credit and deserved it. His title song started in a minor key to set the eerie and ominous mood. In addition to "I Want to Go to Hollywood," he wrote "Everybody's Doing It," which had Preysing rationalize his lies to investors. Yeston captured Kringelein's thrill in finally being "At the Grand Hotel" as well as Grushinskaya's surprise at again finding romance in "Bonjour, Amour" after the baron had professed his love for her in "Love Can't Happen," an ambitious and especially majestic melody.

Wright and Forrest still had much to offer. "Maybe My Baby Loves Me" was a scat sensation done by two bellboys. And last but hardly least, Tune certainly wasn't doing Wright and Forrest a favor by keeping "We'll Take a Glass Together."

City of Angels, a witty and hilarious spoof of film noir, won the 1989–1990 Best Musical Tony. Part of the success came from Larry Gelbart's still-sharp wit ("Her husband's name slipped her mind. He's seventy-five.") and David Zippel's especially clever lyrics: Said a disappointed wife to her author-husband, who was selling out: "Your fiction always had a little grit in it, a little heart in it, a little wit in it. It used to be so clear that there was art in it if you had written it. So must you go and spit in it?"

Their work was greatly enhanced by Cy Coleman's smoky jazz-club music. "With Every Breath I Take" almost did take one's breath away, for the melody went high, then perilously low, seemed shapeless, and yet resulted in an intoxicating whole.

But as accomplished as *City of Angels* was, *Grand Hotel* was substantially more ambitious and achieved considerably more.

Falsettos (1991–1992) was another musical that was better left to regional theaters than national tours.

There *are* people who would appreciate a musical about homosexuals, women with children, short insomniacs, a teeny-tiny band—and ill-placed lightbulbs in one's body. There just aren't that many theatergoers west of the Hudson who would buy tickets for such a show. Three or four weeks in a three hundred-seat house would accommodate all who want to know about Marvin, who left his wife Trina and son Jason in order to romance a man named Whizzer.

Big roadhouses of two thousand to three thousand would look awfully empty both in the audience and onstage for this seven-character, unit-set musical. Some would have blanched at the moment in which Marvin, in bed with Whizzer, peeked under the sheets to once again marvel at the majesty of the man.

In terms of Tony history, *Falsettos* was even more controversial than it might have initially seemed. There had virtually been no Tony-winning or nominated musical in which a husband who was a main character had even left his wife for another *woman*.

Adultery? Sure. Littlechap and Guido Contini cheated and Senex wanted to, but all stayed married. (*Oh.*) Captain St. James was cheating on two wives, but didn't plan to leave either. Sheldrake's wife threw him out, but he wanted to stay in the marriage (not necessarily, however, for the best of reasons). But Joe Boyd wouldn't have left Meg for Lola any more than Al Rossi would have abandoned his wife for the Queen of the Stardust Ballroom.

Jerry in *Seesaw* and Sam in *Woman of the Year* had split, but soon returned. Tom in *Golden Boy* and Phil in *Milk and Honey* wanted divorces, but by the final curtain, nether had left home. Nick Arnstein wasn't leaving Fanny for another woman; he simply felt she'd be better off divorced from a graduate of Sing Sing.

Kayama in *Pacific Overtures* offhandedly mentioned "I've left my wife," but she was no one we'd ever met and had no impact on the plot. In other Sondheim musicals, husbands pretty much stay put. Herbie left Rose, yes, but they weren't yet married. In *Company*, Peter and Susan had a sensible divorce that each wanted. Phyllis sang, "Could I Leave You?" and Sally wanted out, but no husband left. Anne ran off with Henrik long before Frederick would have escaped with Desiree.

Out in the hinterlands, people (at least wives) are more interested in stories where men are crazy for women—which is why *Crazy for You* won.

Caroline, or Change (2003–2004) had Tony Kushner of *Angels in America* fame as its book writer/lyricist; Jeanine Tesori, whose *Thoroughly Modern Millie* (2001–2002) won Best Musical and lost Best Score (to *Urinetown*) composed.

They did exemplary work. The show may have suffered with Tony voters because its structure was more in line with an opera than a musical.

There were few "songs" as such, but snippets of melodies and precious few applause buttons.

"Nothing ever happens underground in Louisiana" were the show's first words, sung by Caroline Thibodeaux, a white-uniformed black maid.

Soon after Caroline told us where she was, the show's time frame was established by a washing machine—which proclaimed in song that it was a "brand-new 1963" model. Then the radio joined the washing machine to wonder, "What lies in store for 1963 or '4?"

These appliances "spoke" to Caroline because she spent most of her time alone in the basement and had no one to converse with while working.

That is, until Noah Gellman, the preteen son of the family for whom Caroline toiled, came home from school. He idolized her, partly because his mother had died and his father quickly married her best friend Rose Stopnick, a Northerner whom Noah hated. He needed a role model he could like, and decided to regard Caroline as "the president of the United States!"

The clothes dryer, which also had a voice, did not mistake Caroline for a chief executive. "How on earth she gonna thrive when her life bury her alive?" Caroline even admitted, "I wish every afternoon I die."

Still, Noah insisted that Caroline was "stronger than my dad!" Actually, she had to be, for the thirty-nine-year-old divorced mother of four made merely thirty dollars a week. Rose felt very generous in offering Caroline each meal's leftovers.

Now Rose would give Caroline a chance to make more money. Noah was negligent in removing his change from his pockets, which Caroline retrieved before each wash and saved for him. As Rose told her father on a long-distance phone call, "The Negro maid, she's making bupkes, how does that look leaving change in his pockets, indifferent to money?"

Rose told Noah, "Take your money out of your pockets before you put your pants in the hamper or else Caroline can keep any change that she finds."

Then Rose told Caroline of her plan, blithely singing, "It'll be like a raise." Considering that Noah usually left a quarter or two, that meant a .04 to .08 percent boost each week. Rose added "Keep the change!" as another of her unwittingly condescending remarks.

"I don't want to take money from a baby," Caroline said. But charity began in the Gellman home, for that literally found money allowed Caroline to give her three children at home an extra quarter or two. (Her older son Larry was in Vietnam, proving the point that had been made by Black Panther founder Huey P. Newton and later appropriated by *Hair*: "A black man goes over there to fight a yellow man for the white man who stole his land from the red man.")

Audiences were surprised when Noah *purposely* left change in his pants so that Caroline would have more money. But just when the musical's message seemed to be that the new generation of whites was more sympathetic to the black cause and genuinely wanted to help, Kushner delivered his knockout punch.

Noah's grandfather had given him a $20 Chanukah present, which the lad inadvertently left in his pants. He was in school when he realized his mistake, and frantically hoped he could get home before Caroline got to his pants.

It led to the show's best line, when Noah sang, "I'll sue!" Litigious little kid, wasn't he? The metaphor was clear: whites, even the new generation, wanted to give blacks a little something—but not all that much.

Caroline, or Change at first glance seemed to have neither the big characters nor the big events that musicals once believed essential. But Kushner proved that he could make a story about mere pocket change into a big event. His many uses of the word "change" added layers. Dotty, one of Caroline's friends and colleagues, was changing because she was taking night courses at the local community college. That threatened Caroline, whose attitude toward her changed, too.

"Times change—even here," Dotty said. Rose's father, a liberal Jew from way back, agreed. "Negroes marching! Change is coming!" In fact, a statue commemorating the Confederacy was suddenly missing.

Caroline continued to believe that "Nothing ever changes underground in Louisiana." Life had already ground her down so that, in her eleven o'clock aria, she moaned that she could neither "afford loose change" or change. "Some folks go to school at nights. Some folks march for civil rights," she sang. "I don't. I haven't got the heart. I'm going to slam that iron down on my heart."

So Caroline might not have been as big a character as audiences and Tony voters might have wanted. More likely, she was too much of a reminder of how much whites have failed to help blacks. A 136-performance run was all *Caroline, or Change* could muster, losing five of its six Tony nominations.

The one category in which it won provided another metaphor. Anika Noni Rose, who'd soon become a Hollywood star, landed the Best Supporting Musical Actress Tony for portraying Caroline's older daughter Emmie. As it turned out, Emmie was one of those who stole the Confederate statue, which she helped decapitate. She would be part of the next generation that would make substantial change.

The Light in the Piazza (2004–2005) had Mrs. Margaret Johnson (Victoria Clark) break the fourth wall quite often to tell us what was on her mind.

Now, would she break the heart of her twenty-six-year-old daughter, too?

Back in 1939, at the age of twelve, Clara had been kicked in the head by a pony, which had prevented her from mentally developing. Margaret never forgave herself for not being around when the accident occurred, so she has since kept a watchful eye on Clara. It was a cruel variation on the cliché about locking the barn door after the horse escapes.

In the novel and film on which Craig Lucas and Adam Guettel's musical was based, Margaret never let the girl out of her sight unless someone else was chaperoning. So why did director Bartlett Sher start the show by having Margaret walk alone onto the vast Vivian Beaumont stage? In fact, Lucas's published script specified that they walk on together.

Nevertheless, Clara showed up some moments later and spoke dialogue that didn't remotely suggest a twelve-year-old girl. Only later, when she and her mother were in a museum—where she saw a statue of a naked man and touched its penis in wonder—did she seem like a naïf.

Once outside, a breeze set the plot in motion. It liberated Clara's hat, which Fabrizio Naccarelli, a young Italian, retrieved. Fabrizio was as halting in English as the Johnsons were in Italian, and while he seemed entranced with Clara, Margaret was immediately suspicious of him. She'd heard about young, dashing Italian fortune hunters who'd do or say anything to get to America.

That suspicion wasn't erased after Clara volunteered that their last name was Johnson and Fabrizio asked if they were related to Van. He seemed disappointed after they said no. Did he want them to be next-of-kin because that would suggest affluence, or because he was starstruck and wanted to meet someone, anyone, connected with Hollywood?

Whether Fabrizio was on the up-and-up would soon be gleaned by those fluent in Italian. For after the Johnsons left, Fabrizio sang a song completely in his native language. The rest of the audience only under-stood "Clara" and "piazza."

Was songwriter Adam Guettel sparing us the Italian equivalent of "Your lips, your eyes, your cheeks, your hair, are in a class beyond com-pare; you're the loveliest girl that one could see"? Really, what else could a love-at-first-sight beneficiary-victim sing about?

Perhaps, "Here's my free ticket to America!"

That the song was in Italian kept the vast majority of theatergoers guessing. Those who knew the language, however, learned a good deal just from the title: "Il Mondo Era Vuoto" meant "My World Was Empty." And while Fabrizio did acknowledge that Clara was his own personal "light on the piazza," he did think that their love would be doomed be-cause she was clearly older than his twenty-three years. "She won't love a little boy," he sang.

Little did he know that he was in essence older than Clara. His inabil-ity with English kept him from seeing that Clara was substantially younger in mind.

Fabrizio virtually stalked the Johnsons and was as nice as Eddie Haskell when insisting that they meet his parents. "You can't say no to these peo-ple," Margaret wryly observed to us.

As soon as the families met, Lucas shrewdly established culture clash. When Mrs. Naccarelli went to embrace and kiss Margaret, the Wasp didn't know how to handle this blatant show of emotion. She could only manage to say "Oops!" and returned the unwanted embrace with some quick air-kisses. Clark's body language was eloquent here in further es-tablishing who this Southern gentlewoman was. At other times, she showed her demure side by lightly pressing her hand flat above her breasts.

The big roadblock turned out to be Clara's age. When Mr. Naccarelli learned that she was a few years older than his son, he forbade the union. In 1953 Italy, a man could never be younger than his wife. Clara saw the panic in Fabrizio's face. "He couldn't look me in the eye," she moaned to her mother.

Is that the observation of a twelve-year-old? Clara had some other thoughts not commensurate with someone developmentally disabled. "If I had a child, I would take such care of her," she said. "Then I wouldn't feel like one." When Margaret tried to discourage her from getting in-volved with Fabrizio, she complained, "You're happy to be the one who knows everything I need and has the final word."

So this *could* have been a story about a so-called limited young woman whose parents have become so inured to her not improving that they haven't noticed her improvements. That would explain Clara's most stinging observation: "Daddy doesn't love you. Look for once in the mirror."

Lucas had subtly insinuated a less-than-ideal marriage from the outset when he had us learn that Margaret and Roy had honeymooned here in Florence. Most couples return to their honeymoon spot together. Why, then, had Margaret chosen not to return with Roy?

Phone calls to him revealed that Roy was out of love with her, too. It resulted in Margaret's wondering about their "Dividing Day," Guettel's most far-reaching song. Here she tried to pinpoint when love died.

So Margaret would convince Fabrizio's father to overlook the age difference. She'd learned from her own experience that two "normal" human beings who allegedly knew their own minds didn't have the secrets to marital success. Maybe Clara and Fabrizio *could* be happy. Margaret had a point when she told Roy, "Why can't we hope for once?" By now, Clara was saying more and more observations that didn't sound as if they came out of the mouth of a preteen. Could love be making her blossom?

The less-than-nice part of the story was that Margaret never did come clean to the Naccarellis about her daughter's problems. The closest she came was saying that "Clara is a special child." Those for whom English is at best a second language would interpret that as "she's darling." And Margaret knew that her carefully chosen words wouldn't be interpreted the way she meant them. A case can be made that Margaret Harold Hilled the Naccarellis.

Still, Guettel wrote beautiful music and somehow captured in it the serene feeling that many Americans feel when they reach Italy. It was an ambitious score that avoided conventional A-A-B-A song structures. This did, however, make the score difficult for those who want a show tune to which they can hang on to.

Too bad, however, that Guettel didn't musicalize Margaret's battle with herself to give up her little girl. Given that her marriage to Roy was not suffused in love, Clara was a good love substitute. Did Margaret initially want to stop the marriage so that she wouldn't lose her constant companion? Many parents tend to think of their children as children no matter how old they get; this feeling must be exacerbated when a child is developmentally disabled. A song on this topic would have been the other side of the coin that "Stop, Time," a lovely ballad in *Big*, addressed: how parents "lose" a child every time he ages and matures into a "new" one.

What Guettel did write was enough to win him Best Score and a share of Best Orchestrations. Tony voters appreciated his atypical sound, but they may not have been sure that the average theatergoer would. Better to send them to *Monty Python's Spamalot*.

A musical about a mentally unbalanced woman who endured one of the worst situations a mother can face and eventually had to submit herself to electroconvulsive therapy?

That isn't going to make all that many people sing, "That's Entertainment!" Nevertheless, if we must have such a musical, it should be as accomplished as *Next to Normal* (2008–2009). It won a Pulitzer Prize for book writer/lyricist Brian Yorkey and composer Tom Kitt. But, like *Sunday*, not the Best Musical Tony. And like *Falsettos*, a small regional theater life.

Next to Normal started off as blithely as *Leave It to Beaver*. Diana (Alice Ripley) sang about her husband Dan and her two teenagers: son Gabe and daughter Natalie. "They're the perfect loving family, so adoring— and I love them every day of the week" were the show's first lines. But by the time that song had ended, Diana had contradicted that statement in so many ways that audiences wondered if she even knew how many days there were in a week.

Natalie had given up on her mother long ago, and immersed herself in music. "You play till the strings or your fingernails break," she sang, revealing a lost soul whose spirit had been broken long ago. Even when her classmate Henry tried to involve her romantically, Natalie was reluctant. She'd seen for years where so-called love could lead.

The family problems weren't the result of Dan's lack of trying. Although doctors had described his wife as "a bipolar depressive with delusional episodes," Dan tried to remain patient and optimistic. He still loved his wife, although he remembered "when she was twenty and brilliant and bold"—when both had had ambitions to be architects. After new medications seemed to be working for two weeks, he was singing, "It's gonna be good"—and he believed it, even though audiences had their doubts.

"Do you read obituaries and feel jealous of the dead?" Diana asked.

Whenever Diana faltered, Dan found it within himself to stay on course. Any audience would have gladly voted him Husband of the Century, even though there were ninety-two years to go in this one.

And how about Gabe through all of this? Actually, he was part of the problem, because he'd died sixteen years earlier at eighteen months from a childhood illness. As in the case of many families in which this tragedy occurs, one parent is able to let go and move on while the other cannot. Diana now envisioned what Gabe would have been like as a teen. Both her husband and her son are *there* for her, but in two different meanings of the word "there."

"I've shown you I own you," bragged Gabe. Later, when the electro-convulsive therapy obliterated Diana's memory, Gabe sang, "They've moved me from your memory. I'm still there in your soul."

Diana knew it, too. "What happens if the cut, the burn, the break was never in my brain or in my blood, but in my soul?"

Tony voters were willing to give Yorkey and Kitt a Best Score Tony for the rock music and lyrics that sat well in their characters' mouths. After all, Natalie and Henry weren't the only products of a rock era; Diana and Dan hadn't yet hit forty, so rock was their musical medium, too. And while Yorkey's lyrics were rarely flashy, he told the story in simple and direct terms. Just as Alan Ayckbourn gets laughs in a different fashion from Neil Simon—he relies on situations, not jokes—Yorkey got his points across without using particularly deft wordplay.

Next to Normal didn't have what virtually every Best Musical Tony winner had had: a strong female heroine. From Lilli Vanessi in *Kiss Me, Kate* to Girl in *Once*, most Tony winners had leading ladies who would have taken a bull, a ram, and a devil by the horns: think Anna, Dolly, and Evita. Tony voters had sympathy for Diana, even when she attempted suicide, but they might have preferred a story where she overcame this obstacle, admittedly difficult as it was. Instead she left her faithful husband at show's end—leaving him to cope with the specter of Gabe.

Comedies in an earlier age often opted for a "here we go again" ending. *Next to Normal* could have done without the same concept. To make for at least a somewhat happy ending, everyone sang a song called "Light" in which the line "There will be light" was sung six times.

But it was too little, too light.

The lights came up on a black woman who was simply sitting. That was it: sitting. She wasn't talking to anyone or doing anything in particular. She was just sitting with a cake box on her lap.

But there was a reason for *The Scottsboro Boys* (2010–2011) to have one of the quietest openings of any Broadway musical. Book writer David Thompson and director-choreographer Susan Stroman were giving us enough time to realize that this black woman was Rosa Parks (1913–2005) waiting for that Montgomery bus on which she'd change history.

Ms. Parks stayed on stage throughout, watching the events that followed with great interest. So would any discerning theatergoer. *The Scottsboro Boys* was an intelligent musical about racism in American history and politicians who failed to do the right thing.

The story of this John Kander and Fred Ebb musical was simple, although the famous 1931 case and its multiple trials that followed were not. While Victoria Price and Ruby Bates were accused of soliciting while riding on a train, they blamed nine black young passengers of raping them.

The men tried cooperating with the authorities. One deferentially said, "Anything we can do for you, Sergeant?" in a most polite voice—only to be castigated by his friend: "Take off your hat!" Thompson smartly made his painful point: in those days, a black man always had to intently watch his step; forgetting to include even one respectful gesture to a white man could lead to trouble.

"When I want your opinion," the sergeant snarled to the lads, "I'll give it to you." Audiences laughed because the line was funny, but their laughter sounded hollow and joyless. Any humor was eclipsed by the crowd's realization that this was indeed the black way of life then—and that wasn't funny at all.

Thompson offered a distressing but brilliant line when the youngest of the nine—a veritable child—heard the outrage in a white man's voice that a black man dared to look a white woman in the eye. "Is that what rape is?" the kid asked—showing his innocence and breaking audiences' hearts in the process.

Bates eventually recanted, but the Southern court wasn't willing to accept her revised testimony. What sadness there was in her line, "Why did everyone believe me when I was telling a lie, but nobody believes me when I'm telling the truth?"

After Bates had admitted the truth, what could a bigoted Southern attorney general do but attack the defense attorney for being Jewish? The song that he sang was euphemistically titled "Financial Advice," but a more apt title would have been "Jew Money," a term used twice. So audiences not only experienced bigotry against blacks, but anti-Semitism, too.

Those who feel that "Jew money" sounded too heavy-handed need only examine the actual court records of April 13, 1933. Wade Wright, a county solicitor who was assisting the attorney general, asked jurors "whether justice in this case is going to be bought and sold with Jew money from New York."

Most of the story centered on Haywood Patterson. The irascible judge wanted Haywood to say he was guilty; if the young man did, the judge would be lenient on him. Actually, the judge knew by now that the law had made a mistake, but he couldn't bring himself to admit that. Instead, the men prosecuting wanted to save face by having Patterson say he was guilty so that then they could be the merciful good guys who would grandly let him go.

But Patterson wouldn't. When he was convicted, the judge barked out, "Any last words?" Indeed Haywood had some, but Stroman and Thompson effectively had the judge and every other court officer walk off while Patterson spoke. How true that the last words of a condemned prisoner mean nothing to those who have convicted him. Allowing Patterson to have his say was just a meaningless formality.

The only one who did stay around was Rosa Parks, who intently listened. That was why at show's end, Parks took her stand. (For the record, Parks was not just an arbitrary housewife or maid who refused to move to the back of the bus; she had already served as secretary of the Montgomery chapter of the NAACP. So Thompson had a point when he postulated that Parks's action on the bus could well have been motivated by the frustration she felt at the fate of the Scottsboro Boys.)

If many a serious story is described as "a bitter pill to swallow," *The Scottsboro Boys* was two full tablespoons of horrible tasting medicine. Perhaps that's why the collaborators settled on framing it as a minstrel show. To be true to that format, plenty of corny jokes were required, and this show had them in abundance. That may have been a mistake, for theatergoers may not have known that minstrel shows routinely dispensed groaners. They might have assumed that these zingers were supposed to pass for genuine humor and found the gags too far beneath them to laugh. They might not have even caught the cleverness of one phrase: because minstrel shows always began with the line "Gentlemen, be seated!" there was great irony later when the judge said the exact same words to those in his courtroom.

This may have been too modest a production to have won Best Musical even if it had been running. Able set designer Beowulf Boritt didn't have much of a budget, so he opted for a bunch of chairs and placed them in intriguing positions. Stroman used those chairs most inventively when one of the lads escaped; she made them into a sinuous maze.

Kander's music was outstanding, melodious, and memorable. The opening number, beautifully orchestrated with banjo and tambourines by Larry Hochman, was not just a toe-tapper, but a both feet tapper. Kander captured the exhilaration of young people making their first real train trip in "Commencing in Chattanooga." Then he conveyed the pseudoelegance of "Alabama Ladies," in which Price and Bates put on the dawg to seem refined.

What a jewel of a beautiful song was "Go Back Home," as the lads dreamed of being set free. When they had reason to believe that they'd soon be released and their troubles would soon be over, they joyfully celebrated in "Shout!" But audiences knew that they were only at the beginning of their torturous journey.

A song about an electric chair harkened back to the torture scene in Kander and Ebb's Best Musical *Kiss of the Spider Woman*. Its vamp sounded perilously like the one for "All That Jazz," too. "Nothin'" was reminiscent of "Mister Cellophane," as Patterson, in his first court appearance, became the "shufflin' Negro" that whites had expected him to be. And needless to say, this wasn't the first Kander and Ebb musical to use a framing device—*Cabaret*, *Zorba*; *70, Girls, 70*; and *Chicago* did too—which made the convention seem worn.

But the fourteenth Kander and Ebb creation to reach Broadway would almost inevitably have them repeat themselves a little. Broadway and Tony voters should have been more grateful that they also repeated their oft-displayed bravery in choosing subject matter and expressed it with their customary excellence.

The Scottsboro Boys set a new record for Tony futility. Although Kander and Ebb's *Chicago* and *Steel Pier* had respectively gone zero for eleven, the team eclipsed those defeats with a zero for twelve showing for *The Scottsboro Boys*. "At least Fred wasn't around to see that," said Kander of his collaborator who had died on September 11, 2004.

But of all the shows that have proved to be too good for the average man, the most mystifying failure is *She Loves Me* (1963–1964). Most everyone who l-o-v-e-s musicals adores the Jerry Bock–Sheldon Harnick–Joe Masteroff masterpiece. And yet, four first-class productions—two on Broadway, two in London—have produced more red ink than is on the cover of the original cast album.

Perhaps nice *shows* finish last, too.

At least Maraczek's Parfumerie was doing well. It was Budapest's premier purveyor of soaps, salts, and perfume. Clerks Georg Nowack, Ilona Ritter, and Ladislav Sipos, and delivery boy Arpad Laszlo took genuine pride in their work. Steven Kodaly (Jack Cassidy)? A little less.

They were loyal to Mr. Maraczek. Steven Kodaly? A lot less. Although he was ostensibly involved with Ilona, he was sleeping with Maraczek's wife. Trouble was, Maraczek assumed Georg was the one cuckolding him.

Early in the show, before Maraczek suspected that, the strife between Georg and Maraczek was simply over a music box. Maraczek thought it would be a good seller while Georg didn't. That incited one of musical theater's favorite devices: from Sky versus Nathan to Higgins versus Pickering, betting has always been useful to a plot.

Enter Amalia Balash, looking for a job. She said that she'd had "five years' experience" in sales before amending that with "five years and eight months." Masteroff proved here that Amalia was honest. Most job applicants would have rounded it off to six years (or ten) to aggrandize themselves.

Georg said no position was available, and Maraczek initially agreed—before challenging her to sell the music box. Amalia got off to a bad start, telling a woman that it was for candy. When she opened it and it began playing its tune, Amalia had to change her tune. She rallied, and explained that, yes, it *was* a candy box meant to alert would-be munchers to eat "no more candy."

So Maraczek won the bet, and Georg had an immediate reason to dislike Amalia. Her chronic lateness was another reason.

Best of all was the way that Masteroff cleverly added another reason. Maraczek had chided Georg for not correctly filling tubes of Mona Lisa cold cream, which had leaked. Later Masteroff showed Amalia and Ilona dealing with Christmas items. Said Amalia, "It's certainly a pleasant change. For the last month, I've done practically nothing but fill those darn tubes of Mona Lisa." Imagine if Georg had known that! He'd have had yet another piece of evidence to use against her.

But he loved her, and she loved him, although neither he nor she knew it. They were secret pen pals who had fallen in love through their letters.

Soon they planned to meet. Amalia confessed to Ilona "I Don't Know His Name," and Ilona was delicate in the way she cautiously advised her.

Most of the characters were nice to each other. How they mourned when Maraczek fired Georg on a trumped-up charge; by now, the husband was convinced that Georg was his wife's lover. Sipos went with Georg to the restaurant where he was to meet his pen pal, peeked first, and didn't know how to tell Georg that Amalia was there.

Masteroff was skillful in how he made Sipos break the news. First: "She looks like someone in the shop," then "Miss Balash." And when Georg said that he didn't think Miss Balash was attractive, Sipos said, "If you don't care for Miss Balash, you're certainly not going to like *this* girl."

Once he looked, Georg was devastated, of course. But now that he knew something Amalia didn't, his frustration got the better of him. He went in the restaurant simply to annoy her, and they fought so much that the headwaiter came over and chided "you and your husband" for creating a disturbance. Such warring people just *had* to be married.

Amalia continued, anyway, with her rant against Georg. "Shall I tell you what I see?" she asked. "A pompous, petty tyrant. I see him ten years from now selling shampoo," she said, because she knew "what he is." Amalia was so nice that even in anger, she chose to say "he" instead of "you." It hurt a little less that way.

That speech got him to go. Now Amalia was alone, and of course her "Dear Friend" would not show. She was devastated as the curtain fell.

What both didn't know was that the detective that Maraczek had hired indeed confirmed that his wife was cheating on him—with Kodaly. That information—and the knowledge that he had been so unfair to Georg—made him shoot himself. Luckily, he only grazed his arm.

And that was as depressing as *She Loves Me* ever got. A happy ending was in store for Georg and Amalia, as well as Ilona, who got a new beau, and even Arpad, who got Kodaly's job.

In *Into the Woods*, Sondheim had Little Red Riding Hood ungrammatically insist that "Nice is different than good." In this case, they were one and the same. The Bock and Harnick score was, to quote one of the latter's lyrics, "a little like the voice of God." Bock gave the ideal Middle European feel in songs as disparate as Maraczek's "Days Gone By" and Amalia's "Dear Friend," and had his melody soar near the end of "I Don't Know His Name."

"Sounds While Selling"—in which clerks and customers interacted—

showed that Harnick was innovative as well as skilled. Most lyricists would have written a list song with clever rhymes for various soaps and beauty products. Harnick instead had the inspired notion of letting audiences hear snippets of conversation, making for some fun non sequiturs: "I would like an eyebrow . . . under my . . . chin."

Has any musical been more generous in giving each of its four leads a second-act showstopper? Amalia's "Ice Cream" was a response to Georg's being nice to her for the first time. Georg got the title song, in which he realized that Amalia was beginning to see him differently. Ilona's "A Trip to the Library" had her meet her new beau and Kodaly's "Grand Knowing You" was his grand exit in which he predicted that all Maraczek employees would one day be working for him. *She Loves Me*, instead of catching musical theater's most contagious disease—second-act trouble—only got better as it went along.

So why didn't it win? One reason was the fate that all the musicals in our next chapter endured, too.

CHAPTER THREE

*

The Party's Over: The Best Musical Tony Losers That Were Lame Ducks on Awards Night

She Loves Me did set one unfortunate record. It was the first Best Musical Tony nominee that had already closed before the awards were dispensed. Or, as they say in politics, a lame duck: one who's no longer in the running.

The 1967–1968 season was the first in which two lame ducks appeared: *Illya Darling* and *Hallelujah, Baby!* The latter won—the only time a lame duck did. Every other time, voters preferred to give the award to a show that could use the business. Why promote a product that customers can't buy?

But most of the lame ducks were, to be frank, not worthy of a Best Musical prize.

Its opening number stressed that life had its ups and downs, lows and highs. That was certainly true of this musical known as *Seesaw* (1973–1974).

"Nobody's goin' anywhere. Nobody's gettin' anywhere," the usually perky Dorothy Fields dourly expressed in her opening song. Had she written these lines in Detroit after *Seesaw* had opened to lackluster reviews? By the time it reached New York, Michele Lee, not Lainie Kazan, was playing dancer-drifter Gittel Mosca.

That was the first decision made by new director-choreographer Michael Bennett, who respectively took over for Edwin Sherin and Grover Dale—and, for that matter book writer Michael Stewart. Although Bennett didn't do much actual writing, he wasn't above taking credit for the book.

Bennett certainly proved Fields's lyric wasn't necessarily so: he was indeed going places. He'd win his second Tony for *Seesaw*'s choreography. How he would have loved the directing trophy, too. But Bennett knew he wouldn't get it—not after his former collaborator Hal Prince had turned that unworkable flop *Candide* into a hit.

Actually, Bennett came close to doing the same. Helping him was one of his favorite performers: the also-getting-somewhere Tommy Tune, yet another Detroit replacement (for Bill Starr). Tune played David, a dancer who yearned for the day that he could become a choreographer. That certainly happened for Tune—and then some, as his four eventual Tonys for choreography would attest.

In fact, Tune was more of an overachiever than his character: he's also won three Tonys for directing and two for acting—including this featured role in *Seesaw*. Considering that his first Broadway gig was in *Baker Street* in 1965 as "one of the Killers," he made good on the dictum stated in *Seesaw*'s big second-act number: "It's not where you start, it's where you finish."

Although New York gave *Seesaw* some bad reviews, *Seesaw* criticized New York, too. The seventies were dark times in Times Square, so the show commented on it in hopes that audiences would laugh at each urban atrocity. But how much mirth was there in one of the first stage directions: "Three tough-looking muggers enter. Two of the muggers grab Jerry Ryan and the first mugger holds a gun and reaches for Jerry's wallet." After they bolted, "Jerry looks around, but no one is in sight"—including the police, for whom he meekly called.

And to think that he'd just phoned Gittel Mosca, whom he'd met at a party, and had now invited to dinner. She, however, wouldn't be surprised when she had to pick up the check; she'd long ago established her own everything-happens-to-me persona. Regarding her ulcer: "Some people gotta jump off a roof to kill themselves. All I gotta do is eat one French fry."

Gittel was threatened that Jerry was a lawyer, and automatically assumed she wasn't right for him. "When you're born on Southern Boulevard in the Bronx, that's it for life," she myopically insisted. She certainly had survival skills (especially with bedbugs) and was intent on keeping a promise to herself that she "wouldn't sleep with God Almighty on the first date." And yet, Jerry's offhand mention of his birthday was enough for Gittel to make an exception. (Frankly, she was just as glad to have the excuse as he was.)

Give Jerry credit for waiting at least until morning to pour out his problems to her. His marriage to Tess was over because her father "took me into the firm, made me a partner, bought me a $60,000 love nest, which happened to be right next to his. A marriage tends to get a little shaky when the husband has to keep saying 'Thank you' each day."

He needed something new—such as Gittel. She worried, not because he was on the rebound, but because she was an all-encompassing fatalist: "I wonder why everything's gonna fall apart," she stated in what would become a self-fulfilling prophecy. Then she sang, "He's good for me, but I'm not good enough for him."

Why not let Jerry be the judge of that? But *Seesaw* had class distinctions on its mind. By 1973, that was a tired topic. So when Jerry was invited to a party that would be replete with lawyers, Gittel asked, "Am I what East Sixty-third expects you to be with?"

She didn't attend. Audiences preferred Ella Peterson in *Bells Are Ringing*, who came to just such a party and conquered her nervousness as well as the guests.

Jerry had his faults, too. He delayed telling Gittel that his divorce was final—lest she want more of a commitment. But she found out before he could tell her.

Not-so-good properties had all too often gone to the threadbare I-was-gonna-tell-you device—usually when creators could think of nothing better to do. But even the non-nominated *Subways Are for Sleeping* let audiences see well in advance that the heroine had planned to tell the hero the truth. Here, after Gittel had confronted Jerry, we had to take his word for it that he'd planned to come clean with her. Where was Jerry's song in a previous scene where he confided his plans to us so that we'd know he was on the level?

It's said that "they all go back to their wives," and indeed Jerry did. He believed Tess when she said that her father would no longer rule their lives. Gittel realized—or rationalized—that she was "way ahead" for having had this relationship.

The musical in which love was the main ingredient had for decades involved two couples for whom we came to care. It was a structure anointed by Rodgers and Hammerstein starting with Curly and Laurey, Will and Ado Annie, and continuing with Billy and Julie, Carrie and Mr. Snow, then Emile and Nellie and Cable and Liat. It had been a favorite of Tony-winning romantic musicals, too, from the first winner (*Kiss Me, Kate*: Fred and Lilli, Bill and Lois). So why didn't *Seesaw* have another couple?

Because the secondary character was gay. David didn't even get a last name, let alone a boyfriend. Although Bennett and Stewart were openly gay, even they didn't believe that 1973 Broadway audiences were ready to deal with two men in love. That would have to wait literally until a year and a day later, when a minor musical called *Sextet* started previews.

Stewart and Bennett's solution was to have David all consumed with his choreographic career. And while he was openly out, he was not quite proud. He mentioned that his father was more of a cook than his mother— "which is why I'm in a little bit of trouble today."

Putting David in a healthy gay relationship might have made *Seesaw* seem adventurous—enough to allow it to edge out *Raisin* as Best Musical. *Raisin*, so named merely to acknowledge (and capitalize on) its source material, *A Raisin in the Sun*, was at least a musical with serious and good-natured intentions, but it wasn't universally acclaimed and was beatable.

Yes, its characters took a courageous stand against racism at the final curtain, which was much more satisfying than seeing Jerry and Gittel, a couple for whom we were rooting despite the odds, break up. But the considerable number of gay Tony voters just might have tossed their votes to *Seesaw* if a relationship between David and a beau had been included and intelligently handled.

They called it *Cyrano: The Musical* (1993–1994), but *Cyrano: The Popera* would have been more apt. This Dutch-concocted entertainment certainly took its lead from the British megamusicals and looked woefully derivative.

This was not the first Tony-era musicalization of Edmond Rostand's 1897 verse drama. In 1973–1974, *Cyrano* received only two nominations: for star Christopher Plummer, who won, and Leigh Berry, his Roxana, who lost. There was no nomination for Anthony Burgess's literate book or Michael Lewis's more-than-acceptable score, which included "You Have Made Me Love," Roxana's ballad to Christian, one of Broadway's most beautiful unknown songs.

Twenty seasons later, *Cyrano: The Musical* received Best Musical, Best Book, and Best Score nominations for work that was far inferior to the previous *Cyrano*. It also got a Best Costume Design nomination, about which few would quarrel; the Dutch producer Joop Van Den Ende spent money as if he were Alexander H. Cohen. But even with the esteemed Sheldon Harnick lending a hand, *Cyrano* was dull.

* * *

In 1967, twenty years before they'd rewrite *Anything Goes*, Timothy Crouse and John Weidman were seniors at Harvard University writing the one hundred and nineteenth annual Hasty Pudding show.

A Hit and Myth took place in Beotia—pronounced B.O.-sha—a mythical Greek town in which a troupe of vestal virgins resided. These were not the best of times for the group. "In fact," sneered one of the Beotians to the head of the virgins, "I hear things are so rough that you're taking one- or two-timers. . . ."

The lowering of standards eventually went from Beotia to Broadway. There would have been a time when *Tango Argentino* (1985–1986) would have come to Broadway as an interim booking. A theater that had just seen the closing of a long-running hit and was marking time until a new musical took residence would take it in for a two- or three-week engagement. Now even a lame duck dance show had a shot at a Best Musical Tony.

And a genuine dance show that was still running just might *win* the Best Musical Tony as *Contact* did in 1999–2000. Providing the small amount of dialogue and the structure was the aforementioned John Weidman. What's more, among the three shows that *Contact* bested was a lame duck. And yet, only months before, tickets had been scarcer than ladies' room stalls before a Wednesday matinee.

That was when *James Joyce's The Dead* (1999–2000) opened at the 138-seat nonprofit Playwrights Horizons. Once this white-hot show moved to a 1,040-seat theater, a playgoer could find enough tickets at TKTS on any night to make his high-school reunion into a theater party.

The writers didn't provide the advance excitement. This was colyricist and composer Shaun Davey's first New York production. Although colyricist and book writer Richard Nelson's plays and adaptations appeared both on Broadway and off-Broadway, he'd never had a true hit.

Many assumed that Nelson would have one when he was asked to add a book to the through-sung London hit *Chess*. Instead, his libretto received plenty of criticism and was often cited as the reason for the musical's quick Broadway flop and no Best Musical Tony nomination.

The excitement for *James Joyce's The Dead* stemmed from the lead. Oscar-winner Christopher (*The Deer Hunter*) Walken would star. The rest of the cast was solid, too: Blair Brown, Sally Ann Howes, and famous ghost-voice artist Marni Nixon. Add in *Side Show* twins Alice Ripley and

Emily Skinner and recent Tony winners Stephen (*Angels in America*) Spinella and Daisy (*The Secret Garden*) Eagan. And who wouldn't want to see Brian Davies, who originated both Rolf in *The Sound of Music* and Hero in *A Funny Thing Happened on the Way to the Forum*, but hadn't appeared in New York for more than a quarter century?

Then theatergoers found it at best a lovely mood piece at a family Christmas gathering at which—as all of us know from experience—not much ever happens.

Walken, as the unhappily married Gabriel, took time out from his malaise to sing "Hail and cheer to our three graces" in honor of his Aunt Julia, Aunt Kate, and their niece Mary Jane (respectively played by Howes, Nixon, and Skinner), who had done the cooking. Howes, once glamorous and now oh-so-matronly, poignantly underlined one of Lorelei Lee's truisms: "And we all lose our charms in the end." Still, when Julia was commended for the way she used to sing and Howes said, "It *was* a lovely voice, wasn't it?" audiences had to acknowledge that it still was.

Much sadder was watching Mary Jane, smiling at Gabriel's toast but all the while realizing that she was fast turning into her maiden aunts.

Most of the numbers were performance numbers that the family sang together. True, such numbers in *Follies* are among the score's most exciting, but Davey and Nelson weren't up to Sondheim's standard, and couldn't have been expected to be. Not until the final half hour did the show deign to deal with numbers that drove the plot or explained it.

James Joyce's The Dead made its points quietly, and just as quietly disappeared. Even the boutique recording labels that produce most original cast albums rejected this one.

Side Show (1997–1998) started off by having the Geek, the Reptile Man, the Bearded Lady, and their colleagues sing, "Come Look at the Freaks." Henry Krieger's eerie melody showed how inured these people were to their fates. Even the way that book writer/lyricist Bill Russell described them in his script was purposely dehumanizing: he called them "Attractions."

"Colored Spade" in *Hair* shocked a good number of Caucasians who naïvely preferred to assume that blacks have no idea what disparaging names whites have for them. Here, these self-proclaimed "freaks" let audiences see and hear that they knew what "normal people" called them, too. And yet, who couldn't semi-identify with them? Haven't we all felt freakish from time to time? Aren't there many of us who have asked our-selves, as the main characters did, "Who will love me as I am?"

These characters were Daisy and Violet Hilton (1908–1969). In *Up in Central Park*, a 1945 hit, two characters sang that they were "Close as the Pages in a Book." Daisy and Violet were substantially closer, for they were conjoined twins.

The best they could do was join a side show. Their employer was so inhuman that Russell and Krieger wouldn't even give him a name: he was simply the Boss. He blatantly called Daisy and Violet "monsters" when entrepreneurs Buddy and Terry came around, and unfeelingly asked for "two bucks for ten minutes" to see "total exposure of the fleshy link."

Daisy and Violet, respectively played by the fetching Emily Skinner and Alice Ripley, were quite attractive (as opposed to the real Hiltons, who were on the dowdy side). Buddy saw the twins as an economic op-portunity, while Terry first and foremost regarded them as human be-ings. "There's something about those girls," he said sincerely.

Russell wisely gave them different personalities and, of course, a heightened amount of sibling rivalry. Violet was camera-shy; Daisy was camera-ready. Although Violet ideally wanted marriage and children and was attracted to Buddy, she was realistic about romance: "These are feel-ings you've got to hide," she told Daisy, who wasn't so sure.

At first, Daisy was much more interested in being "worshipped and celebrated . . . pampered and loved" by an adoring public who would ap-preciate her star quality. (Rose Hovick isn't the only person in this book consumed with dreams of vaudeville.) And yet, Daisy would form a romantic attraction with Terry, who was increasingly intrigued and attracted.

For that matter, Violet had a love interest, too, in Jake, a black side show employee. Making him African American allowed Russell to add some pre–civil rights issues; Violet told him that "the world won't let you" love a white woman. Jake had a good rebuttal: "If I can see past your affliction, why can't you see past mine?"

Violet couldn't, and wanted Daisy to give up her dreams of romance. "Leave Me Alone!" established how impossible life was for these two lit-erally living together. And after this bitter fight, they had to entertain the gawkers and insist that they were "two songbirds" with "zero friction."

Buddy and Terry were thrilled with their progress and kissed them. Daisy, ever the flirt, said, "If we always get kisses, I'll even try harder."

And while a kiss would not seem to be much on which to bring down a first-act curtain, under the circumstances, the one between Daisy and Terry was quite dramatic. Think of it as a variation on what Higgins said to Pickering about Eliza's offer to pay him a shilling for English lessons: "If we view a shilling not as a simple shilling but as a percentage of this girl's income, it works out as fully equivalent to sixty or seventy pounds from a millionaire."

Reporters started noticing that there might be something between Daisy and Terry. She joked with a reporter, saying that she couldn't get involved because "I'm already attached."

Robert Longbottom cleanly staged the show on sets of movable bleachers. After the British Invasion in which musicals had a tire ascend, a barricade built, a chandelier fall, and both a helicopter and a mansion rise, *Side Show* seemed to be skimping. Tickets to Broadway musicals were now up to seventy-five dollars, and while audiences never like paying high prices, they don't mind as much when they can see the money on the stage.

That wasn't the main reason that *Side Show* couldn't pass ninety-one performances. The audience was asked to agree with Daisy and think less of Terry for being reluctant to marry a conjoined twin. "Thought you were made of the stuff it would take," Daisy snarled.

Expecting a man to marry one woman and always—*always*—have another one right there is asking quite a bit of audiences. (And Stanley and Stella Kowalski thought *they* had in-law trouble.)

Russell should have had Daisy take a higher road. Sample dialogue: "I understand, Terry. I know it's a great deal to ask you to marry me. So instead, let me thank you for taking us away from the freak show and getting us into vaudeville. You made our lives so much better than they were, and I'll always love you for it." That would have been better than demanding, "Who is the freak here? The coward? The lout?"

If Daisy had been forgiving and gracious, audiences would have cried as copiously as an aging athlete who announces his retirement at a press conference. The decision that Russell made to conclude his show probably prevented it from becoming a popular success. Not that *Side Show* would have won Best Musical in its season of *The Lion King* and *Ragtime*. Still, if Russell had taken the time to rewrite, *Side Show* might have instead been delayed until the much weaker 1998–1999 season. With a more poignant ending, it might have beaten *Fosse*, the de facto winner over *The Civil War*, *It Ain't Nothin' But the Blues*, and *Parade*.

* * *

Parade (1998–1999) began the same way as *1776*, with a military drummer confidently playing. There was, however, a profound difference between the musicals. *1776* glorified those who forged a country that would offer liberty and justice for all. *Parade*, taking place 137 years later, showed that liberty and justice weren't always available to all. In the case of Leo Frank (1884–1915), anti-Semitism played the main role. Long before Hitler would persecute six million Jews, the people of Atlanta greatly mistreated one.

Leo, a longtime Brooklyn resident, had accepted a job at his uncle's pencil factory in Atlanta. Soon after he met Lucille Selig (1888–1957), they married. Book writer Alfred Uhry, the Georgia Jew who had written about a far more benign Atlanta in *Driving Miss Daisy*, took great dramatic license by changing one fact; he had Frank come to work for *her* uncle.

This was the backstory to April 26, 1913: Confederate Memorial Day, on which Atlanta always hosted a large parade. "Why would anyone want to celebrate losing a war?" Leo exasperatedly asked Lucille. He instead went to the factory to catch up on work, for Leo believed that a husband should be a good provider. Lucille admitted to herself that he was as "loyal and stable as any tree," but she wished that he'd be a better provider of sex.

En route, Leo passed the parade and wondered, "How Can I Call This Home?" He definitely felt like a fish out of water—but soon he would be placed in a fishbowl for all of Atlanta to see, as his name became inextricably linked with Mary Phagan.

Phagan (1899–1913) was a teen at the parade who innocently flirted with a young man named Frankie before deciding to go to the factory to pick up her dollar and twenty cents week's pay. Leo, the only executive around, gave it to her. Later she was found murdered, and janitor James Conley implicated Leo as the killer. Uhry stated that Conley had escaped from a chain gang, and was told that he'd be returned to it if he didn't tell all he knew.

Instead, Conley told all that he could invent.

Conley was black—a color not often welcomed in the early twentieth century South. And yet, at least in this case, a Jew was even more distrusted and hated.

That Leo wanted the crime kept out of the papers made the police suspect him. His motivation was to protect the factory, but in the rush to judgment, motives and facts weren't considered important.

Uhry interrupted the scene in which Leo was interrogated by having Mrs. Phagan arrive and say, "My daughter didn't come home last night." After the policeman said, "May I have your name, ma'am?" Uhry ordered a blackout, because he knew we'd inferred the mother's identity.

He should have kept writing. Having Ms. Phagan learn of Mary's fate while being face-to-face with the alleged killer would have been far more dramatic. The ensuing dialogue would have been more painful for an audience. Uhry's not writing it seemed like a pulled punch.

Composer-lyricist Jason Robert Brown erred by starting the next scene with reporter Britt Craig singing "Big News." Audiences inferred that Craig was talking about the Phagan murder. Actually, he wasn't yet aware of the crime; he was being sarcastic and complaining that nothing of substance ever happened in Atlanta. ("A kitten up a tree . . . the mayor's mother broke her toe.") Given that the Confederate Memorial Day Parade had just occurred, Craig should have referenced that in his song. Having him sing during the parade that *at last* there was some news would have helped.

However, setting up Craig as a frustrated newspaperman was a good idea, for it showed that he'd jump on any big story—which he'd soon get via Leo and Mary.

Pressure from the press caused Governor John Slaton to tell his district attorney Hugh Dorsey, "We gotta get to the bottom of this fast. You got a lousy conviction record, Hughie. How long do you think they're going to keep you in office if you let this one wriggle off the hook?"

So Leo was taken to jail, where Lucille immediately came to see him. That he was even *suspected* of murder filled him with righteous indignation. He was also repulsed by his surroundings. "Do you have any idea what spending the night here would be like?" he asked Lucille. Little did he know what audiences did: Leo would spend every night for the rest of his life incarcerated. Lucille, however, was still confident that this miscarriage of justice would be quickly rectified.

When she approached the authorities, she was full of umbrage. "But you don't say he's innocent," one responded. "I have nothing more to say," Lucille stated, acting haughty to show how insulted she was. That was read as evasive. Again we saw how the Franks didn't understand the severity of what they were facing. Leo was innocent in two ways: not only guiltless but also naïve.

Lucille said she wouldn't attend the trial because she couldn't face

67

Mary's mother. After Leo insisted that she had to attend for his sake, she found the courage to agree. But Uhry neglected to show the two women confronting each other.

At the trial, each witness was shown to have his own agenda. As Meredith Willson wrote in *The Music Man:* "Mass 'steria! Animal instincts!" Young Frankie reported that when Mary said she was going to get her pay, he said, "At least let me come over there," which she deemed unnecessary. This made him seem heroic, protective, and smart enough to see danger when she couldn't. What we'd actually heard him say to her was "Okay. See you around."

For the funeral, Brown aimed high by writing a melody that started out as a dirge, became a hymn, and then a cry of anger: "It Don't Make Sense." But to Leo, it *didn't* make sense. The ill wind that kept Leo in jail allowed Craig to flourish. The reporter admitted that Leo "saved my life."

Aside from one perfunctory "leading the witness" rebuke, the deck was stacked against Leo. Conley sang a gospel song without singing the gospel truth. To cope with her intense sorrow, Mary's mother rationalized that she did the right thing ("My Child Will Forgive Me") and yearned for the day when they would be reunited in heaven. As the hymn-like three/four time song continued, audiences increasingly felt her pain and mourned for her until she reached the last word of the song—when she looked at Leo and spat out the word "Jew!"

The most galvanic song had the factory girls sing that Leo was always trying to seduce them. In describing how Leo would say "Come Up to My Office," Brent Carver suddenly became the evil man they were describing—a lecher who sang his song of seduction replete with ominous bass notes and sinuously deft dance steps. It wasn't the real Leo at all, so the contrast was startling.

The big second-act opener had two blacks—he a shoe shiner and she a maid—glad to see that a white man would meet the hanging fate that so many of their people had come to know. Eerie, but understandable.

Not unlike the Baker in *Into the Woods,* Leo learned that "It Takes Two" to achieve a goal. Lucille approached Governor Slaton at a party. She interrupted him while he was flirting with the ladies, suggesting that he more than Leo was more likely to be involved with a sweet young thing. The song "Pretty Music" came to an end just as Lucille told Slaton that she was "Mrs. Leo Frank." The dead silence was potent. He didn't ask what she wanted, causing her to say, "You are either a fool or a coward."

That might have caused Slaton to do nothing, but he did relent a bit and commute Leo's sentence to life in prison. Given that Leo was at last allowed outside, Lucille decided on having an outdoor picnic to celebrate "a momentous occasion." In a nice Uhry detail, she brought her wedding china for the food.

Tony voters who scanned their programs in advance for a song list may well have been nodding when they saw "'All the Wasted Time'—Leo and Lucille." Sure, husband and wife would ruminate about the lost years that he'd spent in prison.

Brown was wiser. The wasted time to which he referred was the period before the murder, when the two spouses took each other for granted and didn't appreciate what they had. It was a sobering message for audiences whose marriages might have been on automatic pilot for some time, too.

And just as in *The King and I*—when the two lead characters had their greatest moment of happiness ("Shall We Dance?") before disaster struck (the captured Tuptim was brought in to face the king's justice)—Leo and Lucille had their last happiness before being parted forever. The first "I love yous" we ever hear them trade come fewer than ten minutes before the final curtain.

That Leo's prison was "minimum security" meant that breaking into it was easy, too. A lynch mob, furious with Slaton, arrived one night, abducting Frank and hanging him.

It was a dour ending to a musical. Uhry and Brown would have done better to have an epilogue such as the one seen in *Ragtime*. There, characters came forward to say what had eventually happened to them. *Parade* would have benefitted from our hearing that in 1982 an eighty-three-year-old former office boy implicated Conley as the real murderer; he said he'd seen him with Mary's dead body, but that his mother didn't want her fourteen-year-old son to get involved. Leo Frank was pardoned sixty-five years after his horrific death. Hearing this information wouldn't have made for a happy ending, but at least it would have been a happier one.

Parade played its scheduled limited engagement of eighty-five performances at the heavily subscribed Lincoln Center Theater, and had been closed for more than two months before Tony voters got their ballots. Enough voters chose Uhry for Best Book and Brown for Best Score—but they gave Best Musical to the revue *Fosse*.

* * *

Speaking of revues, the one mistake that so many make is not letting us get to know the characters as people. Who were the characters in *Blues in the Night* (1982–1983)? Woman number one, Woman number two, and Woman number three. Were they numbered in importance to the show? Social standing? Bank account balances?

In both *Tintypes* (1980–1981) and *A Grand Night for Singing* (1993–1994), each of the five performers was called "Performer." *It Ain't Nothin' But the Blues* (1998–1999) had eight cast members each called "Performer."

Quilters (1984–1985) took pains to name one character "Sarah," but six others were called "Daughter," three were called "Musician Daughter," two were called "Musician Son," while one was simply "Son." If a mother can't even bother to tell us her children's names, we're not going to be emotionally involved with them.

What's often been said about Best Musical Tony winner *Ain't Misbehavin'* is that director Richard Maltby, Jr., made it more than a revue by creating *characters* to sing Fats Waller's songs. Nell Carter played a woman who believed that concept of the Big Beautiful Woman, while equally ample Armelia McQueen was a little less secure. Andre De Shields was the dangerous man who was no stranger to drugs. Charlaine Woodard was the accomplished nightclub singer. Ken Page upheld the notion of the jolly fat man and was the official Fats Waller stand-in.

Indeed, many subsequent production have listed "Andre," "Armelia," "Charlaine," "Ken, and "Nell" as the characters, although other performers were playing the "roles."

Michael Leeds, who both wrote and directed *Swinging on a Star: The Johnny Burke Musical* (1995–1996), knew that character anonymity was one of the pitfalls of the celebrate-a-songwriter revue. So, for the most part, when chronicling the career of Johnny Burke (1908–1964), he not only gave his performers names, but characters to play, too.

A look at the program showed that in the opening sequence alone, we'd meet Mame, Reginald, Flora, and Cleo, the last of whom owned and emceed a 1929 speakeasy. She was about to introduce a song by a new songwriter. "What's the kid's name?" she had to ask her bandleader, who remembered: "Johnny Burke."

Clearly, however, this scene was set before October 29, when the Depression began and Leeds took audiences to the Bowery. Although here he didn't give his characters names, he gave them specific identities to play: The Polish Gentleman, The Housewife, and The Homeless Man, who was glad to find one red cent on the street. It was enough for him to sing "Pennies from Heaven."

Leeds then segued to a 1935 radio show. The announcer said, "We celebrate"—and was then purposely interrupted by the Harmonics, a girl group that smoothly sang "Johnny Burke" as if they were the two most glorious words in the English language, *including* "musical comedy."

The announcer then told us that Burke was "the only man to have five songs in the Hit Parade at the same time." Out came Buddy and Betty, the onstage and offstage sweethearts as well as star Vicky Vovay to do them all. (Truth to tell, Burke's five hits hadn't passed the test of time. Even those with the strongest memories of way back when could at best remember "An Apple for the Teacher.")

Then it was off to 1944 and a USO Show in the Pacific. Michael Mc-Grath was a perfect emcee, with Bob Hope's personality and dash, happy to introduce entertainers Buzz Albright and Lena George. Enlisted men have always loved eye candy, and that was provided by Miss South Dakota, Miss North Carolina, and, of course, Miss Rheingold.

Pulled onto to the stage was one shy GI. "What's your name, soldier?" yielded the answer "Eddie," and "You got a girl?" was answered affirmatively. Eddie got the chance to sing "Polka Dots and Moonbeams" to his girl back home before everyone got to sing that year's Oscar-winning hit: "Swinging on a Star."

Act two began in 1950 in the Hotel Roosevelt Ballroom in Akron, reminding us of when such cities still had nightclubs and populations that could afford and sustain them. "Imagination" and "It Could Happen to You" were two hits featured here. Then we returned to 1942 and the filming of *The Road to Morocco*, for which Burke had provided lyrics to James Van Heusen's music. And while the surnames Crosby, Hope, and Lamour weren't used, was there any doubt of the identities of the Bing, Bob, and Dorothy whom Leeds had named?

Leeds finished up with "Today: The Starlight Supper Club, Manhattan," a stand-in for the Rainbow Room, which was still in operation when *Swinging on a Star* was produced. (Akron isn't the only city that can no longer afford such clubs.) That it took place in the present underlined that Burke had written some standards: "But Beautiful," "Misty," and "Pennies from Heaven," still sung, to quote one of its lyrics "all over town."

So Leeds wasn't content to simply do one song after another, but found a novel way to track Burke's entire career: by answering the journalists five Ws of who, what, when, where, and why.

When a large picture of Burke flew in at show's end, audiences had already come to know him. A picture is said to be worth a thousand words; here a thousand words and lyrics and more than three dozen melodies had created just as good a picture of Johnny Burke.

So what, you say? *Swinging on a Star* didn't do any better at the Tonys than *Blues in the Night*, *Tintypes*, *A Grand Night for Singing*, or even the non–lame duck revue *It Ain't Nothin' But the Blues*. All got shut out from winning a single award.

Yes, but those other shows were produced in seasons when the Tony committees were desperate to fill the Best Musical category. On the other hand, the 1995–1996 season in which *Swinging on a Star* was produced had no dearth of high-profile shows. That the nominators chose *Swinging on a Star* in lieu of *Big*, *Victor/Victoria*, or *State Fair* showed their admiration for its having achieved its goals while the others, in their estimation, hadn't.

The nominators' choice also led to a witty display ad in the *Times* from spurned *State Fair* producer David Merrick: "When the Big Victor is announced, it won't be Fair."

All right, you say: explain the success of *Swing!* (1999–2000), which was hardly a lame duck on Tony night; it wasn't even halfway through its thirteen-month run, and it had twenty-seven performers called "Performer."

The key word is "twenty-seven." When that many people populate a musical revue, audiences don't expect to get to know anyone. Only the intimate revue seems to make that promise. Think of various parties you've attended. At a big, loud, and crowded one, you might have a good time, but you might not get to know anyone, or even expect to. But at an intimate dinner party, you'd assume you'd get to know at least a few facts about a few people.

Swing! however, offered a much bigger band and markedly more dance, allowing for much more to see and hear. Of all the revues named earlier, *Swing!* was not only the most populous—with more performers than all the others combined—but it also was the only one to have both a Best Director and Best Choreographer nominee: Lynne Taylor-Corbett. It was a great, big Broadway show that didn't happen to have a story line, that's all.

* * *

Bringing up the rear in the 2011 2012 Best Musical Tony race was *Leap of Faith*. Jack Newton was as phony as his new name: Jonas Nightingale. He claimed that he was a Man of God, but we'd seen too many preachers with feet caked with the dirtiest clay to believe that he was.

When Jonas got stuck with a broken truck in Sweetwater, Kansas, he told his entourage to "Rise Up!" and soon he had them doing just that in song. "I can make the rain appear," he sang to one of his confederates, before he shrugged and winced as if to say, "Do you think I can get anyone to believe me?" Given that he was a charlatan and his employees knew it, why did they sing "Rise Up!" when they really should have wised up?

"All we need is one score," Jonas said. So did *Leap of Faith*. Alan Menken's music was his dullest ever, even when he paraded out gospel numbers. Glenn Slater's lyrics had an occasional turn of phrase. "A fox like you don't fool a chick like me," sang a woman, before later adding, "You're like an open book that I put down by chapter two."

This woman was Marla, a combination of two characters that Janus Cercone had created for her 1992 film: Marva, a waitress, and Will, a sheriff who'd harass Jonas. That made for a nice surprise when Cercone and cowriter Warren Leight had Marla reveal to Jonas that she was Sweetwater's sheriff. But the book writers weren't wise to include the plot point that the town was experiencing a drought and that Jonas would claim to bring rain in a mere three days. One would expect professionals working in theater to have at least heard about *The Rainmaker*, if not *110 in the Shade*.

As Jonas, Raul Esparza worked hard and deserved a Best Actor Tony nomination. He sang strongly and brought to life the one-dimensional character. After Jonas was warned by one of these confederates that "These people have nothing!" he smugly grinned in case-closed fashion before exclaiming, "Exactly!" and drooling over the prospect of fleecing pigeons through "religion."

Like mother, unlike son. Jake, Marla's preteen who had been in a wheelchair and could not walk since an automobile accident had injured him and killed his father, needed to believe in Jonas. A more convincing scenario would have a lad who'd been so damaged from the accident that he couldn't remotely believe in anything any longer and would see through Jonas. But the story needed a believer, and Jake served.

Jonas asked Marla how much time had passed since the accident.

When she said she didn't know, he pressed her, and she admitted, "Three years, four months, and eight days."

The cliché that people calculate time so precisely is among literature's least convincing. The "x years, y months, and z days" structure is usually used to spur a cheap laugh; here, it was meant to show how deeply devastated Marla was, but it only wound up seeming phony. The writers would have done better to have Marla pause and somberly say, "It'll be three years on Thursday." But they were clearly desperate enough to include most anything that popped into their heads—such as having Jonas tell his followers, "Get out there and save their goddamn souls." It was meant to get a laugh of surprise because it incongruously mixed religion with profanity. It didn't.

Jonas worked in tandem with his sister Sam. She was cute, but the audience disliked her because she was sneakier than her brother. In advance, she did research on the townies which she relayed to Jonas through the earpiece he was surreptitiously wearing. When he came out with salient facts about them, the poor souls believed that he'd received his information from God.

"If he's a man of God, why does he need money at all?" Marla asked her duped townspeople. But her skepticism wasn't strong enough to keep the lonely widow, sex-deprived for a thousand days, from accepting Jonas's proposition.

Ah, well. Many good women have fallen for many bad boys. Utterly unconvincing, however, was the scene that took place après sex. Jonas stepped out of the house just as Jake wheeled by. The two guys had a long conversation—so long, in fact, that Marla came to the screen door where she listened to them. Why she didn't feel the risk of her son seeing her in Jonas's house? Never in the entire show did the kid find out about it, which made for a very strange red herring.

Back to business. Jonas insisted about the Sweetwater citizens that "If they don't get their miracle, they don't believe enough."

For a minute, *Leap of Faith*'s theme seemed to be that while Jonas had no affinity with matters of religious faith, he could give Marla the faith that she'd love again. As arresting a theme as that would have been, it wasn't exploited.

En route, *Leap of Faith* wanted to get its audience involved. At one point, it encouraged everyone to raise his arms; at another, to clap in rhythm—and to fill collection baskets. And when precious few theatergoers applauded in response to the question, "Anyone here believe in God?" they found that they'd been outfoxed when Jonas drawled, "I see we have a few out-of-towners here."

At one point, Jonas asked the audience, "Do you believe?" No, not when Jake started walking, the rain began falling, and he and Marla became a couple.

And yet, one of Jonas's associates said that everyone should appreciate the man. "We'd be on the street in rehab without him." It's the same type of thinking that gets people to say bad shows should stay open because so many people would be out of work if they closed.

But close is what *Leap of Faith* did after only twenty performances. Despite Jonas's proclamation that "Miracles happen every day," they appear with far less regularity on Broadway.

CHAPTER FOUR

*

You're Gonna Be Popular: *The Best Musical Tony Losers That Learned That Running Longer Is the Best Revenge*

We hear that when halftime arrives at the Super Bowl, an inordinate number of television viewers go to the bathroom, causing toilet-flushing to reach its apex.

During the Tony Awards broadcast, that would happen each time Isabelle Stevenson came on. She'd tell about the good deeds done by the American Theatre Wing, from educational programs to free tickets. From 1965 to 1998, Stevenson served as president of the Wing, which had been intertwined with the Tonys from the beginning. She became its chairwoman until her death on December 28, 2003.

This was some decades after she'd appeared in an edition of *Earl Carroll's Vanities*. (For those of you who *did* stay around to watch Stevenson's Tony speeches, can you picture Isabelle Stevenson singin' and dancin'?)

Stevenson represented the old guard of the Tonys, and when she died at 90, she may have left at the right time: a bit more than six months after *Hairspray* won. With the *possible* exception of *Billy Elliot* (2008–2009), she probably wouldn't have enjoyed any of the subsequent Best Musical Tony winners: *Avenue Q* (2003–2004), *Monty Python's Spamalot* (2004–2005), *Jersey Boys* (2005–2006), *Spring Awakening* (2006–2007), *In the Heights* (2007–2008), *Memphis* (2009–2010), *The Book of Mormon* (2010–2011), and *Once* (2011–2012).

Actually, Isabelle must have been unnerved as far back as *Hair* (1968–1969), with all its profanity, civic disobedience, and, of course, nudity. Needless to say, she couldn't relate to those characters who staunchly believed that marijuana was one of God's creatures.

The Biltmore Theatre, in which Mae West's *Pleasure Man* was shut down by the police, forty years later was the same theater to show full frontal nudity onstage.

Pleasure Man ran two performances. *Hair* amassed 1,750 and became the longest-running show that the Biltmore Theatre has ever had.

Hair had great impact, and not simply because of the rock music it introduced. It set the tone for the way that many shows would now come to Broadway. After Joseph Papp produced *Hair* to inaugurate his new Public Theatre downtown, it caught the eye of Michael Butler, a civilian who loved it so much that he decided to bring it to Broadway. Thus, he introduced the word "move" to a producer's vocabulary. Up until then, the theatrical luminary most likely to have used "move" was the director when he blocked his actors.

In terms of the Tonys, Butler moved it too late, opening the show two weeks after the deadline. Isabelle and her cronies must have breathed a sigh of relief. If it had been eligible for 1967–1968—that notoriously weak *Hallelujah, Baby!* season—it might have amassed enough votes to win. A year later, it was easy to brush it off as yesteryear's news while *1776* was the most recent musical to open.

But *Hair* ran longer. So did many other Best Musical Tony losers.

Only one show, before it closed, became the longest-running musical in Broadway history without the benefit of a Best Musical Tony Award: *Grease* (1971–1972).

Every other musical in the Tony era—*My Fair Lady, Hello, Dolly! Fiddler on the Roof, A Chorus Line, Cats*, and *The Phantom of the Opera*—had won the Best Musical Tony years before it set the record.

Grease lost every one of its seven nominations to *Follies, Two Gentlemen of Verona, Inner City*, and the revival of *A Funny Thing Happened on the Way to the Forum*. All four of those musicals rang up 1,389 performances—about 40 percent of what would become *Grease*'s then-record 3,388-performance stint.

Like *Follies, Grease* used a reunion as its jumping-off point. Jim Jacobs and Warren Casey took a look at Rydell High School's Class of 1959. But instead of showing us what the kids had become for better or probably worse in thirteen years, they spent fewer than ten minutes at the reunion, then flashbacked to high school days and never returned to 1972.

That was much more fun for the average theatergoer than *Follies*.

Not that the audience for each was remotely the same. *Follies* brought in the traditional longtime theatergoer who remembered the Berlin, Fields, Gershwin, Harburg, Kern, and the DeSylva, Brown, and Henderson songs that Sondheim expertly pastiched. *Grease* catered to those born during or after World War II. The older ones now had enough money to spring for a fifteen dollar theater ticket; younger men decided that just this once, they'd splurge and really impress a date (and perhaps afterward get what Kenickie got from Rizzo).

Most Tony voters found it crass and vulgar. Granted, the kids at Rydell High weren't as belligerent as the hippies in *Hair*—but voters weren't sending out welcome wagons. They were frustrated, for as 1972 began, *Hair* was winding down and would soon close. Now Broadway could get back to being Broadway.

But only twenty-three days before *Hair* shuttered on July 1, *Grease*, which had been slowly building a downtown audience, moved to the Broadhurst. Suddenly rock music had a new Broadway life.

In a way, *Grease* was more threatening than *Hair*. While both had songs that centered on dropping out of high school, most of the *Hair* characters seemed to be over eighteen, even well into their twenties. They were young men and women now, on their own, out of their parents' houses. No one ever mentioned a mother or father, for each kid had passed the point where parental authority was an issue.

The kids in *Grease* were still technically kids, under eighteen, although pushing it. While the musical never showed us a parent, the kids often alluded to them. Marty, one of the Pink Ladies (named for the cocktail, no doubt), mentioned that her mother would "kill" her if blood from an ear-piercing got on the rug. After Doody mentioned that his mother had made him a lunch, Roger sneered, "You mean your old lady dragged her ass out of bed for you?" Replied Doody, "She does it every year on the first day of school." Thus, we got the picture of a lower-middle-class household and a mother who wasn't Maria von Trapp.

Because the kids were younger than *Hair*'s, *Grease*'s less-than-lofty language—*snatch, shit, tit, gang bang*—may well have struck Tony voters as worse than *Hair*'s even more plentiful undeleted expletives. "Eat me!" hadn't before shown up in a Broadway musical. Some Tony voters might have even been upset by "Get bent!" until they realized that this was a euphemism for "fuck you!"—which would soon appear here, too. That

Marty—a Pink Lady—said it proved something that adults enjoyed saying at the time: "Today the girls are worse than the boys."

Marty even alluded to a teacher's sexually harassing her. Today such claims come as often as sunrises, but they were unheard of then, especially in what was supposed to be a nostalgically fun show. It may have been Marty's word against his, but later in the show, we did witness a middle-aged deejay trying to seduce her.

Into this maelstrom came young and innocent Sandy Dumbrowski, straight from a parochial high school. Although these were the days when parents tended to side with teachers in any dispute that their children would have with them, Sandy's father disagreed that her wearing patent leather shoes prompted boys to stare at them in order to get a peek at her panties. (Hmm, *Grease* began its life in Chicago; so did *Do Patent Leather Shoes Really Reflect Up?* a far less successful later musical. Did the authors of that show get the idea from this line in *Grease*?)

Sandy's summer vacation was a memorable one, because she'd met Danny Zuko; the two flirted and had had some fun times, although Sandy never let the romance get very far on the sexual barometer. Now she was surprised to see that he attended Rydell as well—and that he seems to have lost interest in her.

He hadn't. But his fellow Burger Palace Boys were right behind him, and in teenage union there was strength. Danny couldn't possibly show that any girl had any sway over him.

Sandy would. She challenged him when he mocked jocks: "They can do something you can't do." The next morning, Danny tried out for the track team and made it.

This plot twist must have pleased Isabelle and many other female Tony voters. As was always the case in musicals, the female was rehabilitating the male. Sarah did it with Sky, Maria with the Captain, and even Maria in *West Side Story* convinced Tony to stop the rumble.

Anyone who assumed that this was the first stage in Danny's rehabilitation was dead wrong. Danny quit the team. He returned to killing time with the Burger Palace Boys, whose "occupation" of stealing hubcaps was the closest they would ever get to winning silver medals.

And while Sandy initially railed against the Pink Ladies for "trying to make me look like just another tramp," she eventually decided that it was the best way to land her man. She became "a greaser's dream girl. A wild new hairstyle, black leather motorcycle jacket, skintight slacks, and gold hoop earrings," said Jacobs and Casey's stage directions.

They had a little more to say: "Yet she actually looks prettier and more alive than she ever has." Audiences agreed, while Tony voters probably didn't. Some of the latter must have recoiled in horror when Sandy then punched Patty Simcox—the nicest (if most pretentious) kid in town—and soon after said the now de rigueur "Fuck you!"

The Tony nominators couldn't have been pleased, but they had little else from which to choose. There were *Follies, Dont Bother Me, I Cant Cope* (yes, no apostrophes), and *Two Gentlemen of Verona*—the latter of which, yes, had rock, but with a more innocent sound.

What else could be the fourth nominee? Seven other of the season's new American book musicals had averaged fewer than twenty-two performances each. Two Israeli-themed shows managed a 159-performance average, but these goodwill imports were never taken too seriously at Tony time.

There *was* one other musical, and it was a certifiable hit: *Jesus Christ Superstar.* That the Tony committee chose *Grease* instead suggested that they preferred blasphemous low lifes to what was then considered a blasphemous approach to sacred material.

Say what you will about *Grease*, the craft in its lyric writing was substantially above Tony winner *Two Gentlemen of Verona*'s. Most every rhyme was perfect and virtually every accent was on the right syllable.

This may be a component of its marathon success; theatergoers have an easier time at musicals when they can understand the words, and rhymes help them to do so. One reason why *Spring Awakening*, the 2006–2007 Best Musical Tony winner, only ran a fourth as long (and in a smaller theater than any of the four *Grease* played) is that it had about five dozen imperfect rhymes. Every time an audience can't understand what's being said, that takes away a tiny bit of its enjoyment. The infractions add up; people can't get as involved in what's happening, and when they leave the theater, they decide the show was "all right," although they might have found it splendid had they been able to understand the words.

But *Grease*'s perfect rhymes may not have been the words that Tony voters most noticed.

Stephen Schwartz admits it. He didn't plan to attend the 1972–1973 Tony Awards, although his score for *Pippin* was one of the show's eleven Tony nominations.

"In those days," he said, "nominees actually had to pay for their tickets. So I decided not to go. Eventually [Tony Awards producer] Alex Cohen called to say that he hadn't yet received my check. I told him, 'I'm not paying seventy-five bucks to see Steve Sondheim win a Tony.'" Cohen thought all nominees should be in attendance, so he waived the price of Schwartz's tickets. Nominees have been comped in ever since. So Schwartz attended and indeed saw Sondheim win a Best Score Tony for *A Little Night Music*, which also won Best Musical.

Schwartz also had to witness Bob Fosse winning two Tonys, for *Pippin*'s direction and choreography. This had to be galling to Schwartz, because he and the legendary stager had not gotten along during rehearsals and tryouts. Perhaps that was another reason why he didn't want to attend. Schwartz certainly had the money. Although one doesn't get über-rich from writing an off-Broadway show, *Godspell* had given him a steady income for almost two years when the 1972–1973 Tonys rolled around, and he'd had five months of solid royalties from *Pippin*.

Add in fifty-one more months of royalties after that. No, *Pippin* couldn't best *A Little Night Music* at the Tonys: the ever-growing reputation that Sondheim was acquiring had to be acknowledged by giving him a hat trick of three consecutive Best Scores. But *Pippin* outran *A Little Night Music* by more than a three-to-one margin.

Although Pippin was the son of Charlemagne, head of the Holy Roman Empire in the late eighth century, Schwartz and book writer Roger O. Hirson wanted contemporary teens to identify with the lad's aimlessness: Pippin went to war with men, to bed with women, and used revolutionary means to right what he perceived were his father's wrongs. Nothing stuck. And yet, when he was given the chance to rule, his head was uneasy when he wore the crown. En route, he got a little nonhelp from his nonfriend the Leading Player (Ben Vereen) who encouraged his suicide.

Then Pippin met Catherine, a single mother. Soon he saw the value of mentoring a child and making him and his mother happy. Pippin came to realize that being a spouse and parent may mean an unexciting day-to-day life, but it was nonetheless a worthy and noble one.

Schwartz's work was, as one of his songs went, "extraordinary" from his dazzling opening, "Magic to Do," to a finale, which started in a most atypical waltz tempo. His ballad for Pippin, "Corner of the Sky," wistfully contained the longing and urgency that searching teens have. "Spread a

Little Sunshine" was sinuous in establishing Fastrada, Charlemagne's second wife—the one who marries only for better and never for worse.

Back to *Spring Awakening*, which used the same anachronistic rock approach—it took place in the 1890s—and had a similar theme about kids trying to find themselves. So why did it run less than half as long in a theater with 350 fewer seats?

To be fair, *Spring Awakening* was more difficult for audiences. Stephen Sater's adaptation of Frank Wedekind's controversial 1891 play included masturbation, a father sexually abusing his daughter, masochism, sadism, suicide, and abortion. While *Spring Awakening* complained about "The Bitch of Living," *Pippin* heard his grandmother celebrate life by singing, "Oh, it's time to start living"—her paean to enjoying life to its fullest.

But while the average theatergoer doesn't know what music sounded like in *Pippin*'s ninth century, he does have a sense of what music in *Spring Awakening*'s nineteenth century sounded like. *Pippin* was more stylized: it didn't rely on realistic sets and costumes; *Spring Awakening* did. As for the book, only *Follies*' libretto has been more unjustly maligned. Hirson's took audiences everywhere they needed to go and made firm points along the way.

Did Pippin himself ever feel satisfied? Whether he did or not, the show that bore his name certainly satisfied audiences from the end of 1972 to the middle of 1977. When it closed at 1,944 performances, only six musicals had ever run longer.

The Best Little Whorehouse in Texas (1978–1979) wound up running three times longer than Sondheim's Tony-winning masterpiece *Sweeney Todd*. Sanitizing a potentially unsavory subject did the, you should pardon the expression, trick.

Book writers Larry L. King and Peter Masterson, along with songwriter Carol Hall, worked hard to normalize the Chicken Ranch as "a green Texas glade where the trees were as coolin' as fresh lemonade."

They elevated their characters, too. Miss Mona (Carlin Glynn) stressed that there was "nothin' dirty goin' on" and insisted that her employees keep their "language clean." More to the point, there was to be "no whips or rough stuff" and "no three or more in a bed."

After Miss Mona had accepted a new applicant—only called Shy, a name that hardly suggested a prostitute—she sang to her, "Girl, You're a

Woman," concluding with the line, "Girl, I think this is your lucky day." It was delivered in the same way an executive says to the new college graduate he's interviewing, "Well, you're a bright lad. Can you start Monday?"

The Chicken Ranch customers were football players from Texas A&M University who had just won their biggest game of the year. Thus, we didn't think of them as sleazy, but just as young, spirited kids, some of whom were having their first sexual experience. Undoubtedly, the Chicken Ranch accommodated late-middle-aged men who were cheating on their wives, but the musical never dwelled on them.

In fact, the person who looked the most foolish was the one who wanted to close the house. The authors' take was that TV muckraker Melvin P. Thorpe was really out to make a name for himself.

It was all undistinguished fun, especially thanks to Tommy Tune's inventive staging. With not enough of a budget to hire a stage full of chorus girls, he had yokes built for the ones he had. Then he had a doll suspended on each side, so one chorus girl would come across as three. What had been a liability had suddenly become an asset.

None of this was enough, however, to unseat the prestige and achievements of *Sweeney Todd*. *Whorehouse*'s presumed second-place finish was apt.

At 5,461 performances when it closed, *Disney's Beauty and the Beast* (1993–1994) has played the most performances of a musical that did not win the Tony; however, it never became the longest-running musical Tony loser while its curtain was up. *Mamma Mia!* will surpass it if it can stay around until February 2015.

In one way, *Disney's Beauty and the Beast* will probably never be bettered: in its ratio of performances that a Best Musical Tony loser played compared to the number that the Best Musical Tony winner amassed. With Stephen Sondheim's *Passion* running a mere 280 (at a theater with 650 fewer seats), that ratio stands at more than nineteen and a half to one.

So how could *Disney's Beauty and the Beast* lose? This one's a real head-scratcher. Clearly it would have been more welcome on the road—as it was for years—than *Passion*, which never had a single road company.

That *Beauty*'s tale was more upbeat would seem to have been an asset. An angry prince who was seemingly doomed (as was everyone who worked for him) redeemed himself. Compare this to what *Passion* offered: a reclusive woman who fell so hard for a man that she stalked him incessantly.

We were never on her side, and when she won out, we weren't particularly happy that she did.

Did the voters feel that the sixty-four-year-old Stephen Sondheim wasn't getting any younger and that this would be his last new musical on Broadway? (In fact, it was.)

Still, there's no denying that word on *Passion* during previews wasn't strong and that audiences were laughing in the wrong places. The show had less than zero youth appeal, of which *Disney's Beauty and the Beast* had plenty.

That Disney wanted its name as part of the title might have alienated some voters. Why couldn't it just be *Beauty and the Beast?* Tony winner Tom (*Fiorello!*) Bosley—a TV icon from *Happy Days*—had an important role, but one would never know it from the advertising. The company was implying that it and it alone wanted to be the star. But so did David Merrick on *42nd Street*, and *that* won the Best Musical Tony.

Was it that the show looked cheap? That was unexpected from a company that had the deepest of pockets. The many old-fashioned backdrops appeared to have been taken from a warehouse where the sets from old Shubert operettas had gone to die. If we couldn't depend on Disney to challenge the look of the British megamusicals, who could we rely on?

Perhaps the voters didn't want to vote for such a literal translation of a popular film. Composer Alan Menken, now collaborating with lyricist Tim Rice since the death of longtime partner Howard Ashman (1950–1991), did add seven songs to the nine he wrote for the original film. And yet, it still seemed that the beloved 1991 film—the first animated film to be nominated for a Best Picture Oscar—had all too literally been plunked on a stage.

If these were mistakes, Disney learned from them. Three and a half years later, when it opened *The Lion King*, it ensured that it resembled the film as little as possible. It wound up winning the Best Musical Tony—unfortunately in the season that *Ragtime* should have won.

In the fifties and sixties, parents gave their opinions to their children about rock 'n' roll: "Your music won't last."

They were right about such songs as "Teach Me How to Shimmy," "Shoppin' for Clothes," and "D. W. Washburn." Other songs, such as "Hound Dog," "Loving You," and "Jailhouse Rock," have mostly survived because Elvis Presley recorded them. However, "Kansas City," "Stand by Me," and "Dance with Me" have stayed around.

And while it's unlikely that no bride or groom has chosen "Poison Ivy," "Yakety Yak," or "Charlie Brown" as their first dance as man and wife, many a married, divorced, or single person who grew up in the fifties and sixties has certainly enjoyed hearing these songs again three decades later. By 1994–1995, these middle-agers were affluent enough to buy theater tickets—which is why *Smokey Joe's Cafe* (1994–1995) was a smash.

Stephen Helper and Jack Viertel's original concept was to have a cast of nine sing three dozen songs by Jerry Leiber and Mike Stoller. There was an occasional tangential link: after Victor Trent Cook demanded of B. J. Crosby "Treat Me Nice," she sneeringly responded, "You ain't nothin' but a hound dog."

No generation throughout history has been as intent on keeping youthful as the baby boomers. Songs that are as far off as their youth are greatly welcome. And because boomers had been reared on rock concerts in arenas, a Broadway house was much more intimate and offered better sight lines to see a set that would have fit in a U-Haul.

Any note that was held for an inordinate length of time got cheers. But just in case the audience wasn't inclined to applaud in rhythm at the finale, "Stand by Me," each cast member walked to the lip of the stage, raised his hands high over his head, started clapping in rhythm, and gave the audience a curt nod of the head—the universal symbol, "Now you have to clap in rhythm, too."

In their opening night reviews of *The Music Man* in 1957, critics noted that the audience clapped in rhythm midway through "Seventy-six Trombones." None mentioned that Robert Preston walked to the lip of the stage and demanded that it happen. The audience applauded in rhythm because it *wanted* to clap.

Decades ago, longtime Broadway observer Howard Gradet postulated a theory: one cannot go forty-eight hours without running into a reference to *The Wizard of Oz*.

He's got a point. In the next two days don't be surprised if you hear someone quote or paraphrase from the beloved 1939 film. It might be "lions and tigers and bears," "Pay no attention to that man behind the curtain," or "We're not in Kansas anymore." Many a boss will be referred to as "The Wicked Witch of the West," and on the day she or he is fired, employees will gleefully sing "Ding-Dong! The Witch Is Dead."

No question, however, that running into a *Wizard of Oz* reference every two days has become substantially easier since *Wicked* became the runaway hit of 2003–2004.

Writer Gregory Maguire had to be grateful to MGM makeup artist Jack Dawn (1892–1961). If Dawn hadn't thought to put Margaret Hamilton in green facial makeup for her role as the Wicked Witch of the West, Maguire might not have had his life-changing novel.

Like all of us, Maguire had known the film since childhood. He, however, had a good deal of sympathy for a girl who was born with green skin. Someone with that affliction would be shunned by kids and adults. Wouldn't that be enough to turn a person antisocial?

In 1995, Maguire brought his feelings to light in *Wicked*. He named the girl Elphaba after L. Frank Baum's initials, and, to stack the deck more against her, made her illegitimate. The book caught the eye of composer-lyricist Stephen Schwartz, whose Broadway career had started off strong: he wrote the title song to the 1969 comedy *Butterflies Are Free* before unleashing three smash hit musicals: *Godspell*, *Pippin*, and *The Magic Show*. The four racked up 7,643 perfomances.

The next three—*The Baker's Wife*, *Rags*, and *Working*—amassed a total of twenty-eight performances, with the first of the trio not even making it to town.

Not that Schwartz was hurting; he'd won Oscars for his contributions to *Pocahontas*, *The Hunchback of Notre Dame*, and *The Prince of Egypt*. But Broadway wouldn't have been surprised if he'd never had another new musical on a New York stage.

Schwartz, however, had the resiliency of the unsinkable Molly Brown and the smarts of Mayer Rothschild. He entrusted Broadway neophyte but Emmy-nominee Winnie Holzman to write the book. The result was a musical that has already doubled the run of his previous long runner, *Pippin*. Indeed, the possibility exists that *Wicked* alone will outrun all six of Schwartz's previous Broadway attractions lumped together. (Look for that to happen in 2022—and don't bet against it.)

So how did this juggernaut *not* win the 2003–2004 Best Musical Tony? Most everyone thought *Wicked* had it in the bag. But a hole might have been poked through the bag on May 12, 2004, at John's Pizza, a restaurant on West Forty-fourth Street. There the producers of *Avenue Q* threw a pizza party for the out-of-town Tony voters. *Wicked* and no other musical thought to do so. Suddenly two hundred or so road voters felt very important and appreciated. Some traded their votes for a slice or two of pepperoni—or even plain.

Make no mistake about it, *Avenue Q* was an excellent musical. When it stopped giving Broadway performances in September 2009—and immediately resumed them off-Broadway—only seventeen Broadway musicals had run longer.

So perhaps it wasn't the pizza. After all, *Avenue Q*'s reviews were stronger.

A look at *Wicked* does explain why its reviews were mixed. The opening number, "No One Mourns the Wicked," was strangely somber sounding. Given that everyone in Oz once joyously sang "Ding-Dong! The Witch Is Dead" after the Wicked Witch of the East had died, why did they drone such a doleful song after her terrifying sister had been killed?

This was ameliorated, however, by the Good Witch's entrance in a bubble, as Billie Burke had arrived in the film. Kristin Chenoweth looked to the bubble born as Galinda—not Glinda, as we'd known her all our lives. (The reason for that would eventually be explained.)

Galinda flashbacked to the exposition on how Elphaba (Idina Menzel) was born green. Holzman condensed Maguire very well here and throughout the show. Soon we were at, as everyone sang, "Dear Old Shiz," the university that both Elphaba and Galinda were attending.

("Shiz," however, is a funny word that sounds perilously like a profane one. How surprising that set designer Eugene Lee didn't add a horizontal banner that said "Shiz University," so that the audience would immediately know that Shiz was a school.)

Elphaba was enrolled primarily to care for her sister Nessarose, who has lived her life in a wheelchair. If that sounds dour, Holzman made the character far less severely impaired than Maguire, who made her armless.

Holzman also offered a new spin on the language of Oz—including a number of made-up words ("rejoicify") that added a syllable here, a syllable there. What a shame that choreographer Wayne Cilento couldn't find an equally distinctive style in how Ozians moved. Joe Mantello fared better as director. It wasn't a superbly inspired staging, but it got the job done in George Abbott fashion.

Galinda was furious that she'd been assigned Elphaba as a roommate; as the most popular girl in school, she felt entitled to someone "better."

This incited Elphaba's anger and magic powers, which teacher Madame Morrible noticed. She told Elphaba that she just might be useful to the Wizard of Oz. That gave Elphaba something to live for, and Schwartz the opportunity to write one of the show's strongest songs. "The Wizard and I" made us immediately and squarely land on the character's side. Menzel's astonishing delivery added to the glorious experience.

Galinda's first steps to becoming Glinda came from Dr. Dillamond, literally a goat, albeit a learned one, who, like all animals in Oz, could speak. He mispronounced Galinda as Glinda because some force was causing animals to lose their powers of speech. Elphaba decided she'd help him when she met the Wizard.

Pretty Galinda was pursued by two students, Fiyero and Boq. She was more interested in the former, so she told the latter to be nice to Nessarose. Boq did, figuring that his gallantry to the physically challenged girl would impress Galinda and she'd come to love him. We would see.

Galinda decided to teach Elphaba how to be "Popular." Schwartz once again proved that he was still the best Broadway had in writing a bubbly and bouncy pop song that also served character. Galinda did like to "flounce," as she said, and the melody did, too.

But how many theatergoers picked up that after Galinda sang of wanting to give Elphaba "personality dialysis" the next line contained "a pal, a sis[ter]"? That was awfully hard to understand, especially at the breakneck pace the song kept.

And yet, Schwartz was delightfully clever near the song's end. Galinda insisted that Elphaba would soon cease to be "dreary who you were" before having to admit "are." Then she rhymed "were" with "popu-*ler*," the way many people tend to say it, before correcting herself to "popu-*lar*," to rhyme with "are."

When Galinda and Elphaba met the Wizard, the latter showed him her powers, putting wings on a monkey (and reminding audiences of a vivid image from the 1939 film). This wouldn't be the only monkey they'd encounter; when the Wizard showed both young women a cage's worth, Elphaba inferred that he and Madame Morrible were behind the plot to rob animals of their powers.

This Wizard belied what Frank Morgan had told us in the film: that he was "a very good man" who was "a very bad wizard." *Wicked*'s Wizard was bad on both counts.

Galinda knew it, too. But she wasn't the type to fight the establishment. Elphaba was, and soon became an enemy of the state, which made Ozians think that she was a "Wicked Witch." That Elphaba decided to escape only exacerbated the belief.

Here Elphaba flew. Although almost a half century had passed since Mary Martin had zoomed over and across the stage as Peter Pan, the decision here was to simply hook Menzel's back to apparatus that had her fly upward, but nowhere else. Just as *Miss Saigon* had disappointed many with its vertical-rising helicopter that did not fly across the stage, many of *Wicked*'s theatergoers had to be frustrated that Menzel made essentially the same trip.

Act two made a solid political commentary: a corrupt government can make its citizens believe what it wants. Galinda showed more spirit than expected when she officially changed her name to Glinda in order to honor Dr. Dillamond. These were all smart choices, as was the one that turned Boq into the Tin Man. When he finally realized that his attention to Nessarose would *not* make Glinda love him, he abruptly broke Nessarose's heart—making her magically take his from him. It's why she became known as "the Wicked Witch of the East."

Morrible was more horrible, for she arranged for a house from Kansas to come to Oz via a tornado, specifically to kill Nessarose. (Not unlike Hamlet in *Rosencrantz and Guildenstern Are Dead*, Dorothy Gale made only a cameo appearance.)

Fiyero came to love Elphaba, making him the Wizard's enemy, too. After he was captured, Elphaba tried her magic and turned him into a scarecrow; thus, when the Wizard's soldiers stabbed him, it had no effect.

What of the Cowardly Lion? Elphaba had protected a lion cub way back when, and that led to his being coddled throughout life. The message was that everyone must let a child face adversities at times or else he'll never grow to face reality. However, not having him as a main part of the action seemed wrongheaded.

The most important message of all was that Elphaba and Glinda came to respect and love each other—that each had changed the other "For Good." Thus, teenage girls—especially ones who hadn't yet found any degree of popularity—attended *Wicked* time and time again, because they loved hearing that hate at first sight could be turned around one hundred and eighty degrees.

And while we all knew before we entered the theater that the Wicked Witch dies, Holzman and Schwartz made us believe that Elphaba's death was a carefully planned ruse.

But why, when the Wizard mentioned "philanthropists," did he pronounce it perfectly? Considering that the Wizard we'd always known had said, "Back where I come from there are men who do nothing all day but good deeds. They are called phil-er-phil-er-er—good deed doers," *Wicked*'s Wizard should have had trouble with "philanthropists," too.

During Thanksgiving week, 2009, *Wicked* was the first show to gross more than two million dollars for eight performances. This record was smashed in five weeks' time during the always white-hot Christmas-to-New Year's week, but the following September (thanks to higher prices, of course) it eclipsed that mark.

So without a Best Musical Tony and some nagging problems in its book and songs, how has *Wicked* done so exceptionally well?

Perhaps because none of us can go forty-eight hours without being reminded of *The Wizard of Oz*—and we'll take this opportunity to be near it once again.

Mary Poppins (2006–2007) told the truth when she told the Banks family, "I wasn't born just one minute before I walked into your home." She'd been around since P. L. Travers had created her in 1934 as the nanny to the dysfunctional Bankses.

She'd reached her apotheosis in 1964. Walt Disney made his film version with Julie Andrews in the first of her two significant nanny roles. Forty years on, a musical version would open in London, where it would run three years—less than half of the Broadway run. Mary said, "I'll stay till the wind changes." She lasted 2,619 performances.

Mary didn't only have that famous English reserve, she was also a genuine dispenser of tough love. When little Julia Banks said, "I'm not sure I like strawberry ice," Mary responded, "I'm not sure I care."

Frankly, Mary's personality could have used some spoonfuls of sugar. Yes, what she ultimately gave Julia was a flavor she liked, but Mary did make the child think that she'd have to endure a taste she didn't.

Although Mary said, "There's no one as hard to teach as the child who knows everything," audiences were in their rights to ask, "What about you?" When the Banks children challenged her with, "You think you know everything," she responded, "I could not agree more."

At one point, Mary left without telling the kids. Fraulein Maria did that, too, but she had good reason: she felt she was coming between the Captain and his fiancée. Mary's decision seemed somewhere between arbitrary and mean. When she returned, Michael asked, "How do I know you won't leave again?" Her less-than-satisfactory answer was "You don't."

As a result, the musical was a jolly holiday *despite* Mary. She had about as much patience as a hand grenade whose pin has just been pulled. A score that has substantially more than a truckful of sugar didn't really suit her sour personality. There's an apt four letter word to describe Mary: pill.

Most of the Sherman Brothers' film score remained, including that one named for a word that really is quite atrocious. (They didn't invent it; the brothers picked it up from an already recorded pop song of the early fifties.) Buttressing the score were new songs by George Stiles and Anthony Drewe. One was terrific, and inspired by Mary's measuring tape that decreed that she was "Practically Perfect."

Mary deemed herself as "fairly pretty." So was the show. A set designer can never go wrong by designing a black, white, and gray set that will then change into an identical one in color. Bob Crowley knew that, and did it well when Bert took us into his paintings. Even Queen Victoria got into the act. The spectacle was probably the closest we'll ever get to that 1903 *Babes in Toyland*. And, in an era where audiences saw many performers wearing cheek microphones, their seeing cheeks adorned only with muttonchops was a refreshing change.

"Anything can happen if you let it" was the show's big message. So did coproducers Disney and Cameron Mackintosh not "let" it win Best Musical?

Some Tony voters are always reluctant to award Best Musical to a show with secondhand music. Increasingly, however, these voters were getting little choice. As of *Mary Poppins'* opening, seven of the previous nine Best Musical Tony winners had included songs that had been heard, either in part of in full, long before they'd hit Broadway.

Others Tony voters resented Disney's success, not to mention Mackintosh's. Independent of each other, they can now boast of having sponsored five of Broadway's eight longest-running productions. The resentment may have doubled when these two giants joined forces to produce *Mary Poppins*.

In fact, umbrage against producers may have cost many shows their Best Musical Tony Awards as we will see in the next chapter.

CHAPTER FIVE

*

Step to the Rear: *The Best Musical Tony Losers That May Have Suffered Because of Their Producers*

Spending twenty-five million dollars on a musical means that audiences should easily see that money on stage. *Shrek* (2008–2009) delivered the goods in that respect: castles, forests, gloriously witty costumes, and a nice large cast. But a price tag of twenty-five million also suggests to Tony voters that they're going to see the best musical ever.

They instead decided that *Shrek* wasn't even the best musical of its season.

It wasn't a bad show. Of course it had a tough act to follow, with that 2001 Best Animated Feature Oscar winner (and its nearly half a billion gross).

That book writer/lyricist David Lindsay-Abaire and composer Jeanine Tesori slavishly followed the film's template made it seem a little dull. Once again, Shrek was an ogre whose lack of looks made people fearful of him, which made him rationalize that he didn't need anyone or anything.

He did step up to the plate, however, when Princess Fiona needed rescuing. She'd always been told that she would be "rescued by my true love," and was aghast when an ogre showed up to save her. In time, she and audiences saw that her true love did indeed save her.

Meanwhile, the evil Lord Farquaad was determined to win Fiona. The lights turned green as he sang "Nobody is ever gonna bring me down" to the melody of "Defying Gravity" from the 2003–2004 Best Musical Tony loser.

This is desperation of the first order. Nine times out of nine point nine, a musical that references and spoofs, however gently, a big hit turns out to be a far less successful show. It signals that it will do anything for a laugh that it can't manage to find otherwise.

There was also too much déjà vu, down to using the ole (and irrelevant) Monkees' hit "I'm a Believer" at show's end.

That DreamWorks could blithely write a check for twenty-five million must have irritated some Tony voters who were also producers. They knew that they wouldn't be able to raise that much even if they'd had the time commensurate with both the London and Broadway runs of *The Phantom of the Opera*. That resentment had to have cost votes.

Tony voters *usually* reward a great show regardless of the producer. But if there's any reason to withhold a vote from a fat cat—or a nasty one—the voters will be happy to check off the box next to another show's name.

The figure of twenty-five million had come into play eighteen years earlier. It was the amount of the advance sale that theatergoers had given Cameron Mackintosh for his *Miss Saigon* (1990–1991) months before it was set to open in April 1991. The word from London was that strong for this show written by the *Les Misérables* team.

Adding to the excitement was that two London cast members would come to Broadway in this update of *Madama Butterfly* set in seventies Vietnam. Lea Salonga would again play Kim, the Asian bar girl who had a child by an American soldier. Jonathan Pryce would reprise his Eurasian "Engineer" who seized the opportunity to be with Kim because her half-American son would help him get to the United States. Said to be most impressive was the scene set on April 30, 1975, when the North Vietnamese controlled the city. A helicopter actually flew in and took away those desperate to leave the country.

Then Alan Eisenberg, the executive director of Actors' Equity Association, was desperate to keep Pryce and Salonga from leaving the country and coming to New York. "The casting of a Caucasian actor made up to appear Asian is an affront to the Asian community," Eisenberg said. "The casting choice is especially disturbing when the casting of an Asian actor in the role would be an important and significant opportunity to break the usual pattern of casting Asians in minor roles."

This became, as they say in Southampton, *quite* the pissing match between Eisenberg and Mackintosh. The producer eventually announced that he would cancel the production and return the twenty-five million.

That made Eisenberg blink—many times, in fact. Denying *Miss Saigon* to the American public wasn't good public relations. What's more, the show could conceivably run a decade, and Pryce and Salonga obviously wouldn't perform it remotely that long. Once they left, there would be plenty of opportunities for Asian Americans.

So Eisenberg and Actors' Equity caved in. But the resentment may well have stayed around when the Tony voters got their ballots. Mackintosh also had the effrontery to charge a hundred dollars for a front mezzanine seat. Not an orchestra seat, mind you, but one in the front mezzanine. (Theater tickets were now more expensive than speeding tickets.)

Why the premium price for *upstairs* seats? The helicopter, it was said, was best seen from that vantage point. Wherever theatergoers saw it didn't matter: the helicopter was nothing special. After all the hype, Tony voters must have anticipated seeing a full helicopter from bubble front to tail fin zooming across the entire expanse of the stage. They *had* to be disappointed when they were given only the front of the machine facing the fourth wall, and rising a not much greater distance as the elevator in *Sweet Charity* had ascended a quarter century earlier.

Actually, the agony on the faces of those who were left behind as this very last chopper left Saigon was more impressive. Human emotion triumphed over and trumped technology.

But the Tony voters gave the Best Musical prize to *The Will Rogers Follies*, a nice enough musical but no world-beater. It managed to run a quarter as long as *Miss Saigon*—the first show to run four thousand performances and not win a Best Musical Tony.

On the other hand, voters awarded Pryce, Salonga, and Hinton Battle (as a GI) Tony Awards. Perhaps *Miss Saigon*'s message was too painful for those who spent the late sixties and early seventies staunchly protesting the war in Vietnam. Those who felt that Americans were victimizing the Vietnamese saw Chris, an American serviceman, ultimately causing a Vietnamese woman pain from which she would never recover.

The Tony-winning *South Pacific* made an easier choice with Lieutenant Cable by killing him. If Hammerstein hadn't, would Cable have done to Liat what Chris did to Kim: abandon the woman he supposedly loved? Granted, the two shows were written more than four decades apart, and *Miss Saigon* did have the benefit of two decades to reflect on its events; *South Pacific* had had only a few years. And yet, one reason that *South Pacific* doesn't seem as convincing today is because the much more honest *Miss Saigon* trumped its Pulitzer Prize–winning ace.

* * *

Although many resented Disney's corporate presence with *Beauty and the Beast*, all was forgiven only four years later, when Disney's *The Lion King* won Best Musical.

How much of this, however, had to do with bigger resentment toward *Ragtime*'s producer?

Garth Drabinsky's publicly owned company, Livent, Inc., built a new theater for his show, and wouldn't deign to use "ordinary" Playbills, but would print his own. Drabinsky also offered a $125 VIP ticket that offered free drinks, access to a private lounge, and bathrooms, he promised, that wouldn't be as crowded.

If the Tony voters were reacting against Drabinsky, that was a terrible shame. *Ragtime* (1997–1998) was the superior musical, thanks to book writer Terrence McNally, composer Stephen Flaherty, and lyricist Lynn Ahrens.

McNally was, of course, the old pro of the group; Flaherty was still in his terrible twos when the playwright saw his first work on Broadway. How well McNally distilled a difficult and long novel in which blacks, Jews, and Wasps suspiciously eyed each other during the opening number, and by show's end formed a brand-new family of five consisting of two Jews, a Wasp, and a black.

Has there ever been a more wonderful human being in musical theater than the character of Mother? (Let's give credit, too, of course, to *Ragtime* novelist E. L. Doctorow.) The average Wasp woman of her lofty station who discovered "a Negro child" in her backyard would have snarled, "Oh, get this filthy thing away from me!" Mother's inclination instead was to provide for both the infant boy and Sarah, his mother. That's not your average New Rochelle housewife today, let alone the 1906 edition. Mother always did the right and noble thing, no matter how many obstacles (such as her husband called Father) were in her way. Late in the show, Younger Brother said, "I have always loved and admired her." You and the rest of us, bro.

There are thousands of love stories in musicals, but has there ever been one with as complicated a past as Coalhouse and Sarah's? He'd abandoned her and she in turn was so despondent that she abandoned their child; eventually there was forgiveness and love was restored. Beautiful.

Coalhouse's car was his tangible proof that he was making it in America. It made him believe that this country keeps its promise that anyone can succeed. There was good reason that his song—"Wheels of a

Dream"—used automotive imagery. When Coalhouse sang to Sarah, audiences reveled in their happiness, and wanted for them what the lovers wanted for themselves.

Alas, that car was one of the prime reasons that some white hooligans were jealous of him. Watching them hack away at the vehicle made for a powerful image. Seeing the result of their destruction was heartbreaking.

Unlike most blacks throughout American history, Coalhouse would not accept what had happened. He delayed marriage to get justice, and Sarah heard that the vice president would make a nearby visit. She sought his help, but this was too soon after the recent McKinley assassination; too diligent Secret Service men overreacted and killed her.

Coalhouse became far from the confident man he'd once been. His resolve to get his justice wound up killing him. How quickly good fortune and life can be taken away; that's America, too.

But there was evidence that America's land-of-opportunity pledge did work. Jewish immigrant Tateh promised his daughter, "apple pie from off a china plate, pretty dresses, pretty dolls." He was able to bestow them all thanks to his native talent and ingenuity in creating movies. The captain on the boat on which Father sailed had told him, "It's men like you who will keep (this country) great." Not exclusively, as we saw.

At least when the 1998 Tonys were dispensed, Ahrens and composer Stephen Flaherty were justifiably rewarded. Interesting that Generation Xer Flaherty, even when he was just starting out in the eighties, composed traditional-sounding theater music. (That's a compliment.)

Flaherty felt no need to write anachronistic rock for a period piece. And so, audiences heard three different classes of people with three distinct musical voices from the early twentieth century: elegant Wasps, freewheeling blacks, and tentatively joyous Jews. He got it stirringly right from each waltz to each ragtime.

Ahrens's work was just as impressive. There was beautiful subtext in "Our Children," as Mother and the Baron sang about their kids bonding, when they were really bonding themselves. "He Wanted to Say"—in which Emma Goldman told us what was on Younger Brother's mind—offered a moment that Bertolt Brecht would have admired (and he was not an easy man to impress).

Best of all was Ahrens's aria for Mother. In "Back to Before" this turn-of-the-century woman realized that she'd found an inner strength that she hadn't known she possessed—and she wasn't going to abandon it now.

The belief that "the first ten minutes of a show are the most important" was substantiated here by Tony voters, who probably chose *The Lion King* because of the thrilling "Circle of Life." Down the left and right orchestra aisles marched a herd of gazelles, a team of giraffes, a flock of birds, a tower of giraffes, a leap of leopards, and an elephant for good measure. But they hardly were actors zipped into animal costumes. Director–costume designer Julie Taymor found a way to merge human with wood, fabric, and Velcro to make variations on centaurs.

After that, however, *The Lion King* was never as impressive. Roger Allers and Irene Mecchi's book was full of fart jokes and a double entendre that, if Walt Disney had been alive to hear it, would have made him fire both writers. For "I need to be bucked up" got the response, "You've already bucked up royally."

Said Tateh, a self-proclaimed baron by *Ragtime*'s second act, "Anyone can get lucky in America."

Now to the most hated producer of them all, one whose personality undoubtedly cost him some votes in Tony races.

In the forties, he was the last-billed producer on four plays. Three of them shuttered in less than a month; the fourth, with the clumsy name of *Clutterbuck*, managed to run six months. But it lost money. After *Clutterbuck* closed in 1950, Broadway had every reason to assume that it would never hear from David Merrick again.

Hardly. Merrick (1911–2000) wouldn't return for more than four years, but he did roar back. He coproduced *Fanny* with Joshua Logan, who, despite having won seven Tonys and a Pulitzer, had to take second billing. Following that, for more than seven dozen productions, Merrick would far more often than not be the sole name above the title.

He was a notorious penny-pincher, an argumentative boss, a megalomaniac, rarely sweet as pie, and often tough as leather. But unlike most producers, many shows that he commissioned and optioned made it to the stage.

Once they did, he had a great time publicizing them. As Jon Maas wrote in the souvenir booklet for *42nd Street*, "David Merrick puts on plays, puts on musicals—and puts on everyone and everything."

No one in his lifetime was as prolific. As many of his *Playbill* bios stated throughout the sixties, "Since *Fanny* opened on Broadway on November 4, 1954, there has never been a week without a David Merrick production on Broadway." That was true until June 23, 1973, when *Sugar*, the sixteenth of his eighteen Tony nominated Best Musicals, closed.

Eighteen out of the thirty new musicals he brought to Broadway means a .600 Best Musical nomination batting average. In baseball, that percentage usually wins division crowns.

On the other hand, no one has ever *lost* more Best Musical races than David Merrick. Of those eighteen, only two won: *Hello, Dolly!* in 1964 and *42nd Street* in 1981.

Why such a low batting average for a producer whose very name defined Broadway from the mid-fifties through the mid-seventies? The answer may be because Merrick was hated, feared, and envied. Recall what he blatantly told the audience in what would be his final Tony acceptance speech: "Imagine what the season would have been without *42nd Street*."

That line, dripping with hubris, might start to explain Merrick's anemic .111 Best Musical Tony wins batting average. Many in the business knew that he had a sign above his desk that read, "It is not enough that we succeed: our competitors must fail."

Would a few more of Merrick's musicals have won the big prize if they'd been sponsored by different managements?

Fanny was a de facto Tony loser in 1954–1955, in the era when only a winner was announced. In essence, Merrick was two for nineteen, for while *Fanny* would have been nominated as Best Musical, it wouldn't have beaten *Damn Yankees*.

The most beloved producer on Broadway (Kermit Bloomgarden, perhaps?) wouldn't have won with Merrick's first Best Musical nominee: *Jamaica* (1957–1958). It got its nod because it was selling well and sported a star who added luster to the Broadway season, Lena Horne. It was written for someone else, Harry Belafonte. Obviously, the leading character was substantially altered. Changing horses in midstream has never been a good military strategy, and it's been just as bad in creating musicals.

Add to this the countless rewrites; for a while, act one ended with the dropping of an atomic bomb. (And you thought that Rose's singing "Everything's Coming Up Roses" was a dynamic first-act curtain.)

Harold Arlen and E. Y. Harburg wrote some solid songs, but Walter Kerr in the *Herald Tribune* distilled the problem in ten words: "Can you make a whole show out of sheet music?" Today, those who backed *Smokey Joe's Cafe* and *Mamma Mia!* would give an unqualified yes, while those behind *All Shook Up* and *Good Vibrations* wouldn't be as sure.

Merrick now had the dubious distinction of producing the musical that had received the most nominations (seven) without winning one.

For the 1958–1959 race, Merrick had the first foreign musical to be Tony nominated. You're naturally inferring it was British; no, French: *La Plume de Ma Tante*.

Some still talk about the first-act finale, in which four monks pulled on ropes to ring bells—only to have the ropes and bells take on a life of their own and control the monks. Otherwise, the show is pretty much forgotten.

Few can quote from it, for it was mostly done in mime, courtesy of the husband-and-wife team of Robert Dhery and Collette Brossard. They played Adam and Eve in one sketch in which the Serpent first approached Adam. Because men are slow to make decisions, he hemmed and hawed and Eve took control, for better or worse.

If *Gypsy*, which Merrick coproduced, wasn't going to be judged 1959–1960's Best Musical, then his *Take Me Along*, which he produced on his own that season, certainly wasn't either.

Take Me Along wasn't the most logical name for a musical version of *Ah, Wilderness!* It had nothing to do with Eugene O'Neill's coming-of-age story about Richard Miller, a sensitive bookworm growing up in 1910 small-town Connecticut. The lad loved Swinburne and Poe almost as much as he loved Muriel Macomber, the girl from almost-next-door. He promised that they'd be married "in only four or five years," the way teens truly believe.

So Richard wanted to take Muriel along somewhere? No. But when a composer-lyricist comes up with a particularly winning song, he often turns it into a title song—and "Take Me Along" was a razzmatazz charmer that sounded turn of the century. Bob Merrill wrote it for Richard's father, Nat Miller and—more to the point—his uncle, Sid Davis (Jackie Gleason).

Sid is a minor figure in *Ah, Wilderness!* providing comic color as the perennial drunk who loves Nat's prim sister and Richard's aunt. Merrill and book writers Joseph Stein and Robert Russell didn't take the easy way out and just lift from O'Neill; they decided to expand the character.

But they occasionally went to extremes. When Sid arrived at the train station from a business trip, an inordinate number of friends showed up to meet him. True, that gave Gleason a star entrance and made him the centerpiece of a choral number, but no matter how beloved a guy is, he wouldn't be greeted by more people than Amanda Wingfield had gentlemen callers.

The Tony voters didn't take enough to *Take Me Along*.

Merrick liked to say, "The only shows I've ever produced have been for adults." Case in point would be *Irma La Douce* (1960–1961), about a French *fille de joie*.

Irma (Elizabeth Seal) was a *poule*—a much nicer word than "whore"— who took on Nestor as a customer until they fell in love. He became her *mec*—a much nicer word than "pimp"—but he didn't like her sleeping with other men. So he donned a mustache and pretended to be Monsieur Oscar, a rich man who gave her five hundred francs nightly just to play cards with him.

In the non-nominated *Tenderloin*, Sheldon Harnick wrote of a prostitution ring, "Everybody's happy; that's the way it stands—just as long as the money changes hands." Not quite true with Nestor; he had to make a living, so he worked at night, which made Irma think he was cheating on her. The same five-hundred-franc note kept getting passed back and forth between them. You'd think Irma would have noticed.

And why didn't Irma see through Monsieur Oscar's disguise? If you had a good friend whom you hadn't seen for a while—and he grew a mustache—the next time you saw him you'd say, "Oh! You grew a mustache" and not "Who are you?" And Irma and Nestor had been far more intimate, so there would be other commonalities that she'd notice.

Peter Brook, who'd directed the Lunts in their last Broadway visit in *The Visit*, showed he was capable of a light touch that made *Irma* a ribald fairy tale. That everyone spoke with a French accent and that the policemen wore capes helped it along. Having Seal on hand—the only woman in a cast of seventeen, and one good enough to best Julie Andrews in the Best Musical Actress race—made it a hit, too. But not a big enough one to become Merrick's first Tony-winning Best Musical.

Six out of the seven New York critics had liked *Do Re Mi* (1960–1961). Only Frank Aston of the *World Telegram & Sun* dissented. Merrick responded by calling his editor to complain—and protested so much that the editor actually dropped Aston's final (and unflattering) paragraph in the next edition.

That's not a way to endear yourself to Tony voters.

So when the 1960–1961 Tonys were dispensed, Merrick had produced two out of the three Best Musical nominees. Despite having a two-thirds chance of winning, he lost to the one he didn't produce: *Bye Bye Birdie*.

However, 1960–1961 was hardly a washout for Merrick. The voters did say that he'd produced the Best Play (*Becket*), and the nominators gave him a special award "in recognition of a fabulous production record over the last seven years."

Still, Merrick, had to have a seven-year itch over not winning a Best Musical Tony. Even in the pre–network broadcast days, it was still the prize to win. Well, maybe next year? No. *Carnival* (1961–1962) was his only shot at the prize, and it certainly wasn't going to unseat *How to Succeed in Business Without Really Trying*.

This time Bob Merrill chose to adapt a recent movie: *Lili*. The title character (played by Anna Maria Alberghetti) was a young innocent who fell upon a flea-bitten European carnival and thought it utterly glamorous. When she met "Marco the Magnificent," she took him at his word that he deserved the title.

He was the bad guy, however, while puppeteer Paul, who had become lame from a wartime injury, was moody but really a good guy.

Gower Champion's staging made it special: curtain up when audiences entered, no overture, man sauntering on stage when the houselights were still up. *Carnival* was well received, especially by the New York Drama Critics Circle, whose members judged it the season's Best Musical.

But that was for the 1960–1961 season; Merrick had opened it a few weeks too late for that season's Tonys. Had he been a little quicker, *Carnival* just might have bested *Bye Bye Birdie*. (It did manage to run more than one hundred performances longer.)

Alberghetti had such issues with Merrick that she put his picture over her toilet. Once, when she said she was too ill to perform, Merrick got her understudy, Anita Gillette, and promoted her not only to the leading role, but also to the press. He made a big deal of the sign painters superimposing Gillette's name on the marquee. Weeks later, Merrick sent a ninety-dollar invoice to Gillette for the painting. "And," Gillette later said, "I actually had to pay it. Equity couldn't do a thing for me."

Deeds such as these keep some Tony voters from endorsing your show. And this was the same season when Merrick pulled his most famous stunt: getting seven people with the same names as the seven theater critics to ostensibly endorse his *Subways Are for Sleeping*.

Merrick then had a fifty-fifty chance to win the 1962–1963 Best Musical race, with two nominees out of four: both British imports, *Stop the World—I Want to Get Off* and *Oliver!* Ironically, the show that won was one that Merrick originally had had under option: *A Funny Thing Happened on the Way to the Forum.* On April 28, 1963, producer Harold Prince went to the podium to pick up his Best Musical Tony while Merrick stayed seated.

Not that Merrick expected *Stop the World* to win. "Commonplace and repetitious" and "overly precious," said two important critics. Although Merrick knew he could use "wonderfully invigorating" in his quote ads, but that one came from the far less powerful Norman Nadel of the *World Telegram and Sun.*

Nevertheless, *Stop the World—I Want to Get Off* became a Broadway hit, as well as a genuine idiom. So how did a show with lackluster reviews close as one of Broadway's fifty longest-running musicals, especially when it was a version of an Everyman-like morality play?

Part of the appeal was that Anthony Newley was starring. (He also staged the musical, and, with Leslie Bricusse, had cowritten its book, music, and lyrics.) Much of the nation knew three of its songs through Newley's recordings: "Once in a Lifetime," "Gonna Build a Mountain" (the last word of which Newley enjoyed pronouncing as "moun-tayne"), and, of course, "What Kind of Fool Am I?" which was covered by dozens of singers.

Newley was Littlechap, a little chap who braved the big, bad world. He and all other characters were dressed for a Pierrot show: a clown show in which performers wear stylized, circus-type uniforms. Thus Littlechap, the show's only man, donned a clown's baggy pants with long suspenders, while every other woman in the cast wore a leotard.

On a set of bleachers in a circus tent, the story was told with a good deal of mime. A bassoon in the orchestra turned out to be a genuine character, representing Littlechap's boss/father-in-law, as it boomed out low notes to suggest displeasure, and high ones to display delight. Littlechap would occasionally turn to the audience and say, "Stop the World!" so that he could stop the show and give us a few interior monologues.

Stop the World remained one of those comparatively few London imports that actually ran longer here, racking up 555 performances on Broadway to 485 in the West End. That's impressive, considering that most theatergoers are women, who couldn't have been pleased with this musical that spoke primarily to a male audience.

Many a man, however, must have nodded in sad acknowledgment when Littlechap, mired in an entry-level job, found that Evie (Anna Quayle), the object of his affection, wouldn't give him a second glance presumably because he was so low on the corporate food chain. This made him want to succeed at any cost. And at this point, Littlechap didn't know that Evie was the boss's daughter, so he couldn't be accused of using her to get ahead.

But get ahead he did. *Stop the World*, instead of using the usual inept son-in-law cliché, had Littlechap working out superbly and winning over his initially dubious father-in-law. There was poignancy at show's end when Littlechap retired and said, "You spend your whole life working hard so you can retire, and the moment you do, the thing you most miss is work."

So *Stop the World* emphasized that the average man is more interested in his career than he is in love—a sentiment that would strike a chord more with 1962 men than 1962 women. The musical not only appealed to the proverbial "tired businessman," but also to male chauvinists, for it was astonishingly sexist even by early sixties standards.

Littlechap was forever disappointed when Evie gave birth to not one but two daughters instead of a son. (Isn't that what ruined Henry VIII? It did in Rodgers and Harnick's quick 1976 flop *Rex*, anyway.) In one sadly shocking scene, Littlechap was about to leave on a business trip, kissed Evie, then his first daughter, but snubbed the second girl, which hurt her immeasurably. On that trip, he began having multiple marital affairs respectively with a Russian, German, and American woman.

So how could this musical succeed? Running expenses. They were low. No one ever changed a costume. Although a dozen sets were routinely needed for most sixties musicals, this got by with bleachers that required little maintenance. At a time when a Broadway musical routinely had fifty in its cast, *Stop the World* had thirteen.

Thus, in an era when the average musical cost $350,000, *Stop the World* came to Broadway for an astonishingly low $75,000. Today, that's a theater party buying premium seats for a hit. But a show can't win a Best Musical Tony with a sexist thrust wrapped in an avant-garde package.

Oliver! had a better chance. This musical version of Dickens's *Oliver Twist* received much better reviews than *Stop the World*, and its score became the best-selling original cast album of the 1962–1963 season, reaching as high as number four on the charts, where it stayed for more than a year. Singers of both sexes flocked to sing "As Long As (S)He Needs Me."

Although Merrick had set a December 27, 1962, opening date, he suddenly announced that he was postponing to January 6, 1963. The show didn't need more fine-tuning; it had had plenty in a long, cross-country tryout. But a newspaper strike was on, and Merrick hoped that it'd end the following week, so that everyone could read the raves.

The strike went on until February, so on January 7, 1963, Merrick bought radio time and read his own review of *Oliver!* It was, as you'd infer, positive. Merrick couldn't buy his way in to becoming a bloc of Tony voters, however, so *Oliver!* lost the race.

Finally, in 1963–1964, Merrick not only won the Best Musical Tony for *Hello, Dolly!* but also his own award as Best Producer of a Musical—a competitive prize that was given six times in the Tonys' first nineteen years, but retired after 1964–1965. For the latter, Merrick won over Ray Stark (*Funny Girl*), Harold Prince (*She Loves Me*), and—here's a surprise—Jean Dalrymple and the New York City Center Light Opera Company (*West Side Story*). *Dolly!* was on its way to outrunning all of those put together, so Tony voters that year had little choice: Merrick had to win.

Besting Stark had to bring Merrick some pleasure. He'd been a coproducer of *Funny Girl* since the days it was called *My Man*. But Stark was the son-in-law of the show's subject—Fanny Brice—so he'd always be the lead producer. Merrick was long past running ideas (and schemes) past a partner. He dropped his option on May 10, 1963—fifty-four weeks to the day before *Dolly!* beat probable second-place finisher *Funny Girl*.

The next Merrick musical was a maverick import. *Oh What a Lovely War* (1964–1965) was as much assembled by improvisation as written. The credits stated that it was "by Theatre Workshop, Charles Chilton, and members of the original cast." But the first-named organization was the real power, for it represented the company that was led by visionary director Joan Littlewood. She'd made this a hit in both London and Paris, and there never was a European hit that David Merrick didn't like.

This too was a Pierrot show, as good a way as any to make a mockery of war. The Master of Ceremonies (Victor Spinetti) took us through a docu-musical in which newspaper clippings were projected by slides and headlines through an electronic ribbon. Add to these the occasional replication of genuine magazine ads ("Beware of umbrellas made on German frames").

The first headlines were sleepy: "Summer, 1914. Scorching Bank Holiday Forecast," "Smith Fouls Carpenter in Sixth Round," and "Opera Blossoms under Thomas Beecham"—just as on September 10, 2001, we were reading "Bermuda Skirted by Storm" and "Censors and Surfers Locked in Battle over Internet Access."

Oh What a Lovely War didn't show much calm before the potent World War I storm. The Kaiser said "War is unthinkable" six lines before a German general was planning strategy. Soon after, the British, who'd been denying even the thought of war, were saying, "In the event of war . . ."

The assassination of Archduke Franz Ferdinand from "the shot heard around the world" gave *Oh What a Lovely War* a chance to show its humor: Austria-Hungary: "You hear that shot?" Serbia: "No." Reid Shelton, later the original Daddy Warbucks in *Annie*, was Austria-Hungary, fitting into Littlewood's plan to have one actor portray an entire nation.

Because old songs from the World War I era were liberally sprinkled throughout the scenes, we could say that David Merrick produced the first Tony-nominated jukebox musical. That would be oversimplifying; *Oh What a Lovely War* was enough of a documentary that period songs seemed right as a way to tell audiences what was then on songwriters' and people's minds. ("Belgium Put the Kibosh on the Kaiser" showed how a little country actually thought it could beat a much larger one.) Most poignant of all was "We're Here Because We're Here." This song we've all taken as silly now had meaning: the men had no better explanation of *why* they were *where* they were.

Some old melodies were refitted with new lyrics. "What a Friend We Have in Jesus" became "When This Lousy War is Over." The lovely Jerome Kern and Herbert Reynolds song "They Didn't Believe Me" instead started, "And when they ask us how dangerous it was, oh, we'll never tell them."

Women were involved, too. A lass sang "I'll Make a Man Out of You," which was a much better approach than "I'll Make an Amputee Out of You" or "I'll Make a Corpse Out of You." Men were made to think enlisting was romantic as well as heroic, but moments after enlisting, they were facing a sergeant-major who told them, "I'm going to be your worst enemy."

Slides of soldiers and civilians confident of a quick and easy victory gave way to slides of horribly wounded and dead soldiers and ordinary people bombed out of their homes. Headlines that crowed "Germans held at Liege; London wild with joy" seemed naïve some time later when the newspapers were forced to relate "59,275 men lost at the Battle of Ypres," "Allies lose 850,000 men in 1914," and "Verdun: total loss 1½ million men."

America stayed neutral, until it realized that war was "good for business" and "advanced scientific discovery." Said one American, citing Woodrow Wilson, "My president is deeply grieved by this war." Britain offered its condolences: "I understand he's a very sick man." The retort was "Yes. He is an idealist."

Mistaken identity has been a backbone of farce since the Greeks and Romans. Here it was much less funny when the British started attacking themselves, thinking that they were shooting Germans. This was one reason why "the average life of a soldier at the front has now advanced to three weeks." And it wouldn't be a war without a chaplain, who reported, "The Archbishop of Canterbury has made it known that it is no sin to labor for the war on the Sabbath."

When it closed after only 125 performances, *Oh What a Lovely War* easily represented the shortest run of Merrick's eleven Tony-nominated musicals. And yet, we could say that Merrick was ahead of his time in producing the show. The month after it closed, Students for a Democratic Society began their own war on President Johnson's Operation Rolling Thunder—and a different kind of thunder began rolling throughout America.

What if Merrick had brought it over during the 1967–1968 season, after protest marches and draft-card burnings had become commonplace? Producers always talk of reaching young audiences, and *Oh What a Lovely War* might have spurred them into buying tickets to a Broadway musical. It also could have won over the easily beatable *Hallelujah, Baby!*

Merrick's next nominated musical involved a war, too—but of lesser proportions. The conflict in *I Do! I Do!* (1966–1967) involved a husband and a wife. His name was Michael (Robert Preston). Hers was Agnes. And yet, when Jan de Hartog wrote his delightful 1951 comedy *The Four-poster*, his script showed that he labeled his characters "He" and "She."

All the better to suggest their universality, my dear. He and She would face the same never-changing, up-and-down aspects of wedlock that every couple has encountered since Adam and Eve became the original He and She.

De Hartog took He and She through thirty-five years, from 1890 through 1925, and saw *The Fourposter* win the 1951–1952 Tony as Best Play. Now, in the 1966–1967 season, Merrick might have assumed that, for the first time, a Tony-winning Best Play would be adapted into a Tony-winning Best Musical.

He certainly assembled the team to do it: Preston (one Tony) as He, Mary Martin (four Tonys) as She, Gower Champion (five Tony Awards and one other nomination) as director-choreographer.

Not that there would be much choreography with a cast of two. Martin and Preston may not have quite cut a rug, but they put a nice dent in it. Preston, while clad in pajamas, did a lovely soft-shoe, too—if a romp in bare feet even qualifies as a soft-shoe.

The book and lyrics were by Tom Jones, the music by Harvey Schmidt. They'd only had one Best Score Tony nomination each, but then again, they'd only had one Broadway musical: Merrick's nonnominated *110 in the Shade* (1963–1964). A better credential was their *The Fantasticks*, which was then just about to become the longest-running musical in off-Broadway history.

After He and She had taken their vows, they sang, "You can throw away your every care and doubt, 'cause that's what married life is all about." Cynics may find that the most inadvertently funny lyric in musical theater history, but most couples probably were that optimistic in 1898.

She was not the only virgin in the bedroom. He was so nervous that he even reached for a nightcap—not a drink, but an article of clothing. Obviously, the two got the hang of it, as was witnessed by their eventually having two children.

Because Jones had expanded the action to cover fifty years, he could only give the newlyweds a half hour to stay deliriously in love. Although the play had shown each of them coming home after a party in a furious mood, Jones told us how it began before they'd left: he couldn't find the clothes he wanted to wear, which led to their discussing each other's "irritating habits": his dirty socks, her inability with money, his atrocious sounds while sleeping, his constantly interrupting her stories, her serving food he dislikes, his hogging the newspapers, and her wearing cold cream to bed.

What married theatergoer couldn't relate? This song—fittingly called "Nobody's Perfect"—started with Agnes stating, "You've changed." She'd said that same line in the play, too, but later and at a far more dangerous point: when Michael had told her that he was having an affair.

De Hartog had him say, "I have begged, implored, crawled to you for a little understanding, warmth and love and got nothing." Jones instead opted for a more cavalier hat-and-cane number, "It's a Well-Known Fact," which Preston was (of course) able to deliver in expert vaudevillian style. The actor's charm allowed Jones to get away with a lyric that was dangerous even for 1966: "Men of forty go to town; women go to pot."

And while Agnes in the play dolefully stated, "You have dismissed me without notice, and I haven't complained once as any other housekeeper would have done," Martin instead got a more joyous way of expressing her feelings in "Flaming Agnes." She took out a flamboyant hat that she'd been saving for an emotionally rainy day—and here was that rainy day.

Michael and Agnes anticipated "When the Kids Get Married," and were eagerly looking forward to their empty nester status. Or so they thought. Preston sang "The Father of the Bride," a song that should have been named for its repeating phrase, "My Daughter Is Marrying an Idiot." But that would have ruined the joke. And as funny as the song was, by its final few lines, Preston had infused it with such emotion that many fathers in the audiences nodded or even shed a tear in recognition.

Jones had Agnes seem more lost than She did in the play. Her deeper feelings resulted in Martin's stirring "What Is a Woman?" which nicely set up a scene that, in the play, seemed to come out of nowhere: Agnes said that she was leaving Michael.

Her dialogue had been particularly hard-hitting: "My life long I've had to be at someone's beck and call; I've never been able to be really myself, completely wholeheartedly. No, never! From the very first day you have handcuffed me and gagged me and shut me in the dark."

Them's fightin' words, and a song expressing them would have been cataclysmically explosive. Jones wisely soft-pedaled these emotions. After Agnes accused Michael of never giving her a gift that was for her and her alone, he had one ready to give her.

But unlike today, when 48 percent of marriages end in divorce, He and She stayed together—although they did agree in their final song, "Marriage is far from easy."

One thing, however, that neither the play nor the musical ever addressed: why did Michael and Agnes never move? Usually when a husband makes increasingly more money—and the script definitely established that Michael did—at least one spouse suggests that they seek more sumptuous quarters. Seems a little odd that they stayed put.

Nevertheless, Jones improved *The Fourposter*, but the Tony-winning Best Play did *not* become the Tony-winning Best Musical. (As of this writing, *no* Best Play Tony winner ever has.) *I Do! I Do!* was perfectly respectable and solid, but it didn't offer the unexpected excitement that *Cabaret* did when it became the first concept musical that worked.

In 1967–1968, Merrick again had a fifty-fifty chance to win the Best Musical Tony, for he had two nominees out of the four: *How Now, Dow Jones* and *The Happy Time*. Actually, he stood an even better chance, because the other two nominees were those lame ducks *Illya Darling* and *Hallelujah, Baby!*

Surely the voters wouldn't say that the Best Musical was one that no one could see. That had never happened before.

How Now seemed less likely to win. Book writer Max Shulman and lyricist Carolyn Leigh relied on topical references to get laughs: Sophia Loren, Gina Lollabrigida, Twiggy, Jean-Paul Belmondo, LBJ, Rudi Gernreich, Harold Pinter, Johnny Carson, Merv Griffin, *Dragnet*, and the commercial that insisted "Only your hairdresser knows for sure" as well as the one for the Dreyfus Fund in which a lion was seen walking through the Wall Street area. (An actor in a lion suit sauntered across the stage.)

And yet, for a show that wanted to be up-to-date, *How* wasn't always "now." The first words of the opening number were obsolete: "The market is a ticker, a slender piece of tape." The New York Stock Exchange had stopped using ticker tape some years earlier—which also made *How Now*'s witty and dynamic logo (a Medusa head topped not by a mass of snakes, but a snarl of ticker tape) passé, too. And Leigh used "gay" in a lyric to mean "bright" and "glowing."

She must have felt au courant, however, when mentioning LSD—the first time it was cited on Broadway, beating *Hair* by about five months. Considering the plot that Leigh conceived for *How Now*, some might have assumed that she'd taken it. Despite Shulman's participation, she must take the blame, for the credits proclaimed it was "based on an original idea by Carolyn Leigh."

Well, it was "original." Nervous Wall Street trader Herbert had told his girlfriend Kate that he wouldn't marry her until the Dow Jones average hit a thousand. (When *How Now* opened on December 7, 1967, the Dow was at 786.) Given that Kate's job had her hourly updating the Dow Jones average on the radio, she was painfully aware that it was nowhere near a thousand, and that she'd probably remain single now and forever.

Then Kate met Charley Matson, a Wall Street trader so unsuccessful that he was about to commit suicide. Kate decided to kill herself too, but before the double suicide, the two would have a one-night stand.

This being musical comedy, one night was enough to get Kate pregnant. Granted, by this time, most women were using diaphragms or taking birth control pills—but not in musicals.

Now Kate "had to" get married, but she couldn't find Charley, so she used her microphone to proclaim to the world that the Dow did indeed hit a thousand so that Herbert would marry her. The lie set off a buying flurry; the truth set off a selling panic.

The show had painted itself into a corner. Herbert certainly wouldn't marry her now. Neither Shulman nor Leigh could find a way out that would make a savvy if tired businessman slap his forehead and say, "Oh, that's marvelous! What a clever solution!" They instead had one of the world's biggest financiers (whimsically named A. K.) save everyone all too conveniently. Equally expedient was Kate's finding Charley.

As for that expected secondary couple: Cynthia, who made her living conducting Wall Street tours, was desperately smitten with tycoon Mr. Wingate (Hiram Sherman).

The fifty-nine-year-old actor was nicknamed "Chubby" for good reason. To be sure, Wingate's success and money were factors in Cynthia's interest, but she genuinely lusted for the guy.

William Goldman in *The Season* said that *How Now* stayed around for months because the title promised a funny evening and "men tend to be interested in the stock market." Yes, but men also liked seeing a young, lovely, and sexy woman genuinely craving an aging, overweight man who looked remarkably like them. Lord knows how many propositions these theatergoers made at their offices the next morning, in those years before "the suits" had to fear suits of sexual harassment.

Cynthia was happy to be kept, but the joke was that Wingate was too busy to visit her. When one executive told him he looked marvelous, he explained why: "Hard work, regular hours, and 200,000 shares of IBM." Once again: men are more interested in career than love.

After Kate began the Wall Street panic, a harried Wingate came to the nest to decompress and have sex. "He's Here," Cynthia sang joyously. But wouldn't you know that after months of hoping that Wingate would show for a little loving, Cynthia couldn't go through with it? In those days, nice girls didn't.

Film composer Elmer Bernstein wrote some fine theater music—unexpected from the creator of the ultrabutch theme to *The Magnificent Seven*, the powerful *The Man with the Golden Arm*, and the haunting *To Kill a Mockingbird*. "They Don't Make 'Em Like That Anymore" had spirit and "Walk Away" was a lovely waltz.

Leigh's lyrics once again showed "signature"—the term lyricists reserve for a wordsmith with a genuine voice. Interesting, isn't it, that the earthiest of musical theater lyricists was a woman? "Run and hock the baby . . . Watch your bloomers, Mabel . . . Like the mustard sells that ham on rye . . . Up your I. G. Farben . . . I've only one word to say: nuts! . . . Where's that trusty old rusty gorilla? . . . Quicker than it takes to swat a fly . . . Time you got off the ropes, kid . . . Only one little slip—and it's showing . . . Or knock yourself off in your neighbor's garage . . . This was your up-and-at-'em day . . . Things are thumbs up; he shows the bums up . . . In the simple opinion of the unwashed dominion."

But Leigh could be plaintive, too. "The clocks don't stop when they ought to stop. They tick relentlessly on," she wrote. It was true for her, too; Leigh had fewer than fourteen years to live, and never had another new musical on Broadway. Although she worked on a musical version of *Smile*, she was replaced by Howard Ashman. Her adaptations of *The Great Gatsby* and *Juliet of the Spirits* went unproduced.

Leigh certainly didn't get a ticker tape parade for *How Now, Dow Jones*. Its fate and Best Musical Tony loss were sealed once Clive Barnes, then the powerful critic for the *Times*, wittily damned it as "How to try at business without really succeeding." Merrick understandably didn't use that quote.

So on Tony night, Merrick undoubtedly pinned his hopes on *The Happy Time*, which had been better received and was grossing more.

Composer John Kander started the show with a glorious swirling waltz, as lyricist Fred Ebb listed the happy times we've all experienced, from the sentimental ("The compliment you once received") to the less lofty ("The lie you told they all believed."). It was sung by Jacques Bonnard (Robert Goulet), who at sixteen had warred with his father, left his French Canadian home, become a photographer, and had since seen the world. Now "He's Back," as the rumbling song went. Jacques's brothers Louis and Philippe, their wives, and the patriarch now known as Grandpere were as welcoming as the reviews for *In My Life*.

Someone was glad to see him: Bibi, Philippe's teenage son, for whom Jacques represented adventure and sophistication. To prove it, Jacques thought Bibi should finally be allowed to attend the nightclub that Philippe owned. Philippe forbade it, but Bibi snuck out that night.

Said Grandpere to Jacques, "You are the Wonder Man who comes in from the Great Wide World! If you raise your hand and point—no matter what direction—he would go."

Bibi's actual teacher was Laurie, who'd been too young for Jacques when he was last in town five years ago. She'd be interested in him now, but she hadn't forgotten that last time he was in town he broke her bike, said he'd fix it, and the next day left.

Is this why Jacques suggested that Bibi take a three-day vacation from school and serve as his assistant? Of course the lad was thrilled, and of course Philippe wouldn't allow it. Bibi blurted out that he wished Jacques were his father, terribly wounding Philippe.

Talk about second-act trouble. Audiences learned that Jacques had returned because a magazine had offered him a contract to photograph his town. This information was divulged in the worst possible way: Grandpere went snooping in his room and found the contract.

Jacques insisted to his father and Laurie that he was back to stay. Could we believe him? Just as being poor is murderously harder after having been rich, living in a sleepy small town isn't easy after experiencing glamorous, exciting, opportunity-filled, liberal cities. And the next moment he was talking of leaving. Not only had he lost confidence in himself, but Tony voters lost confidence in him, too.

Worse, Jacques talked of bringing Bibi with him. Yes, Mame has the right to take Patrick here and there; she's his official guardian. But Bibi has a father. As Grandpere said to Jacques, "You are a thief," and when an astounded Jacques asked what he'd stolen, Grandpere said, "Affection you did not work for. You did not come home to take pictures. You came home to be home. And now you want to take some of that home away with you."

So Jacques turned into an antihero, and Tony voters turned against him. Book writer N. Richard Nash tried to ameliorate the problem a minute before the show ended by having Jacques state that he eventually had his own son. He didn't mention a wife.

Merrick made a rare miscalculation by booking this small story into Broadway's biggest theater: the Broadway. Was that all that was available? No. While he was preparing to bring in *The Happy Time*, he folded his production of *Mata Hari* in Washington. That freed the Alvin Theatre, with 350 fewer seats. Why didn't he take that?

The production, too, was overwhelmed by Jacques's photographs—some of which represented his accurate memories, some that contradicted what he said, and some that exposed the truth. The brainstorm of the show's director-choreographer Gower Champion turned out to be only a nice idea on (photographic) paper.

As Tony night wore on, Merrick had to be buoyed by Champion's winning both the Best Director and Best Choreography prizes; the two times before that Champion had won both—*Bye Bye Birdie* and *Hello, Dolly!*—his musicals had won, too. Since the Best Director prize had been instituted in 1959–1960, all eight Best Director winners had seen their shows win Best Musical.

Not this time. Despite the lovely score, *The Happy Time* lost to lame duck and terribly flawed *Hallelujah, Baby!* It meant well in examining race relations, but Walter Kerr said it best: "With the best intentions in the world is a course in Civics One when everyone in the world has already got to Civics Six."

Hallelujah, Baby!'s composer Jule Styne said, "You always win for the wrong show." Another way of putting it: Tony voters didn't want Merrick to win.

However, that year's nominators did. They gave him a special award—which might too have influenced the voters. ("We're gonna hafta listen to him give one speech; who can bear hearing him give another?")

The next year, Merrick must have felt that he couldn't be denied. *Promises, Promises* (1968–1969) had opened to close-to-unanimous raves.

After a thrilling overture of Burt Bacharach music, Neil Simon's adaptation of the Oscar-winning *The Apartment* started softly. Chuck Baxter (Jerry Orbach) was sitting at a desk, where he took the audience into his confidence.

"The main problem with working as a one hundred and twelve dollars a week accountant in a seventy-two-story insurance company with assets over three billion dollars that employs 31,259 people here in the New York office alone," he said, "is that it makes a person feel so godawful puny."

Many a New Yorker worked in just such a situation (and cubicle) and could relate. Others also empathized when Chuck tried to get the attention of his boss Mr. Sheldrake, who regarded him as Mr. Cellophane.

That is, until Sheldrake learned that Chuck was loaning his apartment to executives and their girlfriends. Then his interest in Chuck increased appreciably. As Chuck said when turning to us and taking us into his con-fidence, "Some married men between the ages of forty-five and fifty-five find single girls between the ages of twenty-one and thirty more attractive than some married women between the ages of forty-five and fifty-five."

The line came courtesy of Simon, who was in top form when adapting the 1960 Oscar-winning film. To be sure, he had Billy Wilder and I.A.L. Diamond's excellent screenplay from which to work. Even a line that sounded like pure Simon actually came from the movie: when Chuck complained to one of his ad hoc tenants that the man had stayed too long at the flat: "Do you know I sat on a park bench until two thirty in the morning in a snowstorm in a London Fog coat? It's for fogs in London—not snow in New York."

But Simon did get audiences to care more about Chuck Baxter by hav-ing him talk to them, and director Robert Moore was wise to cast Orbach against type: for a change, he played a purely nice guy.

Another smart Simon move involved Fran Kubelik, the object of Chuck's affection. She surprised the audience when she blatantly told our hero why she hadn't yet left the office after working hours. "Oh, what's the use, Chuck? I stayed late because I wanted to see you."

Fran went on in that manner for two more sentences before Chuck raised his hand, yelled "Wait! Hold it a second!" and turned to the audience and admitted that Fran hadn't said anything of the kind; he'd simply been fantasizing. We can't say that Fran didn't know Chuck was alive, but when she actually said, "Hello, how are you, Frank?" we thus learned of her low level of interest.

Alas, Fran was in love with Jeff—as in Sheldrake. As in the film, Chuck unexpectedly learned of their romance. Chuck gave Sheldrake a woman's compact that he'd found in the apartment. "I'm afraid the mir-ror is broken," he told his boss. "She threw it at me," Sheldrake explained.

Chuck would see it again at the office Christmas party. He was in high spirits because his promotion from Sheldrake had allowed him to buy a jaunty new hat. When he asked Fran how he looked, she offered him her compact so he could see. When he saw the broken mirror, he knew it was the one he'd found in his apartment—and that Sheldrake was sleeping with Fran.

Like the aforementioned *King and I* and *Parade*, we had devastation after a joyous moment, which had been the office party. "Turkey Lurkey Time" had had the company's workers constantly dancing and interweaving in a figure-eight position. Better, think of the loop that represents infinity, and think of it as continually moving. Perhaps infinity wasn't as long as some theatergoers could have watched "Turkey Lurkey Time," but plenty would have welcomed two or three encores.

It was the brainchild of the increasingly successful choreographer Michael Bennett, who was officially working on his third Broadway musical and was rewarded with his third consecutive Tony nomination—but only his first hit.

Actually, Bennett didn't have much to do. His other big number was barely a dance. It took place in a wine bar which, Simon's stage direction said, was "packed with people." Bennett took that literally. He assembled a group of dancers, smushed them together as tight as they could get, and had them do the latest dance steps, sometimes with a partner, sometimes not. The result looked more like a blob than an assemblage of people, but it certainly mirrored those crowded East Side clubs that the so-called beautiful people were then frequenting. Better still, it once again proved that the best choreography has an idea behind it, and isn't just the movement of arms and legs.

How fitting, too, that these club-dwellers were dancing to Bacharach's music. Wasn't everybody in 1968? Happily, the song wasn't the result of someone's playing a current Bacharach hit on the jukebox; it was one song out of a score of sixteen written by Bacharach and his most valuable collaborator Hal David.

It was their first and only Broadway musical. Most "one-hit wonders" make many attempts to shed the label by try, trying again. The Bacharach and David team instead walked away. Broadway, they'd decided, demanded too much time and effort. When they were in Boston and had assumed they'd written enough, they were asked to come up with a song for Fran and Chuck on the morning after she'd attempted suicide. They reluctantly went to write, but came up with show's most enduring hit, "I'll Never Fall in Love Again." They made it all look easy (as all hit shows do) but still, writing a musical was *hard*.

As we saw earlier, in *The Apartment*, Sheldrake told his wife that he had to take a client to *The Music Man*. Here's an indication that Simon, Bacharach, and David wanted to do something new. They changed the event to a basketball game—probably because mentioning a musical in a musical would seem too self-reverential. It inspired Bacharach and David to write one of their best songs, "She Likes Basketball."

We always hear what a dour and terrible human being Jerome Robbins was, but he certainly isn't exhibiting those qualities here. Maybe his exuberance comes from feeling he has a hit with *Bells Are Ringing*. At far left, Adolph Green is obviously agreeing with what Robbins has to say (or is at least pretending he does) while composer Jule Styne looks a little less sure, and Betty Comden, sitting below, seems less certain still. However, Judy Holliday, sitting closest to the director-despot, has a look on her face that suggests she's eager to learn. Holliday would be the only one of the bunch to win a Tony, too, beating out Julie Andrews's Eliza Doolittle in one of the few victories that *Bells Are Ringing* enjoyed over *My Fair Lady*.

When you see a musical that stars Gwen Verdon and Chita Rivera, you expect to see them dance together. Bob Fosse certainly kept us waiting in his 1975 musical *Chicago*, holding off until show's end to have the two do "The Hot Honey Rag." This followed their hat-and-cane number that proclaimed, "In fifty years or so, it's gonna change, you know." They were speaking about life in general, but it certainly became true of musical theater. No one during *Chicago*'s original run would have predicted that it would become the longest-running American musical to ever play Broadway. But that happened because of a 1996 revival which, in 2011, outdistanced *A Chorus Line*—the musical that had humiliated it at the 1975–1976 Tonys.

What would put such a sour and injured expression on Phil Silvers's face? Someone telling him that she's not interested in money, that's what. Here in *Do Re Mi*, it's Tilda Mullen, who waitresses in an early '60s coffee shop that features folk music. Every now and then Tilda sings a song for the patrons, and Hubie Cram now wants to make her a star. Trouble is, Tilda doesn't have any "Ambition," which, as Hubie is about to sing to her, is necessary in life. Are you surprised to hear that Hubie got his way? Didn't Phil Silvers always? Actually, no—by show's end, Hubie admitted that he was nothing much as a husband or a human being. And that's one reason why *Do Re Mi* failed to win a Best Musical Tony or become a financial success. Phil Silvers was the one person whom everyone wanted to see get away with every scheme he tried.

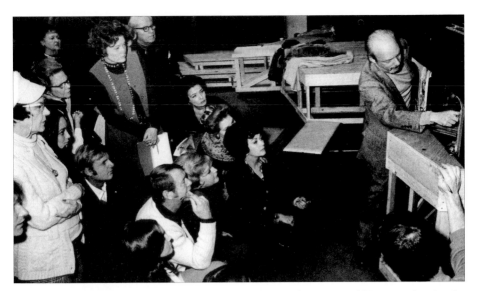

January 9, 1971: the first day of rehearsals for *Follies*. Producer-director Harold Prince is showing the cast and crew how Boris Aronson's set will look and work. Everyone does seem to be quite immersed, and the thought may already be occurring to some that this is not just going to be another Broadway musical. It wasn't, although it certainly didn't impress enough Tony voters to allow *Follies* to emerge victorious over *Two Gentlemen of Verona*.

Here's Fanny Brice with the only man who ever really loved her: Eddie Ryan. Actually, the way that Barbra Streisand is looking at Danny Meehan suggests that she indeed loves him, too. Alas, however, it's not in "that way," partly because Eddie isn't tall, dark, and handsome. Roxie in *Chicago* says that an ugly guy needs a pretty girl on his arm; well, if a girl isn't pretty like a Miss Atlantic City, she requires a knockout, too. Never mind that Nicky Arnstein K.O.'s Fanny in a very different way; had Fanny married Eddie and lived happily ever after, *Funny Girl* would have had an even weaker second act and might not have been even nominated for the Best Musical Tony that it lost to *Hello, Dolly!*

Here's Jerome Robbins in an even better mood when rehearsing *Gypsy*. On the other hand, one must wonder why Ethel Merman is threatening to pour a pot of coffee on his head—while looking gleeful at the prospect. Lane Bradbury, cast as Dainty June, appears to not want to get involved, while Sandra Church, the original Gypsy Rose Lee, seems to be wondering if she should chuck her container of Chinese food at Robbins, too.

Yes, that is Barbara Cook—the 1963 model—on the extreme left, celebrating the opening of *She Loves Me* with producer-director Harold Prince and costars Barbara Baxley and Daniel Massey. The picture was probably taken before they all saw Walter Kerr's review—although, to be fair, it really was the only negative one. However, *She Loves Me* closed the week before the opening of *Hello, Dolly!*—the musical that would best it for the Best Musical Tony.

One really must trust one's director, but Mary Martin looks mighty wary as Gower Champion tries to guide her during rehearsals of *I Do! I Do!* Champion has the look of a man who's dealing with someone past her prime. Actually, Martin had three years earlier had a flop with *Jennie*, and probably was worried about having another. She didn't, for *I Do! I Do!* was a solid hit, although it lost the Best Musical Tony to *Cabaret*.

Virginia Martin and her *belle poitrine* as Belle Poitrine in *Little Me* doesn't seem to doubt what Swen Swenson is telling her: "I've Got Your Number." He's just one in the long string of men who interest her in the 1962 Neil Simon–Cy Coleman–Carolyn Leigh musical. The show received better reviews than *A Funny Thing Happened on the Way to the Forum* had managed to get six months earlier, but by the time the voters got around to casting their ballots, *Little Me* was faltering and *Forum* was still hot; the latter won.

Eugene O'Neill's *Anna Christie* took place in a bar and on a barge—and nowhere else. But whenever George Abbott did a musical, he'd add a scene in a place where his cast could dance: a union benefit, a tribute—and often a ball, including this one "At the Check Apron Ball." Gwen Verdon looks as if she doubts the wisdom for this excuse to dance, but Harvey Hohnecker (who by the end of the '50s would rename himself Harvey Evans) and John Nola look happy to be part of *New Girl in Town*. And while the costumes look just as good as the ones seen in *The Music Man*, that show wound up winning most of the Tonys in 1957–1958, including Best Musical.

So *was* Lainie Kazan too fat to convince audiences she was a dancer, as Michael Bennett alleged when he fired her from *Seesaw*? Judge for yourself here. True, a long skirt can hide a multitude of pounds, and Kazan does appear to be in pain at exerting herself so hard. *Seesaw* did manage a respectable run of nine months—after Michele Lee took over for Kazan, that is—but it couldn't make a loser out of *Raisin* in the 1973–1974 Best Musical Tony race.

Are these the faces of people who expect to win the Best Musical Tony? Gwen Verdon seems bored. Original cast album guru Goddard Lieberson looks genuinely worried. Composer Cy Coleman appears to be holding his tongue while lyricist Dorothy Fields looks resigned to a not-so-happy fate. Actually, *Sweet Charity* had recently opened to reviews that were much stronger than these faces would suggest. But an original cast album recording session, which must be accomplished in one day—and on the cast's only day off—is always wearing. It was an omen: Both the album and *Sweet Charity* itself could never surpass *Man of La Mancha*.

Bacharach's music reflected the comparative youth of the characters. The next "time: now" musical to open after *Promises* was *The Fig Leaves Are Falling*, which also involved marital infidelity. The middle-aged Albert Hague gave his forty-something characters songs that sounded right for their age, but he also gave the cute young thing who started an affair with our hero the same middle-aged sound; that's all Hague could write.

And who'd have expected that Broadway musical rookie director Moore would stage *Promises* so well? Only three years earlier, he'd been a mere supporting actor in Merrick's production of *Cactus Flower*. Then early in 1968, he'd done a superb job directing the landmark play *The Boys in the Band*.

But there was a profound difference between staging a one-set, off-Broadway drama with a cast of nine and a multiset Broadway musical that employed thirty-seven. Moore kept the three-dozen-plus performers and the show itself moving in one of the slickest stagings of the sixties.

He didn't win a Tony, but Marian Mercer did.

Who?

She was Marge MacDougall, a genially tipsy woman who came on to Chuck while he was drowning his Kubelik sorrows. Mercer had only appeared in two Broadway shows (and would be seen in only four more). She had all of twenty-three lines in one scene, twenty-one in another, and shared a single song with Orbach. With a slightly glazed smile and a coy demeanor, she and Moore let subtlety rule the scenes, unlike the vulgar and overdone character that Katie Finneran created in the 2010 revival, although she won a Tony, too. To date, it's the only role that has provided two different women with Best Featured Actress in a Musical Tonys.

Promises was en route to 1,281 performances—which at the time would make it Merrick's second-longest-running show, right behind *Dolly!* of the five dozen or so he'd brought to Broadway. So Merrick must have thought he had the Best Musical Tony wrapped up. What was his competition? *Zorba* was a disappointment; *George M.* was drawing to a close. Yes, there was *Hair*, but Tony voters wouldn't go for that.

So on the morning of March 16, 1969—the day of the Tony deadline—Merrick was probably confident. Yes, one final show would open that night, but it was that musical that had bombed in New Haven and dealt with, of all things, the signing of the Declaration of Independence.

The next morning, you could have knocked Merrick over with a boa. Keith Edwards, whose father Sherman conceived *1776* and wrote its score, says, "For a solid week after the show had opened to raves, Dad sat at the dinner table every night and read every word of those reviews to us."

Merrick didn't make the trip to the Edwards's home to hear them. After his enemies saw *1776*, they must have danced in glee around their desks for at least twenty minutes. This wouldn't simply be a vote against Merrick, but a vote for a superior musical. *Promises* was fun, yes, but *1776* made one proud to be an American, was surprisingly suspenseful, and far more moving.

From 1957–1958 through *Promises* in 1968–1969, Merrick had only missed having a Best Musical nominee in 1965–1966 (when he at least had three of the four Best Play nominees, and won for *Marat/Sade*). Now, however, four seasons would pass before he even had another candidate.

When *Sugar* (1972–1973) was nominated, Merrick obviously had no illusions that it would beat either *Pippin* or *A Little Night Music*. He might have even assumed that it could finish behind *Dont Bother Me, I Cant Cope*. Indeed, Merrick had gone so long without a hit musical that the Tony committee may have thrown him a nomination because its members felt sorry for him.

Sugar itself was pretty sorry. The musical version of Billy Wilder's *Some Like It Hot* managed to become one of those Broadway shows that runs more than five hundred performances, barely ekes out a profit, and always has available a pair of prime orchestra seats on Saturday night.

The new title *Sugar* suggested that book writer Peter Stone, composer Jule Styne, and lyricist Bob Merrill were placing the emphasis on the character that Marilyn Monroe had played in *Some Like It Hot*. Wonderful as Monroe was (and no other adjective will do), the story is simply not Sugar's. The focus must always stay on Jerry the bass player and Joe the saxophonist, respectively played in the film by Jack Lemmon and Tony Curtis.

They had the more dramatic story. Joe and Jerry not only witnessed the 1929 St. Valentine's Day Massacre in Chicago, but they were also spotted by the killers. Soon they were on the run to avoid being rubbed out. Jerry and Joe were so desperate that they took the only available jobs they could find: playing in an all-female orchestra, which meant that they had to dress appropriately.

At first, Merrick didn't buy the oh-so-expensive rights to *Some Like It Hot* but the German movie that had provided Wilder and collaborator

I.A.L. Diamond with their inspiration. But the German film didn't have the added aspects of the gangsters chasing Joe and Jerry. Thus, Merrick's book writers—first Michael (*Hello, Dolly!*) Stewart and then George (*The Seven-Year Itch*) Axelrod—were prevented from using that delicious complication. After reading two dull scripts from two unhappy authors, Merrick finally decided to purchase the rights to Billy Wilder and I.A.L. Diamond's screenplay. As the old saying goes, "When you buy cheap, you pay twice."

Styne and Merrill reunited with director-choreographer Gower Champion; a year earlier, they'd all created *Prettybelle*. It was an ambitious musical in which the title character, played by Angela Lansbury, bedded most every minority member in a small Southern town, in recompense for her late husband's bigotry that had terrorized them. It died in Boston, which didn't embrace its unconventional nature.

Merrick preferred to think of his songwriters as the *Funny Girl* team and his director-choreographer as the one who'd staged his *Hello, Dolly!* Besides, a musical of *Some Like It Hot* would not be the least bit controversial, but simply great fun.

Sugar was portrayed by Elaine Joyce (who, twenty-seven years later, would become the fourth Mrs. Neil Simon). Styne had discovered her at a party and was convinced that she'd be wonderful. He would be proved wrong. Robert Morse and Tony Roberts would do respectively better as Jerry and Joe.

Stone didn't clear up one of the film's oddities: early on, Joe and Jerry talked endlessly of how impoverished they were, and yet when they decided to dress as women, they suddenly acquired an extensive female wardrobe right down to pajamas. How or where did they get these clothes? Only Wile E. Coyote's easy access to Acme equipment during his Road Runner pursuits seemed as expedient.

Styne and Merrill offered an additional lapse in logic. Jerry and Joe were first seen in drag at the train station where they sang to everyone on the platform, "Hello, world! They call us Daphne and Josie!" Given that their lives were at stake and they were desperate to leave town unobtrusively, why did they draw attention to themselves?

No one can accuse Styne and Merrill of being unwilling to work. Granted, they did try to recycle "A Temporary Arrangement," which they originally wrote for *Funny Girl*. Merrill gave Styne a slightly changed lyric for "My Nice Ways," which he'd written for *Breakfast at Tiffany's*. Otherwise, they wrote more than a dozen unused songs for the tryouts, which were among Merrick's most trouble-plagued. That so many cast members came down with hepatitis was so well known that it actually was mentioned on TV's *Hollywood Squares*. The stages of Washington, Toronto, Philadelphia, and a hastily added Boston were littered with discarded music, including a Carmen Miranda parody for Joe, Jerry, and Sugar. Someone probably realized that *Sugar* took place in 1929, when Miranda was just starting her career in her native Brazil and was still a decade away from the United States.

Merrick fired set designer Jo Mielziner and brought in Robin Wagner. He canned Stone, who went to the Dramatists Guild—an organization that Stone would later head—which prevented his ouster. Pop singer Johnny Desmond, playing gangster Spats Palazzo, was fired in Toronto. Bert Michaels, who was associate choreographer, dance captain, and performer—before being fired and then rehired—suggested his old tap teacher Steve Condos be cast, for tapping could stand in for machine-gun fire. Champion went for it.

A character named Joker Gomez was dropped and one named Knuckles Norton was added. Frankly, they were the same character, but Equity rules say that if a producer replaces an actor, his contract must be honored. If authors write him out, that's a different (and less expensive) story. Knuckles was the way Merrick extricated himself from the ruling.

We could say that Mielziner, Stone, Michaels, Desmond, and even "Joker Gomez" had Tony-voting friends who refused to vote for *Sugar*. But even if it had been a top-notch musical comedy, it wouldn't have beaten the classy *A Little Night Music*.

But as much hell as *Sugar* caused Merrick, there'd be almost as much for his next—and final—Best Musical Tony loser. At least *Sugar* ran and even paid back its investment. *Mack & Mabel* (1974–1975) closed after sixty-six performances, making it Merrick's fifth-shortest-running musical to reach Broadway. Only *Maria Golovin* (a small opera), *Vintage '60* (a small revue), *Pickwick* (a big import), and *Breakfast at Tiffany's* (a big disaster) amassed fewer showings in New York. With its November closing, *Mack & Mabel* was long gone by Tony night. To be sure, many who saw and loved it have kept it alive and propelled it even past cult status. After all, how many sixty-six performance American musicals get *two* productions in London's West End?

The same team that ten years earlier had had such a success with *Hello, Dolly!* created it: Merrick, book writer Michael Stewart, songwriter Jerry Herman, and director-choreographer Gower Champion.

All but one of them was Tony nominated. And the loser was . . . ?

CHAPTER SIX

✳

It's Smarter to Be Lucky Than It's Lucky to Be Smart: *The Best Musical Tony Losers That Encountered Unexpected Circumstances*

The reign of Clive Barnes as chief critic of *The New York Times* was a mere ten years—1967–1977—but that was enough time for him to destroy the traditional Broadway musical.

Every president must have a platform, and so must the nation's most powerful theater critic. Barnes's plank was that musical theater should reflect the music of the times. Thus, he believed that the distinctive sound that Broadway had always enjoyed now had to give way to rock.

When Barnes got the job, he'd just passed forty—the time when a midlife crisis often strikes. Perhaps Barnes needed to feel young, and the best way he could do that was to identify himself with so-called young music.

This came to a head in 1974–1975, the season in which both *The Lieutenant* and *Mack & Mabel* opened. Both were commercial flops, but in what was perceived at the time as a bad season, they were both up for Best Musical Tonys.

But *The Lieutenant* was also up for Best Score, while *Mack & Mabel* wasn't.

The Lieutenant's window card boasted "Brilliant rock musical!" (Lewis, *The Record*), "If you never see another show, you must see this one" (*L.I. Press*, with no critic mentioned), and "A striking, fiercely stimulating musical evening"—attributed to *The New York Times*, again with no critic's name attached.

The theatrically savvy will smile. Clearly if Barnes had written that, *The Lieutenant's* producers would have named him. Did a second-string critic or *Times* mailroom employee utter this?

Actually, after *The Lieutenant* had opened on March 9, 1975, producers Joseph S. Kutrzeba and Spofford J. Beadle had much from Barnes to quote: "The music is attractive and supportive. Although described as 'rock,' it in fact covers a lot of territory including old-fashioned vaudeville and even a touch of a comic barbershop quartet. The lyrics, while a few of the rhymes are occasionally agonized, tell the opera's story with clarity and punch."

Were *only* "a few" of those lyrics "agonized" in this nine-performance flop?

It was the work of Gene Curty, Nitra Scharfman, and Chuck Strand. None had ever done a Broadway show, and none would ever do another. Director William Martin did have Broadway experience—as assistant to the producer of *Noel Coward in Two Keys* in 1974.

Choreographer Dennis Dennehy, however, had already appeared on Broadway in *Heathen!* the Hawaiian musical that had opened and closed on May 21, 1972. In it, he'd played four roles—Kaha Kai, the Chanter, the Mugger, and one of the Girls and Boys of Past and Present. Despite his not snagging one of the four Tony nominations that *The Lieutenant* enjoyed, Dennehy was assuaged by Drama Desk's nod for Outstanding Choreography. He returned to Broadway twelve years later as choreographer for *Late Nite Comic*, which would run less than half as long as *The Lieutenant*.

Of *The Lieutenant*'s eighteen performers, twelve had never appeared on Broadway, and eleven never would again. One in the latter category, however, would meet with great success: Eddie Mekka became Carmine "the Big Ragu" Ragusa on *Laverne & Shirley*.

That's a very different role from the one Mekka had in *The Lieutenant*. In his Tony-nominated performance, he was the no-name title character. However, only those who'd neglected news since November 12, 1969, wouldn't have known that he was William L. Calley, Jr., a second lieutenant in the Vietnam War who'd been charged with ordering his men to murder civilians, resulting in hundreds of deaths.

That the show closed on March 16, 1975, was ironic: that was seven years to the day that Calley had ordered his men to kill.

The Lieutenant's overture sported lazy guitar licks and some Jimi Hendrixy riffs. Then came "The Indictment," in which the Lieutenant was read the charges. "Not guilty!" he shrieked.

We flashbacked to the recruiting office that he'd entered years earlier. Easy country music suggested Calley's Southern roots. (He was born in

Florida to a World War II army veteran. Whether Calley's dad staunchly approved of his son's actions or was ashamed of them wasn't mentioned in the musical. It was a missed dramatic opportunity.)

The man who would be Lieutenant sang, "I saw the sign on your door, and I'd like to hear more of what the army can do for me. I've struck out in the insurance line. . . . I can't find a trade where I can make the grade. I got my draft notice late. I'm in a terrible state."

Was his terrible state the result of getting his draft notice late or because he couldn't make it in the insurance "line"? Besides, anyone who'd received a draft notice had no decision to make.

That escaped the lad. "I really need your help," he sang. "My ass is on the line." (Presumably not the insurance one.)

The Recruiting Officer sang in countermelody: "Join the Army. Where can you go? You'd be surprised," he insisted, avoiding the word "Vietnam." Instead the Recruiting Officer promised, "You'll go off to some tropical isle. We'll fix you up in our latest style." (And you thought that army uniforms never changed their look.)

Our future Lieutenant naïvely asked himself "What can I lose?" before adding, "I need a new pair of shoes." If that's the best a character can do to justify his decision, audiences won't have much respect for him. They had less after he sang, "The army could be my pot of gold. I really should enroll."

You don't *enroll* in the army; you *enlist* in the army. Perhaps the lyricists felt that their character was so green he didn't know the correct verb. More likely, they chose "enroll" because they *thought* it rhymed with "gold." (However, does anyone see the army as a "pot of gold"?)

Soon after came some ricky-ticky, silent movie, vaudeville-flavored music, followed by two measures of "You're in the Army Now" and the organ's making klaxon horn sounds—all to indicate the absurdity of the establishment. In *Jesus Christ Superstar*, Andrew Lloyd Webber and Tim Rice took this silly, over-the-top approach in "Herod's Song"—once. But they didn't use it for Pontius Pilate, whom they took seriously. *The Lieutenant*'s creators often used ridiculous-sounding music in order to mock the military in a much-too-simplistic approach.

Three Generals sang "Look for the Men With Potential," lamenting that the new draftees didn't seem to be contenders for Officers Candidate School. "Maybe we can scrape up enough," they sang. "Take anyone who's got officer's stuff."

Officer's *stuff*? Meaning "officer material"? By now we knew that the lyricists would take any rhyme that came their way.

Our nameless hero was accepted into Officers Candidate School, where a sergeant gave an insincere "Welcome!" before adding, "We're gonna teach you how to kill." The lyric was set to a gritty rock melody, which didn't suit a member of "the greatest generation" who had presumably been born no later than the thirties. His sound should have reflected his era.

Broken piano chords resulted in the new lieutenant's admitting, "I was so enthused . . . but now I'm a bit confused." He confessed that "I always wanted to be a leader instead of just the following kind."

"The following kind"? Not "follower"? Yes, for "kind" would rhyme with "It's weighing heavy on my mind."

"I Don't Want to Go Over to Vietnam," sang the Lieutenant, but that's where he was sent. There the Chaplain eulogized those killed "by a vicious, ruthless enemy." The authors then set the first five lines of the Twenty-third Psalm to music, but apparently found setting the final seven too daunting, for they simply had them recited over music.

Peter Allen got credit and an Oscar for writing a mere one line of "The Theme from *Arthur*"; shouldn't King David's name have been put on the Best Score Tony nomination certificate, too?

The Captain sang that "At 0700 Tomorrow" he would "neutralize the trouble spots." The B-section changed tempo in the way that *Jesus Christ Superstar*'s "Everything's Alright" did. Later, during "Massacre," a music-only piece, the chords sounded perilously like the ones heard in the *Superstar* overture.

The recruits sang "Kill all the V-C" numerous times, with the accent misplaced on the V rather than the C. That made it sound like "Vichy," a word that belonged to a different war.

The Captain, furious at the battle's pace, roared, "What's taking you so long?" The Lieutenant answered in rhyme, "We had to neutralize the Viet Cong." That didn't pass muster. The Captain demanded, "We've got to get rid of all these people."

"What does that mean?" the Lieutenant queried.

"Get rid of them!"

The ambiguous words suggested that killing wasn't the Lieutenant's idea; he'd merely interpreted the words as an order. After the carnage, he ruminated, "Something's gone wrong here. I don't know what, but I got a feeling it's something to hide." Yes, as he later admitted: "These aren't dead soldiers. Looks like a civilian population to me . . . Public knowledge would be a big disgrace. The army would surely lose face."

Well, *those* were two consecutive understatements. The collaborators were more accurate when they wrote, "There'll be hell to pay if it ever gets out."

More ricky-ticky, razzmatazz reintroduced the Captain. "Word got back that things got out of hand," he growled. "You've got to come up with some kind of answer." He and the Lieutenant tried to agree on the number of casualties and compromised on "Twenty-eight," as the song was called.

"You must be wrong," a general roared. Another noted, "Hundreds of bodies were seen from the sky." Another contradicted, "You can't count civilians from up in the sky. He saw twenty-eight." That spurred the song's title line: "Let's Believe in the Captain," with the aside, "And let's be glad he didn't see any more."

"Final Report" had the First General recite, "Friendly casualties were light and the enemy suffered heavily." A GI snarled, "Bullshit! Can't you see them standing there so smug and satisfied knowing all the time damn well—they know damn well they lied," in a textbook example of lyric-padding. The GI vowed to write letters to higher-ups as this long scene ended.

Two years later, the statute of limitations hadn't run out on the ricky-ticky music. "He Wants to Put the Army in Jail," sang a senator, who'd finally deigned to read the GI's letter. We'd had many Lloyd Webber homages thus far; now Rice would get one: "A guy like this is *dane-gerusss*," intoned the First Congressman.

Then came a couplet to which Rice wouldn't have stooped: "I'm sure you'll concur he'll create quite a stir." Again, what a character would actually say in real life was irrelevant; was a rhyme around that we could use?

A worse offense occurred with the Clergyman when he reported receiving an incriminating "letter from a member of my flock. I wrote back and told him, 'Seek the help of the Lord.' Now please excuse me: I'm bored." No, not even the most uncaring cleric would publicly admit to being "bored"—especially concerning such a serious situation.

The Second Congressman sang, "I feel his ghastly story is real." Why not "I believe" or even "I suspect," which offers more assurance than "I feel"? Oh, right: feel/real.

"There's No Other Solution" had the organist play the ominous chords heard in a horror movie when someone walks up a dark flight of stairs. Then came a return to the ricky-tick for the army brass. "This outcry must stop" was followed by two hits on a drum block for comic effect. After "It's possible it may go right to the top" there was a raspberry sound. And after everyone admitted "It's a helluva mess," a circus slide whistle came in.

The three Generals decided, "We'll have to give them someone to try. Why not use the Lieutenant? He's the perfect fall guy!" Indeed he was, considering that he was guilty.

But one general objected: "I'd like to avoid it." The other two cried, "But what can we do? It's part of the game." Choosing "game" was meant to show how little these men regarded casualties, but the word choice was too easy and callous.

The collaborators had a good idea in having the Lieutenant sing the jaunty, "I'm Going Home," full of the joy that returning soldiers feel when they leave foreign soil. The dramatic irony let audiences know that his return would provoke no ticker-tape parade.

Instead, the Three Generals sang, "You're the one we're gonna try for what happened at My Lai." In another melody that recalled *Superstar*'s "Heaven on Their Minds," Three Reporters greeted him as "The Star of the War," their pet name for him. Each took a line, "Was it a thrill? Did you like to kill? Have you had your fill of civilians," in a rare and deft interior rhyme. "Was killing babies all a part of your scheme?"

"Scheme" seems lightweight for a premeditated mass killing. You know why it was chosen: "Did you like hearing them scream?" was the next question.

In "On Trial for My Life," the Lieutenant professed, "I only did the things they taught me. I did my best; look what it brought me," in the show's most deft couplet.

"The Conscience of a Nation" had the Prosecutor singing sanctimoniously about honor. Had the authors finally abandoned ricky-tick when dealing with authority figures?

No. After one verse, they returned to spoofy-sounding music—and inadequate word choice. They reached their nadir here: "He knew what he was doing on that day. You've got to find him guilty in a way."

In a *way*? What happened to "beyond a reasonable doubt"?

Although the composers had been paying homage to Lloyd Webber, they now chose to honor Galt MacDermot. The Prosecutor's address to the jury referenced *Hair*'s "Abie Baby." But the Defense Attorney's "Damned No Matter How He Turned" made him neither effective nor professional: "Something tells me that something terribly wrong is happening here." ("Something tells me"—meaning "I have a hunch"?)

He then sang in the style that rock likes most when underlining a point: falsetto. "It grieves me so to see the army torn apart and another tragedy start." He returned to his normal voice to stress, "What a wonderful choice we gave the man. No matter how he reacted, he'd be damned."

After the Prosecutor demanded, "Find him guilty," the Lieutenant insisted, "I believe I was right," leading to "I just did what they asked of me" before landing on, "I'm not sure I know right from wrong."

The jury members individually cried out "Guilty!" And while some theatergoers reached for their coats, the show returned to the army's recruiting office, where a new young man was interested in enlisting (or enrolling, if you will) although he "was doing fine in the construction line." My, any potential recruit tends to call his occupation a "line," doesn't he? Actually, the authors would have done better in having him say that he was "*on* the construction line."

"Life in the army is grand," the Recruiter assured him, before redundantly adding, "when you're an army man." We were again treated to "We'll fix you up in our latest style, and off you'll go to some tropical isle" and the show ended.

In addition to Best Musical, Best Score, and Best Actor in a Musical, *The Lieutenant* was nominated for Best Book—although there were few lines of dialogue. In 1982–1983, when the equally through-sung *Cats* received a Best Book nomination, plenty of people complained. Why no similar outcry eight years earlier?

Probably because so few saw *The Lieutenant* and weren't aware of it—or because the all-knowing critic from the *Times* had anointed it.

And what did Barnes think of the score to *Mack & Mabel*? "[Jerry] Herman's music is frustrating, as usual. Without seriously comparing him to Irving Berlin, he has a similar instinct for strong, simple melodies and straight-forward (if not particularly clean) lyric-writing."

Michael Stewart's book about Mack Sennett (1880–1960) and Mabel Normand (1892–1930) ran the gamut of early moviemaking. The story began in 1911, when talkies weren't even a dream, and finished in 1938, when cinema had advanced enough to tackle *Gone with the Wind*. It certainly was a colorful era.

Herman was up to creating its music. He started with a bit of the ricky-ticky, silent movie, vaudeville-flavored music found in *The Lieutenant*. Here, however, it felt logical for a silent movie pioneer who was famous for both his Keystone Kops and Bathing Beauties.

Now, decades later, Mack stood by his films in "Movies Were Movies." In a mere twenty-two lines, Herman managed to touch all the bases of the silent movie era: "Cheering the hero . . . hissing the man in the cape . . . Pardner, there's gold in them hills . . . bandits attacking a train . . . one little tramp with a cane . . . Pauline was tied to the track after she trudged through the ice with a babe on her back . . . girls at the seashore . . . Swanson and Keaton and Dressler and William S. Hart."

Add to these "blundering cops in a thundering chase" and "getting a bang out of lemon meringue"—two nifty interior rhymes—and one is starting to wonder why Barnes finds Herman's lyrics unclean.

Soon Mack remembered when he was filming and a delivery girl arrived with his star's lunch. The two squabbled over money, and Mack was so impressed with the delivery girl's fire that he started filming Mabel Normand for the first time.

Mabel was at first reluctant to quit the deli, as was shown in one of Herman's most fetching songs. She watched what Mack had filmed, and decided, "Miss Waitress from Flatbush, get down from up there; you're behaving like some little ass."

Those feelings, however, didn't survive beyond the verse. Soon she was astonished: "Look What Happened to Mabel," she decided. "From now on, this pile of flesh'll be considered somethin' pretty special." And by number's end, we were watching her making movies.

Of course, Mabel had to be grateful to Mack for making it happen, and he had to feel profoundly for the woman he Galatea'd into "somethin' pretty special." But matters weren't that simple, as audiences heard in one of Herman's most beloved ballads: "I Won't Send Roses." Mack explained to Mabel that business would always come first; in addition to roses, door holding, compliments, and birthday celebrations were not to be expected.

"In me, you'll find things like guts and nerve," he sang, "but not the kind things that you deserve." The rhyme seemed clean here, and the use of the words in front of "things"—first the verb "find" and then the adjective "kind"—was deft.

But Herman's last line was by far the most important: "And roses suit you so." There it was: Mack *was* attracted to Mabel, and if he weren't all consumed with making movies, she'd be the one for him. He was telling her not to take personally his inevitable negligence; he was at fault, not she. That kept us from disliking him, because he made clear that she was fully worthy of a man's attention.

Once again, a musical had a love versus career theme. But Mabel tried to appreciate Mack's point of view. She reprised "I Won't Send Roses," starting with "So who needs roses?" as she reached the first of the famous Kübler-Ross "Five Stages of Grief": denial. Once again, Herman reserved his most important sentiment for his last line, when Mabel concluded, "So who wants roses that didn't come from him?"

Already she was more in love than she realized. And why not? He was an achiever. But the theater is littered with female characters who ostensibly love achievers but eventually need to make their love achieve supremacy.

(Remember George Seurat? "They have never understood—and no reason why they should.")

Actually, a career issue started bigger trouble. Mabel wanted to do drama, but Mack replied, "I Wanna Make the World Laugh." In the song, Herman captured some of Sennett's most enduring images: "throw a fish in the heroine's face . . . the guy with the fly on his nose . . . a hero with ants in his pants . . . itching powder and Papa's mustache." Specific images are always best in lyrics, and Herman certainly delivered them here. Cleanly.

Mabel's next song had her reach the second Kübler-Ross stage—anger—as she complained that she wanted to be "Wherever He Ain't."

"I walked behind him like a meek little lamb," she sang. "And had my fill of his not givin' a damn. I'll go to Sydney or Ceylon or Siam," she decided. Triple rhymes are always welcome in musicals, but these three *clean* ones get a little extra credit because they involved different spellings of the "am" rhyme.

Mabel went to work for director William Desmond Taylor (1872–1922), which meant that Mack suddenly needed a new star. He decided that a mere one wouldn't do, which is how he conceived of the Bathing Beauties: "Hundreds of Girls," he sang to a rollicking Herman melody. Mack would film as many as he could " 'till ev'ry fella from Duluth to Atlanta sees all of his fantasies." (Nice, no?)

Of course, by 1974–1975, a Broadway cast with a hundred people, let alone girls, hadn't happened since the 1946 *Show Boat* revival. Gower Champion had only sixteen Bathing Beauties at his disposal. So he and set designer Robin Wagner came up with a floor-to-ceiling corkscrew from which the girls would slide from top to bottom. Then they'd go behind it and scurry back up and come down again. Alas, it didn't quite create the needed illusion. It seemed to us we'd seen that girl before.

Champion might have been better off using a different kind of slide—a photographic one—of a different silent screen lass on the back wall to each beat of music. Or was Champion still smarting from the unwieldy and ultimately unsatisfying use of the photographs that were projected on the back wall of *The Happy Time*?

Whatever the case, Champion couldn't make the Keystone Kops nearly as funny as the silent movie gambols in the original films. He gave us ample chance to compare, because he started act two with a montage of the actual Sennett films. He shouldn't have reminded us how good they were.

Mabel did return to Mack after *both* had reached the third Kübler-Ross stage: bargaining. He promised that, yes, he'd film the drama she wanted to do. Some critics chided Herman for once again delivering a song—"When Mabel Comes in the Room"—in which a chorus celebrated the woman in his show's title. "Hello, Dolly!" set the tone in 1964; even teens in the throes of Beatlemania allotted one of their eighty-nine-cent purchases to Louis Armstrong's surprise hit.

"Mame," although not nearly as successful as a pop record, was an even greater production number because Mame Dennis had actually achieved something unprecedented to warrant the excitement of the men and women around her: she'd survived a fox hunt on the plantation's most ornery horse and had got the town's biggest catch to propose to her.

Dolly, on the other hand, was simply returning to a restaurant where she'd been a customer. Had she been that good a tipper?

Now Mabel was returning to the studio where she'd been a genuine star. Her friends and colleagues had much better reason to welcome her return than Dolly's. Two decades later, Andrew Lloyd Webber, Don Black, and to some degree, lyricist Amy Powers, would successfully musicalize this same moment in *Sunset Boulevard*, when Norma Desmond returned to her old haunt in "As If We Never Said Goodbye." They instead took the moment from her point of view.

Herman's heroines, however, usually basked in admiration; yes, Dolly had sung the first chorus of her number but then the waiters took it from there. Mame just listened and smiled. So did Mabel.

Still, the song had resonance; we've all known the jubilant feeling of greeting and old friend or coworker after too long an absence. If Herman had written this song before "Dolly" or "Mame," he and it would have been greatly lauded, for both melody and lyrics are as accomplished.

Mack was a tiger that couldn't change his stripes. Soon after he started filming Mabel's drama, he conceived of the Keystone Cops and turned it into a comedy. The Keystone Kops would turn out to amuse millions, but not Mabel. Hence, the fourth Kübler-Ross stage: depression.

That brought her back to Taylor, who turned her into a heroin addict. When he was murdered, she became a prime suspect. The result was Herman's best torch song, "Time Heals Everything." Mabel sang bravely about Mack before succumbing during the last line, "but loving you," and reaching the fifth Kübler-Ross stage, acceptance.

Mabel died, and Mack eventually realized what he'd lost. "I Promise You a Happy Ending," he decided, "that has you loving me loving you."

Doesn't quite work, does it? Stewart's rash of supporting characters didn't help. Lottie Ames thought she was first in Mack's eye until Mabel came into the room. To balance this, Stewart wrote Frank Wyman, the budding writer who loved Mabel. These were standard romantic complications that you'd expect to find on any Hollywood lot, be it factual or fictitious. Stewart also included someone resembling Fatty Arbuckle to make some funny faces and do some pratfalls—but not, for better or worse, the act that got him into serious trouble.

The result, however, was that the actors in these roles didn't have much to play. Stewart was so busy trying to make a riveting story for Mack and Mabel that he neglected to flesh out these other characters.

The tale was actually a small one at heart that might have done better as a chamber musical dealing with Mack, Mabel, and Taylor. But the *Hello, Dolly!* men weren't chamber-musical types. A small approach would have definitely eliminated "Hundreds of Girls," and losing such a fetching song would have been a major loss.

Nevertheless, in the ensuing four decades, while *The Lieutenant* has rarely if ever resurfaced, *Mack & Mabel* has reappeared with regularity. Virtually every revival involved significant work by Stewart or, after his death in 1987, others. By now it's had more surgeries than Joan Rivers has had on her face.

The score stayed as is, and continued to shine. "Time Heals Everything" became a cabaret perennial. Torvill and Dean won a gold medal after ice dancing in the 1982 World Figure Skating Championships to the original cast album's overture. In the 1997 film version of *Love! Valour! Compassion!* one man was shown deciding on which original cast albums to take for his weekend away. He selected the smash hits *Evita* and *Funny Girl*—and *Mack & Mabel* (and rejected *Cats*).

But the 1974–1975 Tony nominating committee seemed ashamed of the traditional Broadway musical and had to show how avant-garde and smart it was to agree with Barnes—by choosing not only *The Lieutenant* but also *A Letter to Queen Victoria* for Best Score. Snubbing Herman implied that his brand of catchy melodies and smart *and* clean lyrics were no longer welcome.

And yet, in 1974–1975, Stewart got a nomination for a problematic book, while Herman didn't for his extraordinary score.

Time heals everything, but not this. The snub virtually made Herman a hermit. Stewart had to talk him into doing his next show, *The Grand Tour.* Although it did get him a 1978–1979 Best Score Tony nomination—probably as a consolation prize for the previous slight—the show ran five performances fewer (sixty-one) than *Mack & Mabel.* Just as it's harder to be poor after being rich, Herman had to face facts: after 5,135 performances in the sixties, he had 127 showings in the seventies.

He'd go out with a winner, *La Cage aux Folles*, which got the Best Score Tony for the 1983–1984 Tony-winning Best Musical. Herman was only fifty-two at the time, but he was content to leave Broadway. No one likes a poker player who wins a big pot at eight o'clock, loses a fortune by nine, wins big again at ten—and then rushes home.

Herman's first Tony-nominated Best Score in Best Musical Tony loser *Milk and Honey* (1961–1962) began with "Shalom: the nicest greeting you know." It did signal a nice greeting for Herman's Main Stem career.

Too bad, however, that "shalom" also means good-bye—which Herman prematurely said to Broadway.

Mack & Mabel was one reason why.

* * *

Peter Stone, the librettist of *Skyscraper* (1965–1966), would later admit that he made one mistake that kept the musical from becoming a hit.

Producers Cy Feuer and Ernest Martin had offered him two ideas for new musicals. One was Elmer Rice's 1945 hit *Dream Girl*, about a woman who was having hallucinations, however benign; the other concerned a home owner who staunchly refused to sell to developers, which kept them from erecting a profitable building on the site.

Said Stone, "It occurred to me to put the two stories together."

More was less, as each story diluted the other. Composer James Van Heusen and lyricist Sammy Cahn's dull score didn't help.

And yet, *Skyscraper* received a Best Musical Tony nomination.

A gossip columnist may have been responsible.

Dorothy Kilgallen had been writing "The Voice of Broadway" for the *New York Journal American* for twenty-seven years. Since 1950, she'd become even more famous, thanks to her stint as a panelist on the TV game show *What's My Line?* Now, when Kilgallen either spoke or wrote, people all over the country listened.

On October 21, 1965, Kilgallen attended a preview of *Skyscraper*. She was a patron of George Junior Republic, a charity for underprivileged children that had chosen the show as its annual theater party benefit.

Broadway had always had a gentlemen's agreement with columnists that they would not comment (at least not negatively) about a preview. But Kilgallen was no gentleman. For her, the word "preview" contained the word "review."

The next day, Kilgallen gave her opinion of *Skyscraper*, although the musical's official opening night was still twenty-two days away. Her lead—"I wish someone would pass a law making it illegal for a columnist to see a Broadway show before its official premiere"—made Broadway wish the same thing, too.

Kilgallen, however, instead acted as if there were law that demanded that she air her feelings. Her opening statement seemed disingenuous when she felt free to say that *Skyscraper* had "no music to speak of" and that it was a "turkey." She even dismissed Julie Harris as "not a musical comedy performer" when she could have given the two-time Tony-winning dramatic actress credit for attempting something new.

What made Kilgallen's 297-word pan all the more surprising is that she blithely admitted that she had only seen the show's first act. Granted, act one of most musicals tend to be better than act two, but Kilgallen's early exit gave her less ammunition to criticize the show.

Kilgallen might not have specifically known that Stone during the Detroit tryout had replaced seventy-five pages of his script (the average musical has about a hundred and fifty). But she had to have heard that second lead Victor Spinetti had been unceremoniously fired and replaced by Charles Nelson Reilly. A Broadway columnist had to have heard the scuttlebutt—especially one who was married to Richard Kollmar, who'd produced six Broadway musicals.

Kilgallen's Broadway review of *Skyscraper* was the only one she'd ever read. On November 8, 1965, she died under mysterious circumstances. Some say that she was murdered because she'd interviewed Jack Ruby, Lee Harvey Oswald's killer, and was about to divulge what Ruby had to say about John F. Kennedy's assassination.

(An aside, Killgallen's son-in-law at the time was composer Larry Grossman, who'd eventually get his share of Best Score Tony nominations for *A Doll's Life* and *Grind*. When Grossman is asked what he knows about the Kennedy assassination, he turns pale and snaps, "I never discuss that. Never!"

John Wilkes Booth in *Assassins* says of the assassination that "Fifty years from now, they'll still be arguing about the grassy knoll, the Mafia, some Cuban crouched behind a stockade fence." He's right. But could it be that the composer of *Snoopy* knows the whole story?)

The following Saturday, *Skyscraper* opened to reviews that were much kinder than expected. Were the critics overly accommodating to mitigate Kilgallen's journalistic gaffe? Others surmised that the critics expected to see a show as bad as Kilgallen had alleged, and that seeing even a slightly better one caused them to overpraise.

"*Skyscraper* is a joyous, boisterous, brash, fast-moving musical"— Taubman, *The Times*. So said the inch-high headline on the full-page ad that Feuer and Martin placed on page fifty-five of the morning edition of *The New York Times* on November 16, 1965. Enthusiastic quotations from a dozen other critics followed.

The irony is that only six pages away in the same edition was the report from the state's medical examiner that Kilgallen had died "from the reaction of a combination of alcohol and barbiturates."

Skyscraper was alive, however. "Mail orders now accepted for the next fifteen months," the full-page ad confidently said in half-inch boldface print. But it wasn't a good enough musical to last even half that long. Still, when the Tony nominators met, they chose it as a Best Musical nominee over the superior (if flawed) *On a Clear Day You Can See Forever*, and tossed four other nominations its way, too. Were the nominators also overcompensating for Dorothy Kilgallen's not giving it the benefit of the doubt during previews?

Curtains (2006–2007) brought on its own bad luck by choosing the wrong number to represent it on the Tony Awards.

A good showing on that annual TV infomercial can sell plenty of tickets the next day. But if the audience doesn't like the song that supposedly puts the show's best foot forward, people head to different Web sites on Monday morning.

The management of *Curtains* decided on "Show People," which took place after the cast of *Robbin' Hood* saw its leading lady murdered during their Boston tryout. Lieutenant Frank Cioffi (David Hyde Pierce), a musical theater enthusiast, was assigned to investigate. When he discovered that the company was blasé about the fate of the show and their jobs, he expressed shock because he expected more from "Show People."

By number's end, the cast rallied and agreed how fortunate they were. It was a big production numba in the grand Broadway tradition, aggressively orchestrated and ending in (what else?) a kickline.

Tony viewers may have assumed that Broadway was congratulating itself once again. Hadn't they heard too many songs that insisted that there was no business like show business?

In this season of *Spring Awakening*, the Kander and Ebb number made *Curtains* look desperately old-fashioned. There's that truism: an old person doesn't look old until someone young stands next to him.

Yes, they wanted a number that featured Pierce, their ace-trump draw. Then why not "A Tough Act to Follow," the duet Cioffi shared with his romantic interest? In "Show People," he started the number and then yielded the floor to the ensemble.

Actually, *Curtains* should have chosen "It's a Business." Here crass producer Carmen Bernstein made no apologies over mounting a musical in order to make money. "I'm not devoid of culture, but my feet are on the floor," she sang. "I'd do the Kama Sutra with a Richard Rodgers score."

We live in a cynical age. Few theatergoers and even armchair Tony viewers still have stars in their eyes. They might have enjoyed Carmen's audacity: "Yes, green's my favorite color and I don't mean on grass . . . And if you don't like my business, sweetie, blow it out your—business."

Truth to tell, *Curtains* needed more than that. As the show wended its way toward a happy conclusion—meaning that a *critic* turned out to be the murderer—we suddenly learned that Carmen Bernstein had killed her coproducer—who not so coincidentally had happened to be her husband. Cioffi discovered it, and now Ms. Bernstein would have to do the time for committing the crime.

There are tough ladies whom we love to love as well as hate, if only for their determined audacity. Carmen was one of them. We didn't want her to be capable of murder, let alone perpetrate it. That she killed was too much of a downer for a show where every other plot point was working out. It wasn't a time to put a sour taste in our mouths.

That *Curtains* lost was no mystery, but *Dreamgirls* (1981–1982)? This was the first musical to capture three of the four Best Performance awards and not win the big prize.

First and foremost among the winners: Jennifer Holliday as Effie Melody White, the lead singer of the Dreamettes who'd be demoted to backup singer when the Dreams were reconfigured.

Book writer/lyricist Tom Eyen handled that scene brilliantly. Manager Curtis Taylor, Jr. (Ben Harney), told the Dreamettes that he'd signed a contract for better engagements, higher pay, and improved living conditions. Only after they were all excited about the good news did he deliver the catch: Effie and Deena would be changing places. He knew that first making all three women excited would undercut the objections that Effie would now have.

Not quite. Effie became so difficult that she had to be replaced—and once she learned that she was fired, she sang what might have been the first first-act closer in Broadway musical history to get a standing ovation *during* the number: Eyen and composer Henry Krieger's "And I Am Telling You I'm Not Going."

Eyen's skill was apparent even with lesser characters. James "Thunder" Early (Cleavant Derricks) loudly complained that the sandwich he'd ordered wasn't correctly seasoned. That immediately told audiences that he was a star, for only someone of importance would dare to grouse over something so trivial.

Another wise Eyen decision was to mention the Supremes by name as a popular group in order to deflect suspicion that *Dreamgirls* was actually about them. Never mind that audiences immediately inferred that Deena was a stand-in for Diana Ross and that Effie greatly resembled the discarded Florence Ballard. Eyen's blatantly mentioning the Supremes meant no lawsuit could ever hold up in court.

Bennett's staging was spectacular, although never better than the montage of the Dreams' tour. After the trio had performed a number, they disappeared behind a curtain; a voice-over announced their next engagement in a different town, and they immediately returned in completely different outfits. Audiences were silent as they noticed that something was different, but it took them a long second to notice the dresses had changed. The "ooohs" that resulted were particularly awe-filled.

Those who believe "timing is everything" can use *Dreamgirls* as an example. It opened December 20, 1981; *Nine*, which beat it as Best Musical, opened May 9, 1982—the same day as the Tony cutoff. *Nine* was fresh in everyone's minds.

Soon after, managements of shows that had been around a while began reinviting Tony voters to take a second look. This was especially true of those that had seats readily available. *Dreamgirls* didn't have them and lost the Best Musical Tony—an award it didn't apparently need. It ran more than twice as long as *Nine*. The *Dreamgirls* management was probably just as glad to have raked in the extra $70,000 on sold seats than giving them away.

It may also have wished that it had opened in another year—like so many other shows.

CHAPTER SEVEN

*

It Would Have Been Wonderful: The Best Musical Tony Losers That Would Have Won in Other Years

Urinetown (2001–2002) and *The Drowsy Chaperone* (2005–2006) wouldn't seem to have too much in common.

The former musical started with a police officer's bringing a somber-looking man on stage. Although he seemed to be escorting him to jail, he brought him to the piano. The "criminal" was in fact the show's musical director, who began an overture that was clear from its first five dissonant notes that Kurt Weill was being channeled. But Weill and collaborator Bertolt Brecht wouldn't have thought to write a musical in which urination was a big issue—that citizens would have to pay for the privilege to pee.

As money-collector Penelope Pennywise sang, "If you got to go, you got to go through me." But she was only a pawn for mogul Caldwell B. Cladwell.

A champion for the people emerged in Bobby Strong. Unlike other musical theater heroes, Bobby was killed midway through act two. Justice did triumph, however, despite this loss.

The plot and score (by composer Mark Hollmann and book writer Greg Kotis) were in marked contrast to *The Drowsy Chaperone's* score by Lisa Lambert and Greg Morrison and Bob Martin's book. This was a nostalgic tour down memory lane, in which a "Man in Chair" enjoys a bootleg recording of a musical from the twenties. He gets so immersed that by show's end, the cast invites him to be a part of it.

What the dark satire and light-headed romp had in common, however, was that each won for Best Book and Best Score—and lost Best Musical. Undoubtedly, voters thought that *Thoroughly Modern Millie* would have an easier time of it on tour than *Urinetown*. As for *Drowsy*, it had no chance against the juggernaut that was *Jersey Boys*.

Both, however, would have won in other years. So would plenty of other shows.

Today, *Cats* (1982–1983) is a humiliating cliché, but in the 1982–1983 season, it was just what Broadway needed: a show so talked about that everybody knew about it.

Saturday Night Live gave birth to the sarcastic nonendorsement "It's better than *Cats*." This line fit the profile of "no publicity is bad publicity—and bad publicity is better than no publicity." You can be sure that the previous season, *SNL* hadn't mentioned *Nine*.

So *Cats*, with a Barbra Streisand recording of its "Memory" making it even more famous, just had to win the 1982–1983 Best Musical Tony. It came in strong and stayed strong and became Broadway's longest-running production in 1997.

That didn't leave *My One and Only* (1982–1983) with much of a chance. Before it opened on May 1, 1983, nobody gave it *any* chance because of its horrific Boston tryout. At his curtain call on opening night, Tommy Tune had actually apologized to the audience for how bad it was. Peter Stone replaced Timothy S. Mayer as book writer, and choreographers Tune and Thommie Walsh took over the direction from Peter Sellars—and somehow made it a two-year hit.

It was said to be a reworking of the 1927 Gershwin hit *Funny Face*, but it mercifully didn't use its stolen-jewel plot and only took five of its songs: "Funny Face," " 'S Wonderful," "High Hat," "He Loves and She Loves," and "In the Swim."

The last one gave Mayer the idea to make Edythe Herbert a long-distance swimmer: "the third woman to swim the English Channel, but the first attractive one." (Gertrude Ederle and Amelia Gade Corson couldn't have been pleased.)

When Billy Buck Chandler (Tune) spied a look at Edythe, he certainly thought that she was attractive. He was so smitten he didn't have the words. It was the perfect opportunity for him to sing "Blah, Blah, Blah," Ira Gershwin's acknowledgment that most love songs don't have words worth hearing.

Billy was a pilot intent on being the first to fly nonstop from New York to Paris. His mechanic Mickey wasn't happy he was smitten with Edythe; she wanted him to be single minded.

Yes, *she*—although Mickey had a mouth like a sailor with Tourette's syndrome. Her salty language made for a marked difference from *Funny Face*; women certainly didn't talk that way in 1927 (at least on stage).

Now Billy wanted to make his mark for Edythe. But at the party he attended, Edythe was on the arm of Prince Nikki—and under his thumb. He possessed "art pictures" for which she'd posed when she was young, desperate, and starving. So while Edythe sang her own version of "Blah, Blah, Blah" when she first laid eyes on Billy, she had to brush him off with the force of the industrial-strength brushes found in car washes.

However, when Billy mentioned Paris, Edythe begged him to take her with him. Alas, weight was an issue on this unproven transatlantic flight and Edythe was simply too heavy (although Twiggy played her). But he offered to fly her to Florida.

Prince Nikki put water in Billy's gas tank, which caused an emergency stop. He and Edythe enjoyed being alone and did a lovely dance to " 'S Wonderful" in a shallow pool. But Billy was soon depressed at the thought that someone might beat him to Paris.

"It isn't what people think of you," said Edythe. "It's what you think of yourself. All the others don't really care about you. They just want to stare at you and touch you and make money off you."

Now that Billy had heard her values, he was really in love.

They were soon rescued, but one chance remark led to the sort of misunderstanding that always separates lovers in shows like this. Billy decided to concentrate on Paris, and ended the first act with "Strike Up the Band."

Not, however, in the way audiences had anticipated. Instead of an orchestra playing a rave-up march, Tune delivered a half-tempo solo of intense determination. It made for a dynamic first-act curtain.

To escape, Edythe stowed away to Morocco. Billy demanded to know why, and was shown the scandalous pictures. His reaction? "I like 'em!"

He flew over to find her, and once he did, he heard on the news that Charles Lindbergh had landed in Paris. Edythe felt bad.

Billy didn't. He knew he'd done Lindbergh one better by flying *past* Paris to Morocco. "Like you said," he told Edythe. "It isn't what people think of you. It's what you think of yourself."

Cats doesn't look so bad now, does it?

Actually, *My One and Only* could have won Best Musical in many other seasons. It was a terrific song 'n' dance show, with exciting chorus numbers—two of which featured Tony-winner Charles "Honi" Coles as Billy's fashion guru. A highlight was "High Hat," when six foot six Tune danced with shorter dancers; when all danced behind a wall. More Tony voters' hats would have tipped *My One and Only*'s way two years hence, when *Big River* won.

My One and Only was the only semblance of competition that *Cats* had; certainly *Merlin* and *Blues in the Night* weren't contenders. But while few if any begrudged *My Fair Lady* the 1956–1957 Best Musical Tony, two other runners-up suffered that same season.

If *Bells Are Ringing* or *The Most Happy Fella* had opened in 1955–1956, the former might have bested *Damn Yankees* for the prize and the latter certainly would have. No one had to wait until *Dreamgirls* to learn that "timing is everything."

Book writers and lyricists Betty Comden and Adolph Green purposely wrote the show for their old pal who'd costarred with them in their thirties and forties nightclub act, the Revuers. Composer Jule Styne joined them for the third time in what would be nine collaborations.

This one was their most successful. Cinderella tales are almost always welcome on Broadway. To make the connection even stronger, Comden and Green took the last two syllables of Cinderella's name for their heroine.

Ella Peterson (Judy Holliday) worked a switchboard at Susanswerphone, taking messages for clients in those pre-answering machine days. Good soul that she was, Ella became greatly involved with her clients' lives.

First and foremost in her thoughts, however, was Jeff Moss (Sydney Chaplin), who had been half of a Kaufman and Hart–like playwriting team. Since the partnership ended, he hadn't done much.

"What does he look like?" Ella mused. One must wonder, however, why she didn't know. Certainly one of the tabloids must have run a picture of Moss at some opening night or any of the many parties this well-known hedonist had attended. Comden and Green should have established that Jeff was extraordinarily camera-shy and never allowed his picture to be taken.

They did think to include a marvelous moment where Ella was about to give Jeff a wake-up call—but not until she put on makeup. Although he wouldn't be able to see her, she still wanted to look her best for him.

Ella's musings about Jeff became one of the best opening songs a musical theater heroine has ever had: "It's a Perfect Relationship." Ella was resigned that he'd always be "just a voice: Plaza 0-double-four-double-three . . . I'll never meet him, and he'll never meet me."

There wouldn't be much of a show if that were the case.

Alas, Jeff didn't respond to his wake-up call—and he did have an important meeting with a producer—so Ella went to his apartment to awaken him. She pretended to be there by mistake, and identified herself as Melisande Scott. Of course he wanted to throw her out, but she stayed long enough to prompt him to work. Ella revitalized him so much that he came to love her.

Unlike Cinderella, who had time run out on her, Ella eventually felt guilty that "he's in love with Melisande Scott; a girl who doesn't exist." So like that fairy-tale princess, she took her leave but didn't leave as much as a shoe behind her.

Not only that: Ella decided to quit Susanswerphone. "I'm Goin' Back (to the Bonjour Tristesse Brassiere Company)" was a showpiece that demonstrated Holliday's talents as well as conveyed Ella's bravery in the face of adversity. But after this extraordinary eleven o'clock number, Jeff found Ella at the eleventh hour and Cinderella wound up getting her prince.

Styne wrote sparking music. "Hello, Hello There," in which Ella taught Jeff to talk to strangers, is probably the only charm song set to an oom-pah-pah waltz. Comden and Green provided witty lyrics. In "Is It a Crime?" Ella fantasized that if she had relayed an important phone call with life-or-death information to Romeo and Juliet, "Those two kids would be alive today!"

One scene that paralleled Cinderella's getting all spiffed up led to "Mu-Cha-Cha"; Ella was so delighted at how she looked that she was ripe to dance. (Her dress, of course, was red, for that is musical theater's most valuable costume: Molly Brown, Nancy, Dolly, Desiree, and Cassie have worn various shades of it).

Comden and Green never had a problem creating colorful characters: Claire deLoon in *On the Town*, Rodney Gender in *Billion Dollar Baby*, and the Wreck in *Wonderful Town*. Here, to ameliorate Sue, the all-business owner of Susananswerphone, they gave her a flamboyant boyfriend in Sandor. He adopted a mittle European accent and grand gestures befitting the president of Titanic Records.

Alas, it was a front. Sandor was a bookie who'd use Susanswerphone to take racehorse bets over the phone. "It's a Simple Little System," he sang, where classical musicians' names substituted for racetracks: Beethoven was Belmont Park; Puccini, Pimlico; Rachmaninoff, Rockingham.

What luck that the man who wrote "Hallelujah Chorus" had a name that started with "H," for otherwise one of the great lyric jokes of all time—Q: "What is Handel?" A: "Hialelah! Hialeah!"—wouldn't have worked.

No one can ever say for sure who writes what in any musical. But one can easily picture Styne, Comden, and Green discussing the song and Green, a classical music maven, jumping off the couch with the "Hialeah-Hallelujah" joke?

Then there was Dr. Kitchell, an arguably mentally disturbed dentist who was thoroughly uninterested in his profession because he preferred to write songs on his air hose. (Comden said that her own dentist was the inspiration, although he merely used his air hose to accompany music that was playing on his office radio.)

Coincidentally, *Happy Hunting*, the Ethel Merman musical that opened eight days after *Bells Are Ringing*, actually had music by a dentist. Harold Karr, DDS, had traded in his periodontal scales in favor of music scales. (Some would argue that Dr. Kitchell's songs were better.)

And let's not forget *Bells Are Ringing*'s two standards: "Just in Time," in which Jeff expressed his appreciation for all Ella had done for him, and "The Party's Over," in which Ella had to face that the person Jeff had come to love wasn't who she was at all.

Comden and Green would write sixteen shows for Broadway (including *Bonanza Bound*, a 1948 out-of-town closing), but this would be the only show that would yield two hit songs. That might have meant a good deal more if their rival *My Fair Lady* hadn't yielded five.

When *Bells Are Ringing* closed, only ten book musicals had ever run longer. Holliday's winning Best Actress in a Musical over Julie Andrews in *My Fair Lady* may have been a consolation prize: "We've got to give this excellent show *something*."

* * *

The Most Happy Fella had three hits: "Standing on the Corner," "Joey, Joey, Joey," and "Big D." And yet, none of them was featured in the overture. That had to be a first: what songwriter didn't want to put his best musical foot forward and entice theatergoers into thinking that hits were in the offing even before the show officially began?

Frank Loesser, that's who. He had grand intentions with this show, so he preferred not to display his musical comedy numbas but instead felt the need to establish his more ambitious thrust. His overture sounded sweepingly important and set a loftier tone.

It was Loesser's third consecutive hit. His first two, *Where's Charley?* and *Guys and Dolls*, had opened only 774 days apart. But Loesser needed 1,957 days to open *The Most Happy Fella*—and for two good reasons.

First, Loesser wrote more songs for it (thirty) than the combined song lists of the two shows that had opened before it—*My Fair Lady* and *Mr. Wonderful*. Second, Loesser also wrote the book. Yes, he was adapting Sidney Howard's 1925 Pulitzer Prize–winner *They Knew What They Wanted*, and plays, with dialogue already in place, are easier to adapt than novels.

But Howard had had plenty of speeches about labor versus management, and Loesser had many more decisions to make on how to handle those. Just as with a garden, pruning is not as easy as it seems.

Tony Esposito, the Italian American sixty-something vintner on a business trip, was attracted to Amy, a much younger waitress. He left her two atypical tips: his bejeweled tie pin and a note. Amy sang what it said: "I don't know nothin' about you," one of musical theater's most beautiful songs, which manages to be both quiet and deliver a lightning bolt at the same time.

The note's sincerity made Amy ignore the broken English. She wrote back. Tony's vineyard workers were there when the postman arrived with her letters—as well as missives for Farnsworth, Van Pelt, Sullivan, and Herbie Greene. "Say, who's Pearl?" the mailman freely read off a postcard.

These were inside jokes, for all were names associated with the production: Ralph Farnsworth (Cook; Bus Driver), Lois Van Pelt (Neighbor Lady), Jo Sullivan (Rosabella), and Herbie Greene (musical director), who at the time was actually dating a woman named Pearl.

When Tony read that Amy—whom he preferred to idealize as Rosabella—wanted a picture, he was devastated. Who'd want to look at someone old and fat, who was gray where he wasn't bald? However, with his handsome foreman Joe planning to leave his employ, Tony asked him to take "a pitch"—meaning "picture," which was the best that Tony could do in his immigrant's English.

Tony was, then, no match for that expert dialectician and grammarian six blocks away: Henry Higgins. Neither was *The Most Happy Fella*. It lost all six Tonys for which it had been nominated, which, at the time, set a sad record. It was also the first money-making hit that was a Best Musical Tony Loser. That's what happens when you open only fifty-one days after *My Fair Lady*—even if you have a more romantic and heartwarming ending than "Eliza, where the devil are my slippers?"

So at 676 performances, *The Most Happy Fella* could manage only a fourth as long a run as *My Fair Lady*. Thus, if any musical were to be recorded in its entirety, it would have to be *My Fair Lady*. But Columbia Record producer Goddard Lieberson instead waxed *The Most Happy Fella* on three long-playing records and packaged them in an impressive-looking box.

Granted, the sheer amount of music and number of songs necessitated more than one disc. But Lieberson could have easily put the songs on only two records. His recording the show virtually word for word was the greatest compliment that a record-setting Tony-losing musical could get.

While *Gypsy* was too good a musical to finish third in the 1959–1960 race, *Once Upon a Mattress* was much too good a show to finish fourth.

William and Jean Eckart were extraordinarily gifted set designers. How gifted? Walter Kerr's review of *Mame* didn't begin with praise for Angela Lansbury, Jerry Herman, Bea Arthur, or book writers Lawrence and Lee. Instead, he spent his first two paragraphs celebrating what the Eckarts had achieved. How many set designers can say that?

Once Upon a Mattress, a fractured fairy-tale version of *The Princess and the Pea*, was the Eckarts' sole venture into producing. With the then still hot George Abbott agreeing to direct, $100,000 was easily raised.

Sound frightfully low? As it turned out, $20,000 of it wasn't even needed. The result was not only a well-received musical, but also a perennial.

Give the Eckarts credit, too, for not throwing in the towel when the musical was constantly evicted by theater owners who felt that they could make more money from other shows. The same weekend that the 1959–1960 Tonys were dispensed, the Eckarts were moving *Once Upon a Mattress* into the fourth of the five theaters that it would occupy. The show didn't win any Tonys, but the Schumer Theatrical Transfer Trucking Company gave the Eckarts a special award for giving them so much business. *Mattress* actors were less grateful; they would often carry protest signs to fight their evictions: "A house! My kingdom for a house!"

The mute King Sextimus probably would have given his kingdom for a house, too—if it had been situated far away from his wife. He was horribly henpecked by the very aptly named Queen Aggravain. She was played by Jane White, a black woman—and even the daughter of NAACP founder Walter White—in Broadway's first use of color-blind casting.

Throughout the musical, Aggravain barked out orders while Sextimus and their son Dauntless stood silently and helplessly by. Nothing would change, the legend went, until "the mouse devoured the hawk."

Audiences may well have been ahead of the kingdom's inhabitants. Some inferred that "the mouse devours the hawk" was a metaphor for mama's boy Dauntless finally standing up to his very vocal and all-controlling mother.

Much easier said than done. Dauntless wanted to find a wife, but Aggravain kept making impossible demands of any candidate, as shown in a scene written in the style of that favorite fifties form of entertainment: the TV quiz show. When the newest would be princess couldn't answer "What was the middle name of the daughter-in-law of the best friend of the blacksmith who forged the sword that killed the dragon?" once again Aggravain got to mother-smother her darling baby boy. Sang Dauntless, "I lack a lass, alas, alack," in the first example of some excellent wordplay from lyricist Marshall Barer.

Barer and his two colibrettists Dean Fuller and Jay Thompson established that Aggravain was sorry that her favorite candidate doesn't quite qualify: "If I were only twenty years younger," she moaned. Given that she took herself out of the running, Aggravain said that any contender for her son's hand "must be a real, genuine, bona fide princess, just as I was."

The queen not only wanted to control her kid, but the kingdom as well. Thus, until Dauntless married, every other citizen would be denied the chance to wed, too. As a result, the ladies and knights sang, "Nobody's getting any." That might sound a tad ribald and out-of-place in what seemed to be a fairy tale. But Barer showed us that we had the dirty minds, not he or his knights or ladies, when he added the word "younger" to the line.

Then entered Winnifred, the gawky, gangly, too tall lass who wasn't ashamed to say that she came from the swamps of Farfelot, a part of the world that made Aggravain look down her eyes, ears, nose, and throat at her. Class distinction—an important theme in musicals of an earlier age when immigrants needed to feel equal to the sons and daughters of the American Revolution—came into play.

Winnifred claimed to be a princess. She sportingly tried to guess which of the assembled would be the lucky person to get her. "Hey, nonny, nonny, is it you?" got many a "Hey, nonny *no*" in response. When Winnifred reached Dauntless, however, he'd already become so taken with her that he could only nervously answer, "Nonny, neeny, noony, nonny, noony, neeny"—a nice parody of Jonathan Winters's 1958 novelty hit, "Ne Ne Na Na Na Na Nu Nu."

Aggravain remained repulsed by Winnifred, but Broadway would be as impressed as Dauntless with the newcomer who portrayed her: Carol Burnett.

Here's the other side of "timing is everything." No beauty, Burnett was right at home as the ugly duckling who frankly admitted that she was "going fishing for a mate" with "bated breath and hook." And while this joke is clunky when read—because of the difference in the spelling of "bated" and "baited"—it played well aurally.

All this happened in Burnett's first song in which she oxymoronically brayed that she was "Shy." Barer made that word especially pay off at song's end when Winnifed sang that she was "one man shy."

Barer was equally deft in having the Jester sing and do a soft-shoe called "Very Soft Shoes"—apt, for that's what jesters have always been pictured wearing. He told how he went into the family business; his father had "played the palace" and was called "a dancing fool." Considering that a jester was also known as a fool, Barer cleverly riffed on this expression that describes someone who loves to dance.

Aggravain was so threatened by Winnifred that she devised an impossible test for her to pass. She put a pea under twenty mattresses; if it kept Winnifred from sleeping, there would be the proof that she had the sensitive skin that only princesses have.

Such a queen is bound to make enemies. Sir Studley put jousting equipment between the mattresses so that Winnifred couldn't sleep. The next morning, Dauntless was thrilled when he saw Winnifred sleep-deprived. After Aggravain, drenched in flop sweat, tried to talk Dauntless out of marrying her, the lad yelled, "Shut up!"

Everyone in the kingdom was stunned—but that was trumped by

Aggravain's suddenly being struck mute and Sextimus's discovering that he could talk. The king, especially in the mousy guise of Jack Gilford, then delivered one of those rare lines that is guaranteed to get applause from a grateful audience: "And I've got a lot to say!" All theatergoers had felt bad for the indignities that Sextimus had endured all night long. For that matter, what person hasn't endured an analogous injustice from an impossible boss?

Equally wonderful at show's end was a nice joke not found in the script, suggesting that Abbott had thought of it. Winnifred again took to those mattresses and tried to sleep, but still could not. Finally, she reached between them to extricate a tiny object that had somehow got stuck between mattresses six and seven. Then she slept. To paraphrase Henry Higgins, "She *is* of royal blood—and a princess."

But *Once Upon a Mattress* wasn't a Tony winner in any way. For the first and only time thus far, a father bested his daughter, as Richard Rodgers's composer-daughter Mary lost to her daddy's *The Sound of Music*. Ms. Rodgers's score has its assets; Aggravain's "Sensitivity" has to be one of Broadway's few songs written entirely in 5/4. And yet, in an era where pop singers were still looking to record songs from Broadway musicals, *Mattress* got not even one to cover a single song.

Mattress has long since had the last laugh. This variation on the time-honored theme of the country bumpkin bettering the city slicker has since had more than 25,000 productions. Millions more have seen it on television. To be sure, many Best Musical Tony losers have made it to the small screen: videos of original productions (*Into the Woods*) or made-for-TV specials (Bette Midler's *Gypsy*). *Mattress*, however, received three separate television productions: with Burnett reprising her role in 1964 and 1972, and then, with age a factor in 2005, playing Aggravain. It's one of those Best Musical losers that will be with us much longer than many Best Musical Tony winners.

And how's *this* for a fractured fairy tale?

A medieval Baker and his Wife (Joanna Gleason) haven't been able to conceive, and are told by a witch that they have been cursed. They can reverse the spell if they can deliver to her "the cow as white as milk, the cape as red as blood, the hair as yellow as corn, and the slipper as pure as gold."

Before long, they run into the cow that's owned by Jack of Beanstalk fame, the red cape owned by Little Red Ridinghood, the plentiful blond hair that Rapunzel lets down from her tower, and the shoe that Cinderella lost while running from the Prince.

Sounds as if it'd be a laff riot, doesn't it? But composer-lyricist Stephen Sondheim and book writer James Lapine had more on their minds than just delivering belly laughs. For better or worse, they didn't deliver one the entire night in their *Into the Woods* (1987–1988).

Oh, there was plenty of wit, especially in the first act. Little Red Ridinghood's contretemps with Wolf led to her wearing his scalped fur as a stole. Cinderella unceremoniously landed on her gluteus maximus after escaping the Prince. The painful amputations that Cinderella's stepsisters endured in order to fit into the Prince's acquired shoe caused some chuckles—and "ewwwws."

And yet, much of the act one fun was lessened because so much of it took place during late afternoon and dark night in a tree-dominated forest. Comedy plays best when it's brightly lit.

When *Into the Woods* began previews, many theatergoers left after the first act—not necessarily because they didn't like the show. Some had simply assumed that the show had ended. After all, the entire company had just sung how everyone was going to live happily "ever after," so the audience decided to leave the theater and do the same. (Really? Didn't the absence of curtain calls tell them the show must go on?)

The authors decided that just before the song and act ended, they'd have their Narrator state, "To be continued."

Ah, but happiness can be fleeting, can't it? That serious second act showed us what Sky Masterson had learned years earlier in *Guys and Dolls:* "I'm healthy at the moment. It can change."

Now the Baker and his Wife were parents, which brought a new set of problems. "I wish we had more room," she said, undoubtedly not the first spouse to make that remark. But she was better off than Little Red Riding Hood, whose house had been destroyed. The kid was as surprised as any of us who somehow feel immune to disasters. Didn't terrible things only happen to *other* people?

Both Rapunzel and Cinderella had married very well and had the lives of princesses ahead of them. Even Cinderella's stepsisters, who were blinded by birds as retribution for the terrible way they'd treated Cinderella, sang, "We're so happy you're so happy." And odd as that may have seemed, some people *do* act this way: put their real feelings aside, make the best of a bad situation, treat a former adversary as a hero, and live vicariously.

The princes who'd wed Cinderella and Rapunzel found married life a bit bland. Jack found life on the dull side, after stealing a giant's golden harp and other riches and killing him.

If it was adventure they wanted, adventure they got when the Giant's Widow came seeking revenge. Frankly, the lady had a point: Jack had murdered and stolen. Granted, two wrongs don't make a right, but rooting for Jack and his friends to kill the Giantess wasn't easy. Their killing her supposedly meant a happy ending. But the Baker's Wife died and so did Jack's mother and a few others, too.

Sondheim and Lapine wrote with their usual style and intelligence and both got Tonys. But *The Phantom of the Opera*, directed by Sondheim's first great collaborator Hal Prince, couldn't be beaten. But *Into the Woods'* strong afterlife in the amateur market—probably because it offers characters that everyone knows—suggests it would have won in another season.

It was a quick exchange between two people, a line that could easily be lost amid the hubbub of a big party. But those who were paying rapt attention to *Mame* (1965–1966) were impressed at what they learned about the title character in a mere six words.

For in the middle of one of bohemian extraordinaire Mame Dennis's bacchanals, a man fervently asked, "Why don't you marry me, Mame?"

To which she blithely answered, "And lose you as a friend?"

(And can't you hear Angela Lansbury delivering that retort?)

To whichever collaborator came up with that line—be it either Jerome Lawrence or Robert E. Lee, who were adapting their own hit play—credit is due. They showed us in this short exchange that Mame certainly had her chances to marry; she simply chose to retain her independence. For a woman living in the twenties, this was quite daring.

She might have married Zorba, for he certainly had her zest for living. Mame too believed that each day was worth celebrating simply because "It's Today," and that we should "live life all the way." Agreeing with her were the party attendees—"people," as the stage directions stated, "who might be Marian Anderson, Paul Robeson, Lady Mendl, Fatty Arbuckle, Robert Benchley, Texas Guinan, and Alexander Woolcott."

In the midst of this delightful maelstrom came Agnes Gooch, nanny to Patrick Dennis (Frankie Michaels). She'd been entrusted to bring the recent orphan from Chicago to New York to live with his only living aunt.

Mame enrolled Patrick in "the Laboratory of Life" rather than an old-boys' school. Is that where he learned to make a good martini, a talent he displayed to Mr. Babcock, his trustee? ("Stir, never shake. Bruises the gin.") What we did know, however, was that Mame taught Patrick quite a bit, including how to "Open a New Window." In a marvelous musical scene, she showed him what New York City had to offer.

Then Babcock discovered where Patrick was matriculating. He took the boy from her, and we learned just how much Mame cared—for this happened on the day the stock market crashed. "Who gives a damn about money?" she said. "I've lost my child."

Mame's good friend, actress Vera Charles (Beatrice Arthur), got her a job in her "terribly modern operetta," but Mame was no better on stage than she was later as a manicurist. She made customer Beauregard Jackson Pickett Burnside bleed, but he didn't care because he was smitten—so much so that after she'd been fired, he tracked her down. Gooch had a terrific line the moment Beau was out of earshot: "Marry him the minute he asks you." It was that much of a foregone conclusion.

Ah, but not before Mame met and won over Beau's family and friends, not to mention a horse most aptly named Lightnin' Rod. The ornery steed was carefully chosen by Sally Cato, Mame's new archenemy, who'd always assumed that Beau would marry *her*.

Krazy Glue hadn't yet been invented, but Mame found the next best substance to keep her on that horse. It led to everyone literally singing Mame's praises as act one ended—but not before we realized that Patrick felt supplanted. But his love for Mame was so strong that he preferred seeing her happy.

Besides, not too long a time would pass before he fell in love himself and proved that love is blind, deaf, and very dumb. Mame deftly extricated him from what would have been a horrible marriage and set him on the path to a good one.

First, however, she sang the best torch song that an aunt ever sang about a nephew: "If He Walked into My Life," in which she questioned the way she'd raised him. The question resonated with many parents who'd often asked themselves the same questions.

So *Mame* wasn't just gaudy idiocy. It had terrific heart and a winning score by Jerry Herman. It wasn't just his title song that was skillful. Herman knew what to take from the original script. Vera in the play's stage directions was described as "somewhere between forty and death." Herman wisely appropriated the line as one of the zingers that Mame bestowed on Vera during their frank decree of being "Bosom Buddies." Finally, Herman even inadvertently wrote a perennial holiday song: "We Need a Little Christmas," in which Mame cheered up her troops when they most required it. You'll never experience a December when you don't hear it.

In this song and many others, Mame displayed an optimism that was as strong as Don Quixote's, whose musical *Man of La Mancha* prevented her from getting the Best Musical Tony. By amassing 1,508 performances, *Mame* closed as the seventh-longest-running musical of all time—but the first musical to run that long and not get the big prize.

Sometimes a show loses not to a financial juggernaut, but to an artistic one. Superb as it was, *The Rothschilds* (1970–1971) couldn't wrest the Best Musical Tony from the landmark *Company*.

In *Fiddler on the Roof*, impoverished milkman Tevye said, "It's no shame to be poor, but it's no great honor, either."

In *The Rothschilds*, equally poor Mayer Rothschild (1744–1812) proclaimed, "There is no virtue in riches, but there is none in poverty either."

By October 1970, when *Fiddler* had already become Broadway's fifth-longest-running production, Tevye's wry observation had been heard by hundreds of thousands of theatergoers. What was worse for *The Rothschilds* is that it had become a veritable Broadway catchphrase—and one that reminded theatergoers who were at the new Jerry Bock and Sheldon Harnick musical that they had had a greater experience at the team's 1964 smash.

Many felt that the property was doomed, anyway. Audiences may want to be rich and famous themselves, but they don't often get behind characters who simply want to make billions.

That's why book writer Sherman Yellen was wise to stress that Mayer Rothschild (Hal Linden) didn't only want a fortune for himself, his wife, and their five sons. He was desperate to change life not only for the oppressed Jews then living in eighteenth-century Frankfurt, but also forever everywhere else in the world.

So Yellen started with some arresting images. After a business trip, Mayer returned to the Frankfurt ghetto where Jews were forced to live and observe a curfew. Each night at ten, the gates of the ghetto were locked.

Mayer's homecoming included running into schoolchildren whose idea of a good time wasn't rolling hoops. These Christians had learned early on that when a Jew approached a Gentile on the street, he was forced by law to take off his hat and bow low.

"Jew, do your duty!" one kid demanded. A policeman was nearby. Our instincts made us assume that he would tell the kids to disperse and leave the man alone. Hardly. "You heard them," he snarled to Mayer.

Mayer swooped off his hat with an exaggerated flourish, bowed low, and turned his humiliation into parody. No one called him on it, probably because both adult and children realized that what they were asking was wrong.

If that weren't heartbreaking enough, as the kids ran off, one of them crowed, "I get the next one!"

Now after the humiliation came injustice. Being a Jew was costly, for the policeman told Mayer that the money he'd made in a foreign country had to be changed into local currency. He, of course, also served as the money changer and charged Mayer far more than what was fair.

Next, German law would permit only twelve Jewish couples to marry each year. Mayer and Gutele were very much in love, but the quota meant that they would have to wait four or five years.

In a way, Mayer was glad that he couldn't marry at the moment—and not because he'd had the commitment issues that Bobby had shown in that year's Best Musical winner. "I will not allow you to share my poverty," he told Gutele, who wasn't a woman who wanted more money, possessions, and pleasures. She loved Mayer and would be happy in "One Room" with him.

This was a refreshing change. Literature is littered with stories of women who are never satisfied with their homes and/or status in life, but Gutele Rothschild was content. Her husband and sons were the ones who wanted "Everything," as they sang in a powerful song.

Gutele wasn't stupid, but she didn't have the keen vision that her husband had. Her take on the Gentiles locking the gates of the Jewish ghetto was "It means they're locked out." But she knew she was rationalizing; she simply couldn't see anything changing. Mayer could, which is why he became a great character both in history and musical theater.

There was a marvelous moment in "Sons," when Mayer was instructing his four young lads how to do business. He started to sing "When a shopper says" and his son Nathan repeated the same words a beat behind him. We assumed it was the start of a musical round as well as a musical comedy convention, but no: Mayer chided him with "Nathan, listen!" The headstrong son stopped, Mayer continued—and audiences laughed.

Even at an early age, the Rothschild sons showed that they knew how to handle customers. When a housewife wanted a pair of candlesticks, one lad offered her two mismatched ones. "They're not a pair," sneered the housewife—to which the boy said, "You and your husband don't match and you're a pair."

He made the sale.

Honoré de Balzac is usually credited with the statement that every great fortune begins with a great crime. Yellen had Mayer commit a much smaller one to get his business off the ground. He dabbled in rare coins, and suggested to his customers that the ones he purveyed once belonged to Alexander the Great, Julius Caesar, and Cleopatra. His chutzpah impressed avid coin collector Prince William (Keene Curtis), who gave him dispensation to marry.

The song was so clever that Broadway audiences could have assumed that it was in place from day one. Actually, it was written in Philadelphia, proving that Bock and Harnick had the skill to write fast when a new song was needed.

Audiences got some nice dramatic irony when the family drank wine they'd made themselves: the first Rothschild wine. They were celebrating success in business, which led to "Rothschild and Sons," a rollicking song ("There's another firm in the firmament.") that was so good that one wishes it had become the show's title song.

The title *Rothschild and Sons* would have also ameliorated a problem that came up in act two. Because *The Rothschilds* spanned forty-six years—from 1772 to 1818—it had to deal with Mayer's death in 1812. Unlike the creators of *A Class Act*—who had Lehman Engel attend Ed Kleban's memorial service although he'd predeceased Kleban by five years—Yellen maintained historical accuracy. Thus, we had to witness Mayer's death when the show still had a couple of songs and a finale to go.

To be sure, to see the sons succeed without Mayer was important, but audiences could be forgiven for innately assuming he'd be proudly observing his sons' success at the final curtain.

Succeed the Rothschilds did—as many high-and-mighty Gentiles were seen bowing to them. It was a magnificent full-circle finish.

* * *

On August 13, 1997, a small British film opened in America with not much fanfare.

And yet, only 1,053 days later, on July 1, 2000, its musical version opened at the Old Globe Theatre in San Diego. A mere 117 days later, it was on Broadway.

Said its director Jack O'Brien in the published text of *The Full Monty* (2000–2001), "I've always believed that certain productions either 'want' to happen, or they don't, and if a project is lucky enough to be one of the former, from the opening gun there is nearly nothing you can do to stop it."

True enough. But what did stop *The Full Monty* from winning the Best Musical Tony was *The Producers: The New Mel Brooks Musical,* as it preferred to be called. Until then, *The Full Monty* had lived a charmed life.

The film had had a funky plot: six men from Sheffield, England, decided to make money by aping Chippendales dancers. Because they weren't nearly as handsome or fit, they had to compensate by doing "the full monty"—a British expression meaning "going all the way" and taking *everything* off.

Sheffield was once a thriving town, thanks to the steel mills. When they closed, they took a great many jobs with them. The unemployed Gaz didn't conceive of stripping simply for fish, chips, and beer. He was divorced and had child support to pay for his son Nathan. If he didn't, he'd lose his part of the custody, and he loved his son too much for that to happen.

The Full Monty became one of England's highest-grossing films. After its American debut, many interested parties contacted Lindsay Law, president of Fox Searchlight Pictures, which had distributed the film. Can we make it into a musical?

Law called his friend Jack O'Brien, artistic director of the Old Globe and offered him the rights. O'Brien asked Terrence McNally, a four-time Tony winner—two for plays, two for musicals—to write the script. McNally said yes.

Adam Guettel, however, said no when asked to write the score. He suggested non-theater composer-lyricist David Yazbek, who not only agreed but also provided one of the strongest musical theater debuts in years.

He, too, would lose to Mel Brooks for Best Score. Such was the unstoppable power of *The Producers: The New Mel Brooks Musical.*

Yazbek's score was *The Full Monty*'s most impressive achievement. After all, everyone expected McNally to deliver a fine script, which he did, wisely Americanizing the show and setting it in equally ravaged Buffalo.

But who knew that Yazbek had a distinct and unique musical theater voice?

His lyric-writing craft wasn't exemplary. Twice he purported to rhyme "man" with "understand." But at least one of those near-rhymes packed a punch, when the men sang, "I want to understand how I got to be a loser and I used to be a man."

Gaz became Jerry Lukowski, who was as depressed as—well, Buffalo. "It's a slow town when you don't know where to go," he sang. His best friend Dave Bukatinsky sang, too: "I want to feel like the husband instead of the wife." Indeed, Mrs. Bukatinsky had a job. So when Jerry suggested to Dave his plan, Dave dismissed him with "You got your wishes . . . and I got dishes."

This came in a song called "Man," in which Jerry defined masculinity as, "When the beef comes out, you do the carvin'. You hate Tom Cruise, but you love Lee Marvin." Musically, Yazbek incorporated some of Elmer (*How Now, Dow Jones*) Bernstein's butch *The Magnificent Seven* theme, which old-timers had heard in the Marlboro cigarette commercial.

Lehman Engel often told his BMI Musical Theatre Workshop students to "look for humor in dark places." And while Yazbek never took the class—he would have learned to rhyme perfectly if he had he instinctively understood the concept. In "Big-Ass Rock," Jerry and Dave discussed alternative methods of suicide with Malcolm McGregor, who'd just tried to kill himself through carbon monoxide poisoning. When they considered hanging, Dave earnestly sang to Jerry, "And I won't leave you swinging there, twitching like a fish while you claw the air. I'll grab your feet, and pal o' mine, I'll pull real hard and snap your spinal cord."

These are nicely conversational lyrics. So was Malcolm's introspective response at being thrilled at having newfound buddies. "I got a friend, like Carole King or Carly Simon used to sing—I always get those two confused."

Three strippers down, three to go. They approached Harold, who used to be their foreman but now was their equal on the unemployment line. He had a high-spending wife in Vicki, whom Yazbek had gleefully sing, "There's me completely in Prada. And I've got the boots that go with the belt that goes with the bag that goes with my wonderful life with Harold."

Harold didn't want to spoil her bliss by telling her he'd been fired six months earlier. Here McNally added a wonderful line: "It'll kill her," he told the men, before admitting, "Who am I kidding? It'll kill me."

In the film, when Vicki learned the truth, she was furious and threw Harold out of the house. McNally improved this, too, by showing Vicki to be stronger than Harold had assumed. When the repo men came, she showed that she didn't simply view Harold as a meal, clothes, and travel ticket. She would now be there for him.

Back to auditioning. Horse, a black man, sang that "They put my picture on the cover of the Book of Love," but he turned out to be not as well-endowed as white-bread Ethan. Once he pulled down his pants, the six-member troupe was complete.

McNally, a lifelong fan of Broadway shows, knew how valuable a woman's touch was in musicals. He invented pianist Jeanette A. Burmeister to accompany the unsexy sextet. Her attitude not only suggested that she'd seen it all, but that she'd also seen it all through seven or eight reincarnated lives.

Yazbek caught the character that McNally created in such lines as "I was subbing with Stan Kenton in this seedy club in Trenton when I heard my third divorce had just gone through." Add to this "I played for hoofers who can't hoof, I've played for tone-deaf singers. And once when I insulted Frank, I played with broken fingers." (Anyone doubt that she meant Sinatra?)

See? Fresh, conversational images. Compare this to Leo Bloom's images when he said he wanted to be a producer: "Lunch at Sardi's every day . . . sleep until half-past two . . . see my name in lights . . . pockets stuffed with cash . . . a great big casting couch . . . drink champagne." (If the line *were* only "drink champagne"; it's actually "drink champagne until I puke.")

Yes, as Shakespeare wrote, "The devil can cite Scripture for his purpose," and I can, too. But Brooks's lyrics for the rest of the show weren't above this standard. His music sounded derivative, too, while Yazbek's managed to actually *sound* amusing.

Comedy songs don't often have excellent melodies; they're mostly full of quarter notes that are subservient to the lyric. Occasionally, a good tune results: "America," "Bosom Buddies," "You Must Meet My Wife." But for the most part, in comedy songs, the tale wags the doggone melody. And yet, Yazbek's melodies were doggone good, too.

The Full Monty did provide Yazbek with a chance to write a genuinely beautiful song, and he fulfilled the assignment. Malcolm, a mamma's boy his whole life, felt devastated at her funeral. He'd been secretly gay, and had only recently been able to acknowledge that to himself and to Ethan. At the cemetery, when he felt woefully alone, he sang what could pass for a church hymn: "You Walk with Me." And while the song itself didn't move the action forward, it had forward motion in the middle, when Ethan began singing after Malcolm had faltered. Once they sang together, audiences knew that they'd succeed as a couple.

Brooks's ordinary sounding music and pedestrian lyrics were carried to victory on the coattails of his book for *The Producers: The New Mel Brooks Musical*. It also had two stars—Nathan Lane and Matthew Broderick—and the hottest director-choreographer in Susan Stroman. *The Full Monty* couldn't compete in those departments, or in sets and costumes that provided old-fashioned spectacle.

Who'd expect that a musical dealing with the Kennedy and Bouvier families *wouldn't* center on Bobby and Jackie and Jack?

True, Jackie made an appearance—albeit as twelve-year-old Jackie Bouvier—in *Grey Gardens* (2006–2007). So did a Kennedy—but it was Joseph P., Jr., whom his father, Ambassador Joseph P. Kennedy, Sr., had been grooming for president.

Tony voters didn't meet them when the curtain rose. Instead they saw the ramshackle exterior of a house and heard a radio announcer report, "In a statement released today, Jacqueline Kennedy Onassis confirmed that her eighty-year-old aunt Mrs. Edith Bouvier Beale and her adult daughter Edie are living in squalid conditions in an East Hampton estate known as Grey Gardens."

However, the house looked quite elegant when we were invited inside. But that's because we'd been taken to 1941, thirty-two years before that announcement.

The twenty-six-year-old Kennedy was seriously dating the twenty-four-year-old Beale. Her mother, affectionately known as "Big Edie" (Christine Ebersole), was throwing a party, for she anticipated that today would be the day that he'd pop the question.

It would be a gay occasion (in the now obsolete use of the word), so composer Scott Frankel and lyricist Michael Korie wrote mock-ups of popular songs of the day that Big Edie and her pianist would sing to entertain the guests. They sounded like genuine 1941 hits, but their introspective songs for all the Beales scored mightily, too.

Many audience members assumed that the reason that the Beales went from refinement to ruin had to do with Kennedy's being killed during World War II. Obviously Edie was devastated and never recovered.

Not quite. The theory that book writer Doug Wright advanced was that Kennedy changed his mind during the party when he saw an unstable family: a too silly mother who was about to be divorced by her husband and, worse, their carefree daughter who had had a brush with semi-scandal when her bathing suit came undone. As a future president of the United States, he had to be more careful. His dropping Edie, as well as the divorce, caused both Beale women to go to wrecks and ruination.

So in the second act, we saw what they'd become. Big Edie (Mary Louise Wilson), seventy-eight, stayed in bed most of the day, surrounded by her daughter, cats, and raccoons. Little Edie (Ebersole), suddenly fifty-eight, attended to and fought with her mother. The highlight of every day was when a neighborhood teen came by. Neither mother nor daughter cared to acknowledge how far she'd fallen in a spectacular display of denial.

It was a powerful show, but *Spring Awakening* got better reviews. Tony voters might have also felt that watching nineteenth-century German teens suffer wasn't nearly as unnerving as witnessing their peers decline and fall.

Or was *Grey Gardens* with its two sets and nine characters simply too small? Most of the time, the small show doesn't win.

CHAPTER EIGHT

*

Big Fish Eat the Little, Little Fish: The Best Musical Tony Losers That Simply May Have Been Too Small

t's hardly a hard-and-fast rule, but by and large, large musicals do better at winning Best Musical Tonys than small ones.

The Helen Hayes and the Booth—respectively Broadway's smallest theaters—have never had a Best Musical Tony winner originate there. All right, one couldn't expect that either *Romance/Romance* or *Xanadu*, each ensconced at the former, could win the big prize. But *Once on This Island* (1990–1991), the tenant at the Booth, stood no chance against Tony winner *The Will Rogers Follies*, let alone such highly regarded nominees as *Miss Saigon* and *The Secret Garden*. The three walls surrounding the stage got a paint job, but there was little in the way of sets.

The musical's big issue was not one of color, but of shade. In Haiti, dark-skinned blacks are viewed as markedly inferior to light-skinned ones. TiMoune not only was a deeper shade of black, but also an orphan peasant who lived with adopted parents. What chance had she with the wealthy and comparatively pale Daniel Beauxhomme?

Then the gods caused Daniel to have a car accident near TiMoune's home. She was intent on nursing him back to health and believed her love for him would transcend all barriers. Her parents tried to tell her that won't happen. They also proved that making a child feel guilty knew no ethnic boundaries: "What we are, we made you," they sang. "What we gave, you took. Now you run without one backward look."

Stephen Flaherty's melody for the song was so beautiful that one could overlook the guilt-trip message. His work with the other songs was so glorious that he created a musical version of a banquet: one delicious dish after another.

Lynn Ahrens had excellent ideas for songs. "Some Say," in which the natives told the story of TiMoune, noted that tales become distorted from retellings. ("No one knows how the real truth goes. It all depends what you hear from friends.") Most skillful of all was "Some Girls," in which Daniel sang of both TiMoune and Andrea, the high-born woman to whom he was promised. When he expressed his feelings—"some girls you picture; some you hold"—an audience couldn't be certain which woman he was selecting—not until he sang, "Some girls you marry; some you love."

At a party, Andrea makes nice with TiMoune, but her asking her to dance is not a nice one. She knew that TiMoune's primitive dance would alienate the Beauxhommes and that Daniel would have no second thoughts about his marriage.

Daniel succumbed. On the day of the weddings, he continues the practice of giving each peasant outside the church a coin. When Daniel gives one to TiMoune, it's the ultimate statement of the wide difference between the two. TiMoune, who wanted so much more from him, commits suicide.

And yet, the natives found a silver lining around this cloudy plot. They said that TiMoune came back to life as a tree. That may seem to be a happy ending to them, but a Broadway audience has different values. Despite the unconvincing rise-like-a-phoenix ending, *Once on This Island* is a musical that is performed as often or even more frequently than the other three musicals that probably bested it.

But when Best Musical races are on the line, Davids have a harder time killing Goliaths than David did in 1 Samuel 17:1–58.

High Spirits (1963–1964) was actually a small musical masquerading as a big one. And in the early sixties, musicals had to be big to warrant the steep $9.90 ticket price.

"Book, music, and lyrics by Hugh Martin and Timothy Gray," went the billing. Both men later acknowledged that Martin wrote the music and Gray the words for this musicalization of Noël Coward's *Blithe Spirit*.

Martin and Gray only had to write songs for four characters: novelist Charles Condomine; his second wife Ruth; Madame Arcati, a medium who comes to their house to hold a séance and inadvertently brings back to earth our fourth lead—the long-deceased Elvira, Charles's first wife. None of the other three characters from Coward's play sang—neither the Bradmans nor Edith, the Condomines' maid, and ultimately, the show's deus ex machina.

Originally, Madame Arcati chose to play Irving Berlin's "Always" to get everyone in the right frame of mind — that unnerved Charles, for he and Elvira had considered it "our song."

Today, producers would probably license the Berlin song as *The New Mel Brooks Musical Young Frankenstein* (yes, that *was* how it was officially billed) did with "Puttin' on the Ritz." Back then, originality was expected, so Martin and Gray wrote a new song. And yet, they smartly kept to the spirit of the original, as was proved by their title that was synonymous to "Always": "Forever and a Day."

In the original play, when Elvira arrived, Coward had her say, "You called me back." Gray made that the first line of his verse when he had her insist to Charles "You'd Better Love Me" while he had the opportunity. She had no idea how long she'd able to stay, but it turned out to be long enough to cause a rift between Charles and Ruth ("Where Is the Man I Married?") and an eventual reconciliation ("If I Gave You").

In musical theater, there may not be much make-up sex, but there certainly are make-up songs.

Martin and Gray improved *Blithe Spirit* in two ways. First, they had both wives compare notes on Charles's deficiencies ("What in the World Did You Want?"). When the songwriters presented this piece to Coward, he must have blushed from embarrassment and cried, "I should have thought of that!"

Secondly, in the play, Elvira said that before she'd returned to earth, she'd been playing backgammon with a man she believed to be Genghis Khan. That one quip inspired the songwriters to pen an entire number devoted to Elvira's interaction with celebrities who now lived in the great beyond.

"Home Sweet Heaven" was one of Broadway's best eleven o'clock numbers. Tammy Grimes drilled home such witty observations as "The Duke of Prussia (I call him 'Freddy') is living by mistake with Mary Baker Eddy."

Martin and Gray couldn't deny Beatrice Lillie, top-billed as Madame Arcati, her own showstopper. "Talking to You" had her interact with a Ouija board. She even got the planchette to spell out how much it loved her.

Both songs took place outside the Condomines' home, not because they needed to be set elsewhere, but simply to give audiences something new to see. In the sixties, opening up a play was of paramount importance to a musical.

So Martin and Gray cut away to "a road on the heath" where Madame Arcati, established as a bicyclist in Coward's play, was seen pedaling to the Condomines' house while singing about the joys of bike travel. The people she passed en route joined her song, but they weren't needed.

This chorus was also used when Arcati took us to her studio where she taught twenty-four students how to "Go into Your Trance." Martin later admitted that he and Gray would have done better to have Arcati sing this to the Condomines and their neighbors the Bradmans before she started the séance. But again, finding a new location for a big numba was the demand of the day.

Every one of the six daily critics wrote approving reviews, but not raves. Audience members probably liked but didn't love the show; a producer gets more than 376 performances if they do. To everyone, it probably just looked too . . . small.

The Me Nobody Knows (1970–1971) had kids tell of their life experiences in urban ghettos. There was genuine power in the matter-of-fact way they talked about being approached by drug pushers, seeing classmates carry guns, feeling that they had been unwanted, and yet facing life squarely in the eye. "When you're born, they carry you," the kids conceded. "When you're dead, they bury you." They grimly realized, "In between, you're on your own."

They were as intent as Bobby, the main character in that season's Tony winner, *Company*, on "Being Alive"—but in a far more basic way.

Ain't Supposed to Die a Natural Death (1971–1972) was *The Me Nobody Knows* all grown up. Those kids who once had hope had now been replaced by adults, and audiences saw what ten or twenty or more years of living in the same ghetto did to people.

For the first time in Tony history, the book, music, and lyrics were written by a black man. Melvin Van Peebles's *Playbill* bio consisted of only seventeen words: "Jesus, seems you always go out to a coffee break when a black prayer is next in line." On the original cast album, he wrote, "There will be no more minstrel shows."

In the same season when the *Weismann Follies'* elder stateswomen came down the staircase for their grand entrance, Van Peebles's characters made quite a different parade. There was the bag lady; the youths who felt the need to look tough to stay alive; the flashily dressed pimp followed by one of his employees in her enormous wig; the men and women who were old before their time. The Tony era had seen actors play a cow in *Gypsy* and horses in *Hello, Dolly!* Now it was time to put a performer in a rat suit. Why not? A rat was just as much a part of the ghetto as any person.

One man was seen limping, explaining that he'd had a murderously hard day at work, and now no buses were around to take him home. "When you're black," he said, "even waitin' ain't easy. If I stand here, I'm loiterin'. If I walk, I'm prowlin'. If I run, I'm escapin'."

In short order, audiences saw what he meant. A too loud party led to a policeman's shooting before he asked questions. One man started running as fast as he could. "Feet, do your thing," he implored, an expression often fancifully used by dancers. The stakes were much higher here.

His running made the policeman automatically assume that he was guilty. The runner didn't get his day in court, because before he could, he was shot dead on the street.

"He was just a baby!" one woman noted, before a homeless woman addressed not only the policeman, but also the audience. "Put a curse on you," she said, wishing that "rats will come creeping into your children's cribs."

The show was obviously too in your face for the overwhelmingly white Tony voters. The Best Musical nomination was reward enough.

I Love My Wife (1976–1977) concerned wife-swapping.

No: let's use the term that should have been employed all along in this swinging decade: spouse-swapping.

The show was produced in an era when good hard sex never killed anyone. The AIDS crisis, only four years away, is one reason why the show is rarely revived.

The sitcom nature of Michael Stewart's book is another.

Although Tony voters were introduced to eight Trenton natives who'd been friends since childhood, *I Love My Wife* was really a four-person show. It centered on two married couples: Alvin/Cleo and Wally/Monica. The other four cast members were mostly used as a musical quartet that backed up the leads. (And you thought that John Doyle was the first to have actors playing instruments.)

By 1977, baby boomers were now thirty or pushing it. Some had married a bit too early and were now haunted by the thought that there was "Someone Wonderful I Missed," as one of Stewart and Cy Coleman's songs went.

It all started when Monica was reading a "How Sexually Liberated Are You?" quiz in a magazine. "You got this in a supermarket?" Alvin shrieked, remembering that not long ago such a subject would have strictly been under-the-counter.

Yes, times had changed and people were "doing things they never talked about before," as one friend said. The biggest disgrace was to be—imagine!—"thirty years behind the times." So what were these friends going to do about it?

Wally was the most sophisticated of the bunch—or believed he was. "I'm more exposed to the more permissive society than you. I go to New York every third Thursday," he crowed. His song about threesomes made Alvin think that he should indulge. But how could he convince his wife? "No, she'd never go for it," he said, in the way that husbands do, absolutely certain that they know everything about their wives.

Surprise! When Alvin broached the subject to Cleo, he found that she was rarin' to go. The only problem was that she wanted another man while he wanted another woman.

So when their friends came over, Alvin tried to get Wally to leave while Cleo tried to get rid of Monica. In fact, Monica had planned to visit her mother and left to do just that. Alvin quickly suggested that the best solution would instead be some wife-and-husband swapping at some future date.

Such as act two. Of course, by the time the big night arrived, Wally hadn't yet found the nerve to tell Monica how the four would spend their evening. When he finally did, she was furious and called him a "disgusting, lecherous, depraved, filthy beast."

She also felt that the best revenge would be to teach him a lesson by going through with it. What no one banked on was that Alvin couldn't. He: "Monica, you're so soft." She: "Alvin, so are you."

Nothing was left but for Alvin to sing "I Love My Wife." Wally reached the same conclusion, although he and Cleo had seemed to be cavorting quite well. But fidelity is what the Broadway audience wanted to see in order to validate its own beliefs.

While the title song had a pretty Coleman melody, the show didn't include his most impressive music; this was a pop-oriented score that included some country and even early techno-sounds. It did, however, pass muster.

Stewart was adept in his lyrics. Perhaps he'd learned a great deal from writing books to shows with excellent lyrics by Lee Adams (*Bye Bye Birdie*), Bob Merrill (*Carnival*), and Jerry Herman (*Hello, Dolly!*). In celebrating Monica's assets, Stewart had the men sing, "Those aren't just buns; they're cakes." Even better: "Men go ape! Apes go 'Man!'"

But the forced innocence of *I Love My Wife* couldn't compete with the genuine innocence and fairy-tale power of *Annie*. While 857 performances was a better run than nine previous Best Musical Tony *winners* had had, *I Love My Wife* had to settle for a presumed second place in the 1976–1977 Best Musical Tony race.

They're Playing Our Song (1978–1979) could have been an off-Broadway show. It was essentially a two-person musical that Neil Simon based on the then-current up-and-down, on-again, off-again romance between composer Marvin Hamlisch and lyricist Carole Bayer Sager. Simon turned them into successful composer Vernon Gersch and one-hit wonder lyricist Sonia Walsk. Gersch was a bit nerdy and uptight while Walsk was a free spirit.

"No, she wasn't free at all," Hamlisch later said of his former inamorata. "She was expensive. She was a *rich* spirit."

To make the evening seem big enough for the Imperial Theatre, both Vernon and Sonia had three alter egos who were identically dressed and served as backup singers. That swelled the cast to eight. Still, of the nine *off*-Broadway musicals produced in 1978–1979, seven had bigger casts than *They're Playing Our Song*.

It wasn't just love versus career, as we've often seen, but love *and* career. Should you become emotionally involved with your collaborator with whom you're already "married" in work?

And so Vernon and Sonia made a too quick decision to spend the weekend together. That Sonia was on the rebound was an enormous issue. She was always running to her old beau Leon when he was broke, depressed, or suicidal. Her feelings, however, spoke well of her; most lovers who break up say they're going to be friends. Sonia meant it.

When it came to wisecracks, Simon still had a million of 'em. En route to Quogue with Vernon, the car broke down, allowing Simon to have Vernon say "It's the distributor" before clarifying: "The crook who sold me the car."

Actually, one of the most hilarious lines was one that didn't get a laugh from anyone but good songwriters. Sonia, when commenting on her chaotically messy apartment, said, "The only place I have orderliness is with my lyrics."

Truth to tell, Carole Bayer Sager was terribly inept at the lyric-writing craft. Only fourteen lines into the show, she delivered her first half-rhyme ("Learn" and "burned"); in song two came her first misaccented word ("melo-DEE"). So when Sonia later said, "I'll spend four weeks looking for the right words in a song," we realized that she obviously needed more time than that. Although Hamlisch's music was, as always, spritely and melodic, it was bogged down by lyrics that only a boyfriend could love.

In musicals, an unconventional woman always gets to a tightly wound man at least for a while: Lorelei/Gus; Gittel/Jerry; Sally/Cliff. Thus, audiences expected that Gersch would eventually say, "If I know you another fifty years, there isn't a day that'll go by when you won't drive me insane. And I'm still crazy nuts for you." And he did.

The two moved in together. Sonia and her alter egos bought in myriad items, allowing Simon one of his favorite gambits: completely redoing an apartment, as he had for *Barefoot in the Park*, *The Odd Couple*, *The Star-Spangled Girl*, and *God's Favorite*.

Vernon saw her moving in as giving them more chances to write. Sonia soon felt overworked. "We have one relationship too many," he decided, which resulted in their having none at all. But after Sonia had heard that Vernon had been hit by a car, she visited him in the hospital. This being musical comedy, he only suffered a broken leg.

As a present, Sonia brought a toy piano, which inspired his three alter egos to bring out three more. As all four played, the tinny sound was somehow endearing. We may not like synthesizers in our orchestra pits, but we did find a place in our hearts for *They're Playing Our Song*'s onstage toy pianos.

At the 1978–1979 Tony Awards, after Dick Van Dyke had listed the four nominees for Best Actor in a Musical, which included Robert Klein, he announced the winner: "Len Cariou for *Sweeney Todd*." But Klein swears—*swears*—that the actual words that he heard Van Dyke say were "Not Robert Klein."

A Day in Hollywood/A Night in the Ukraine (1979–1980) consisted of two separate shows, with each half as different as, well, day and night.

Day was set in the movie palace once known as Grauman's Chinese

Theatre, but it confined itself to the lobby. Audiences were never invited behind the six onstage doors.

However, above the action was a very small stage on which director Tommy Tune recycled an idea he'd had for a musical called *Double Feature* that had played at the Long Wharf Theatre six months earlier. He had dancers come on, but only allowed audiences to see their feet. It was quite a feat, for crowds cooed with pleasure when they had no trouble guessing that those pedal extremities belonged to Charlie Chaplin, Dorothy Gale, or Mickey Mouse.

Seventeen songs were borrowed from established songwriters, ranging from Harold Arlen to Richard Whiting. A few new ones came courtesy of Jerry Herman as well as cast member Frank Lazarus, who provided music for Dick Vosburgh's lyrics.

After intermission, audiences exclaimed "Ooooh!" While they expected a musical to have a dynamically new act two set, the modest act one setting had prepared them for yet another standard-issue setting. But *A Night in the Ukraine* was to be a hellishly clever Marx Brothers movie that they never made, loosely based on *The Bear*—"the best-selling play by Anton Chekhov, Russia's top gag-writer." So here was "Mrs. Natasha Pavlenko's opulent villa"—a borscht-red set in Tsarist Russia.

Carlo and Gino (Priscilla Lopez)—read, Chico and Harpo—worked for the officious widow. "When Major Pavlenko died," she mourned, "part of me died, too." Carlo offered this solace to the grandly overweight grande dame: "You can still do lots of livin' with what you got."

Samovar the lawyer—Groucho, of course—was willing to share the load with Natasha. He took pride in his shyster status: "I'm wise to all the loopholes," he sang. "I haven't any scroop-holes" was Vosburgh's nifty parody of the type of wordplay that often invaded Groucho's songs.

"Hello, lawyer!" Carlo sang, while playing a bit of Handel.

For a lawyer, Samovar was pretty broke. Major Pavlenko owed him money, which he hoped to get from Natasha. "If I don't have it by tomorrow," he said, "I'll be sent to prison—and I hate living with relatives."

The Marxes often shared the screen with dewy-eyed and dopy lovers, so Vosburgh and Lazarus created two simplistic simps. While Natasha wanted her daughter Nina to marry a certain baron, she said the expected "I don't love him" before singing "The Day I Meet My Lover" with all the "the birds will go twitter-tweet" platitudes.

Mirabile dictu! That very day Nina indeed met her lover: Constantine, a coachman. "What I wanted to be was a playwright," he mourned, "but my first play was turned down yesterday by the Moscow Art Theatre."

He was discouraged, but she wasn't. "You're sensitive and intelligent and witty and kind and truthful," she said of the man who had said exactly fifty-nine words to her.

She later didn't think he was truthful at all when she overheard him saying, "I don't love the little fool . . . as a ruthless fortune-hunter, it's my job to be convincing."

"Oh, Constantine!" she said, coming out of the shadows. "You've broken every bone in my heart!"

But Constantine was only reading his play aloud. Then he sang aloud his song of woe. "Such emptiness now" rhymed with "I'm such an empty mess now."

About 122 seconds later, Nina heard Samovar reading Constantine's play aloud and realized the truth. Oh, and Samovar still had to romance Natasha, whom he praised down to her "pronounced moustacha."

Vosburgh got all the Marxist ingredients: Groucho dictated a letter to the utterly incompetent Chico; Harpo made a mess and then itched to convey that he was bringing an important "mess-itch." Then he upended a bicycle, and darn if the wheels didn't function as a harp.

"It looks like everything turned out all right," Chico sang. Not quite at the Tonys, however. Too bad this one (two?) couldn't have won the prize for producer Alexander H. Cohen, who'd put the Tonys on the TV map by getting ABC to agree to air them.

Cohen never won what he most wanted: the Best Musical Tony. At least he won Best Play in the first year of the national broadcast, in 1966–1967, for *The Homecoming*. Alas, although he followed that with thirty-one more productions, he never won again.

One can hear the producers of *Baby* (1983–1984) telling the cast, "If we don't win any Tonys on Sunday night, we'll close." Translation: "We're closing Sunday." And everyone knew it, too.

Baby (1983–1984) started with a very scientific film of how a sperm fertilizes an egg. They weren't pretty pictures. The term "too much information" hadn't yet come into vogue; if it had, some audience members would have been muttering the three words before act one, scene one started in earnest.

Sybille Pearson's book was set in a New England college. Lizzie and Danny, each twenty, studied there. Around the time that they were born, Alan and Arlene were married. Since then, he was an administrator at the school, while she raised their three children. Now they had just celebrated not only their twentieth anniversary at the Plaza, but also their last kid's leaving home.

Pam and Nick, both gym teachers, were desperate to have a child before her biological clock stopped running. But they, the ones who most wanted a baby, turned out to have the hardest time, while the other two couples who weren't looking to conceive find that they have. Even harder, the nurses had told Pam she was indeed pregnant, only to later admit that they'd made an error. Tests showed that Nick's sperm count was woefully low.

Nevertheless, Nick and Pam spent the rest of the show trying to conceive. They ultimately came to realize that having each other was pretty special in itself.

Danny was no Bobby in *Company*; he *wanted* to get married. Lizzie was the one who said, "Marriage turns talented men into husbands and brilliant women into wives." Not until he gave her a ring and stated that he felt married did she come around.

Another twist: Arlene didn't want this new child, while Alan did. "I'll help this time," he promised. Her response: "You're damn right you will."

As always, Richard Maltby, Jr., had marvelous ideas for songs. "Fatherhood Blues" stated that even men who don't want children are assuaged by the fact that they were able to impregnate a woman. Few spouses would disagree with Maltby's contention that children are "Easier to Love" than a husband or wife is. Lizzie found that having a big belly meant big doses of advice from mothers who talked about labor almost as long as they'd been in labor.

All were set to David Shire's music that nicely reflected the different age groups. The Tony voters gave it no awards, but after that Sunday closing, community theaters made it their baby.

Book writer/lyricist Barry Harman and composer Keith Herrmann teamed to write two one-act musicals that would justify their title *Romance/Romance* (1987–1988). The first one, "A Little Comedy," was the better.

That it took place in late 1800s Vienna allowed Herrmann to write some lovely swirling waltzes and a rousing polka. Alfred, the self-proclaimed "rich, unattached, and reasonably handsome" ladies' man decided that he wanted to be loved for himself. So he decided to "mix with the rabble." There he met a lovely, lower-middle-class miss.

But Josefine was playing the same game. She too had known the high life and rich men, so she dressed down in hopes of having "an adventure." Along came Alfred, pretending to be an impoverished poet.

Harman beautifully captured the thrill of a couple's falling in love and suddenly feeling that there was no one else inhabiting the world. Pervading the piece was great charm, of which few recent musicals could boast. But only minutes before the ending, Harman turned his characters cynical. "I never did trust him," she sang as he sang, "I never did trust her." Too bad, for otherwise "A Little Comedy" would have been a little masterpiece.

The second show, "Summer Share," had Barb married to Sam, while Lenny is Monica's husband. The two couples headed to the Hamptons for a tension-free vacation.

But the best-laid plans didn't include that Sam and Monica, best friends since college, would take the chance to discuss their innermost feelings. Their marriages had become a bit stale, and they took to wondering if they should have wed each other. More to the point: should they now have an affair? Is the angel you know better than the angel you don't?

Harman got Sam and Monica to ask the tough questions, first about flirting, and then about outright cheating. Unfortunately, he wrapped up the problem much too soon and neatly. Nevertheless, while the final moments of "The Little Comedy" sank the show, the last lines of "Summer Share" were charming.

Sam asked Monica, "When you go into Lenny now, you two wouldn't . . . ? Never mind!"

In response, she said, "Darling, don't be silly. Tonight, I'm all yours!"

The Best Musical Tony, however, was all *The Phantom of the Opera*'s.

Cameron Mackintosh had become the premier producer of the eighties and nineties by sponsoring such megamusicals as *Cats, Les Misérables, The Phantom of the Opera*, and *Miss Saigon*. So that his next production was a mere six-person black revue was surprising.

Five Guys Named Moe (1991–1992) was a jukebox musical that actually had songs that once inhabited a jukebox—depending on where you were. For while Louis Jordan had fifty-five records make the top ten—and eighteen reach number one—from 1944 to 1951, these achievements were made on the rhythm and blues charts. At the time, Jordan's work was still considered "race music."

It's one reason why his songs weren't better remembered, and why Mackintosh didn't know them when he sauntered into the Theatre Royal Stratford East to see *Five Guys Named Moe*.

Despite the lofty-sounding name of the playhouse, this was a glorified community theater. So imagine how thrilled its directors were when Mackintosh offered to move the revue to the West End—and then to Broadway.

There *was* a story, however slight. Nomax is in his apartment, still stunned and hurt that his girlfriend has dumped him. He turns on the radio, and the recordings he hears comfort him. They're delivered by artists named Big Moe, Eat Moe, Four-Eyed Moe, Little Moe, and No Moe.

With a book like that, you'd better do something else to add to the fun. So Mackintosh added a pub next door to the Lyric Theatre in London and then a bar that nestled next to Broadway's Eugene O'Neill Theatre. Truth to tell, many theatergoers may have had a better time at the after-party (although it offered neither free food nor an open bar). When a show solely consists of music of another era, people like to recognize the tunes, and not enough knew Jordan's work.

Hence, *Smokey Joe's Cafe: The Songs of Leiber and Stoller* (1994–1995), at 2,036 performances, ran five times as long as *Five Guys*. Baby boomers, now pushing forty, were getting nostalgic for songs of their youth. *Joe's* had them; *Moe* didn't.

It was an offhand remark that Savion Glover made when Public Theatre artistic director George C. Wolfe asked him what he'd like to do at his theater.

Replied Glover, "I want to bring in 'da noise, bring in 'da funk."

They had their title: *Bring in 'da Noise, Bring in 'da Funk* (1995–1996). Now they'd bring in an all-black staff to create a history of tap dancing.

It started with a riff on the Bible: "In the beginning was 'Da beat!" Reg E. Gaines's book then took audiences on the boats that brought slaves to America. There was little that these unfortunates could do to pass the time but dance.

If anyone doubts the power of the arts, he should take a look at the law the South Carolina legislature passed following a slave uprising on September 9, 1739: "The use of any form of drum by slaves is prohibited."

Slavery ended. "Panhandlers used their hands as pans," went a lyric which may have come from any of the three lyricists: Gaines, Wolfe, or Ann Duquesnay. (She, incidentally, appeared in the show and won the Best Featured Actress in a Musical Tony.)

Moving up to the twentieth century, we heard "Arkansas, four, Alabama, one." This was hardly a baseball score. Instead, Duquesnay was citing a litany of how many blacks were lynched in 1916: fifty by her count. ("Assisting persons to escape, five; insulting a white man, two . . .") A dancer then did a cruel parody of a tap dance to indicate a man swinging from a rope.

Hence, the northern migration. We heard black after black glad to be bellmen, waiters, and bus boys. At least in the North they'd stay alive.

But the men who found employment in Chicago factories would "don their workclothes and become part of the machines, surrendering their individual rhythms to become cogs." Even so, they weren't appreciated by the Irish Americans, who saw them taking away jobs; hence, the 1919 Chicago Race Riot.

Better times were ahead in the Harlem Renaissance. Gaines and his lyricists were proud to mention such names as Zora, Satchmo, Ellington, Langston, and Countee Cullen. There was plenty to celebrate—until the Depression.

Hollywood provided some work for the tapper, but more for the black willing to shuffle. Such performers rationalized: "Oh, Susanna, don't you cry for me; 'cuz I got a Rolls-Royce in my drive; six servants servin' me."

That attitude lasted only so long. "Goodbye, Daddy," the next generation said. "Sorry, but you got to go."

When the time came to document the mid-fifties, the three writers weren't afraid to indict Northerners for not immediately taking the stand that the Southerners took. As Duquesnay's character sang, "Ain't nobody draggin' me off no bus . . . I'm tired."

The five tappers acknowledged the Black Power movement of the sixties and the New York blackout of 1977. In the eighties, progress wasn't fast enough, Michaels Jordan, Jackson, and Tyson notwithstanding. "I need some food" was a common cry.

Four black men in four different parts of New York tried to hail a taxi. Glover played the first, who had a hip-hop look and was passed by. He tapped to express his fury. So did the second, a well-groomed student, and the third, who held up an American Express card as an indication of his legitimacy, *and* the fourth, who was reading Colin Powell's autobiography.

The show ended on a more optimistic and powerful note. Each of the cast members expressed his own views:

"The most important thing that I do is be with my family and music, because those are the two things I love very dearly."

"A lot of people that I looked up to when I was younger and wanted to be like are now dead or in jail . . . I wanted more."

"I'm not a lost cause, because: one, my mother, two, you know tap dancing."

"I could be just as mad as I don't know what and then I could start dancing and it'll just—it lightens my spirit."

"Tap sorta saved me. People was I guess out doing what they was doing. I was like the one in dance class."

Here was more proof that the arts can save and enhance lives.

Noise/Funk reached 1,135 performances, making it the longest-running show created by a totally black team. In a year when it wasn't pitted against *Rent*, it might well have won Best Musical.

The 25th Annual Putnam County Spelling Bee (2004–2005) brought everyone back to high school, when the gym was the nerve center of all important activities.

Book writer Rachel Sheinkin didn't have to concern herself with finding the right structure. She'd inherited it from the template that was set at the first nationwide spelling bee held in Washington, D.C., in 1925. Since then, every word has been announced, defined, and used in a sentence before the speller tackles it.

Needless to say, the chosen words were ones that people seldom if ever encounter. What fun Sheinkin must have had in perusing the dictionary, finding "boanthropy" and learning that it means "the delusion that one has become an ox." She must have immediately run to her computer to type *that* one in. Thus, after each contestant asked, "May I please have the definition of that word?" Sheinkin had an automatic punch line every time.

More difficult was getting laughs from each "And the use in a sentence, please?" But Sheinkin succeeded. When a speller asked for a sentence that included "phylactery"—defined as "small square leather boxes containing religious texts traditionally worn on the left arm and head by Jewish men during morning weekday prayers"—she was told, "Billy, put down that phylactery. We're Episcopalian."

We had the suburban elegance of Rona Lisa Peretti, the champ of a previous bee who'd returned for the ninth time to emcee. Helping her was Douglas Panch, a nervous vice principal who was quite unaccustomed to public speaking. In fact, Panch alluded to "an incident" that he'd caused five years earlier. About an hour into the bee, he had a breakdown. Why couldn't he have been characterized as a terrific person, as so many in the education profession are?

Actually, the show was curiously anti-intellectual. William Barfée (Dan Fogler) was myopic, overweight, sloppy, lactose intolerant, and sinus-impaired. Leaf Coneybear contorted his mouth and had a virtual seizure every time he spelled a word. Marcy Park was dour and all business. Chip Tolentino was the shy guy made to look silly when singing about "My Unfortunate Erection."

Logainne SchwartzandGrubenierre was the adopted daughter of two men, Mr. Schwartz and Mr. Grubenierre, who apparently didn't want their names joined together by a hyphen but by a conjunction. Thus what would have been a difficult nineteen-letter-long name ballooned to an even more difficult twenty-two-letter one. To further stack the deck against her, Logainne had a spittle-thick lisp, too.

Only Olive Ostrovsky seemed to be even-tempered and well-adjusted. But why were students accomplished in an academic skill ridiculed as misfits, freaks, and geeks? Kids who are terrific at spelling should have been entitled to admiration.

The best plays offer orchestration of character: a range of different types on stage. *Bee* stacked the deck to suggest that most kids who can spell are undesirable dorks who can't cope with real life and the outside world.

What's more, when Logainne asks for a sentence that used "strabismus" she heard, "In the schoolyard, Billy protested that he wasn't cock-eyed. 'I suffer from strabismus,' he said—whereupon the bullies beat him harder." Must even a kid with a vision problem be mocked and subject to being unjustly pummeled?

None of this bothered Tony voters, who awarded Sheinkin Best Book. But how much did composer-lyricist William Finn have to do with this self-loathing approach? When he won his Best Score Tony for *Falsettos* in

1991–1992—and received no fewer than thirty-seven seconds of enthusi-astic applause he ended his acceptance speech with "I'm a miserable person."

That same year, when a *Theater Week* reporter asked him how he'd describe himself, he said "a big fat Jew." Finn doesn't seem to have much self-respect, so he may not know how to give it to others.

But while we're on the subject of *Spelling Bee* . . .

CHAPTER NINE

*

You Were Good, but Not Good Enough:
The Flawed Best Musical Tony Losers

The contestants in *The 25th Annual Putnam County Spelling Bee* tauntingly sang, "Goodbye! You were good, but not good enough," whenever one of their rivals was eliminated from contention.

Did Tony voters feel the same when voting for *Monty Python's Spamalot* instead of *Bee*?

We're about to embark on our biggest chapter, because—let's face it—most Best Musical nominees were good, but not good enough.

At four performances, *Rags* (1986–1987) remains the shortest-running show to be nominated for Best Musical. That's all the more surprising, given that it was written by blue-chippers. As the ads liked to say, "From the creators of *Fiddler on the Roof, Annie,* and *Godspell*"—respectively book writer Joseph Stein, composer Charles Strouse, and lyricist Stephen Schwartz.

In *Amadeus*, Emperor Joseph II once complained that Mozart had written "too many notes." Strouse didn't write too many; the ones he found were quite beautiful and in tune with 1910 Jewish immigrants. Blue notes, phrases for klezmers to suggest the Lower East Side, and frisson-inducing melodies made this one of the best of his many fine Broadway efforts. Has there ever been a sexier turn-of-the-century song than "Blame It on the Summer Night"?

Schwartz didn't write too many words, but Stein did in creating too many characters. Indeed, there were more main characters than the number of performances *Rags* played.

The story of Rebecca Hershkowitz would have been enough. She and her son David had to leave her village before the pogrom killed them

Strippers, Showgirls, and Sharks

both. (Shades of a *Fiddler* sequel?) When audiences heard that her husband Nathan had come some years before but had not sent for her, they inferred that he would not want her if she found him. He would undoubtedly be an all-American now and embarrassed to see this relic from his past.

Not quite.

But before Rebecca found Nathan, she found work at a factory where Saul wanted to improve conditions. Rebecca doesn't want to make the splash of a wave, but she is intrigued by this man who would. So she allows herself a date with him and her interest grows. That's why she wants to "Blame It on the Summer Night" and not herself.

So the story takes an unexpected turn. A wife is this close to cheating on her husband—right around the time she finds him.

And he *is* happy to see her. The problem is, he's become the type of American she doesn't want to be—the glad-hander, the opportunist, the phony. She's outgrown *him*.

Bella, Avram, Ben, and Rachel had stories, too, and some dovetailed nicely with Rebecca's. But the central story was complicated enough.

Admittedly, Broadway would soon get a megamusical that involved more characters. But *Les Misérables* had a more epic scope, and its through-sung score was novel enough to make an impact.

Too bad. There were some nice messages here. ("In America, they don't make it easy for you, but they let you do it.") *Rags* also reminded us to "Honor thy great-grandfather and great-grandmother." They made the difficult trip and worked in jobs many of us wouldn't consider today. They did the hard work so we wouldn't have to.

One of *Rags*' most poignant moments occurred at the top of the show. After the ship docked, some immigrants got off and were found to be health risks. They were put right back on the same boat on which they had traveled months in steerage. All that distance for nothing! And now the trip back would be worse, because they had nothing to look forward to as they did when they optimistically came here.

And that moment didn't need a single word.

Long after Jewish immigrants came the Chinese immigrants in *Flower Drum Song* (1958–1959). It was a moneymaker for Rodgers and Hammerstein, but the only hit of the six they'd had that failed to become a classic.

That Hammerstein wasn't physically well may have been inferred by

179

his collaborating with journeyman Joseph Fields on the book. Only once during his Rodgers and Hammerstein days had Hammerstein shared book credit, and that was *South Pacific* when he *had* to; Joshua Logan had brought him and Rodgers the property, and co-owned it.

C. Y. Lee's 1957 novel called *The Flower Drum Song* offered different conflicts from the ones the Jews had had. Money wasn't a problem for Wang Chi Yang, who'd emigrated to San Francisco with his large fortune intact. Unlike the Hershkowitzes, he didn't want to become an American, but stayed staunchly Chinese.

Of his two sons, teenager Wang San had easily been assimilated into American life and had discarded all Chinese values. Wang Ta, a bit older, was conflicted between old Chinese traditions and new American ones.

The latter category included Linda Low, the flashy showgirl with whom he was entranced. How carefully he kept her from his father, who he knew wanted him to marry a native Chinese woman from "a house with a high door."

That would seem to be recent immigrant Mei-Li, but she was the picture bride who'd been promised to Sammy Fong long ago. Coincidentally—too coincidentally, really—Sammy was a nightclub owner who was in love with Linda, too.

No matter. The show came to the amiable conclusion that there was worth in both new- and old-world cultures and customs. Along the way, there were some catchy Rodgers melodies, too.

Hammerstein didn't often write lyrics along the lines of "Dong-dong, you're in Hong Kong." He reportedly said, "This is the first lucky hit I've ever had." It ran an even six hundred performances.

He and Fields were lucky to have written it in the late fifties. Not too many years later, many audiences would have blanched at such lines as "She's built like a Ming vase" and "She's one of those local egg rolls." When Mei-Lei's father said of his daughter, "She is as strong as a cow and just as amiable," Mei Lei sincerely responded, "Thank you, my father." The old "L" versus "R" joke was put into play, too, when one of Sammy's Asian showgirls pretended to be Irish and proclaimed "Ellin go blah." Sammy's emcee delivered a joke that bombed, causing him to comment, "Back to the laundry."

Under these circumstances, the observation that Wang Chi Yang said to Sammy Fong could serve as a criticism of the script: "You have an unfortunate way of expressing yourself."

The performer chosen to play Sammy showed that nontraditional casting was still in the future. Caucasian Larry Storch was originally cast, but when he was found wanting during the Boston tryout, he was replaced by the equally white Larry Blyden.

Flower Drum Song lost the Best Musical Tony to *Redhead*, which had a Tony-winning performance by Gwen Verdon (her fourth win in as many tries) and dynamic staging from Bob Fosse. He won a Best Choreography Tony, but didn't win for Best Direction of a Musical, for that category was still a year away. If indeed it had been instituted in 1958–1959, Fosse would have undoubtedly won over the *Flower Drum Song* director who had well overshadowed him when both were Hollywood dancers: Gene Kelly.

No Strings (1961–1962) could be considered an important building block in black musical theater. Granted, the composer *and* lyricist was Richard Rodgers. True, librettist Samuel Taylor had written many a Wasp high comedy. (Exhibit A: *Sabrina Fair*.) Both had represented commercial Broadway for some time, but now they'd write an original musical about an integrated romance.

Barbara Woodruff (Diahann Carroll) was a black New York model who had relocated to a less-prejudiced Paris. David Jordan was a successful American novelist who came to France ostensibly to write. Instead, he lived off his fame and anyone willing to pick up the check.

No character made an issue of Barbara's being black. David was attracted to her, and that was that. The only mention occurred in "Maine," in which David sang about his home state before Barbara mentioned that she came "up north of Central Park." Translation: Harlem.

That Rodgers didn't write "Maine" until the Detroit tryout reiterates that he and Taylor had made a conscious effort not to mention race. Was this evidence of their sophistication, because race didn't matter to them? Did they want audiences to realize that race should be irrelevant?

Or were Rodgers and Taylor playing it safe by avoiding the subject? In an era where homosexuality was still "the love that dare not speak its name," an interracial romance wasn't far behind.

Much was made about exciting Paris keeping David from writing. It turned out to be a convenient plot twist; Barbara could urge him to return to Maine, where he could write without distractions. Barbara wouldn't accompany him—and not simply because Portland isn't as fascinating as Paris or the Pine Tree State has little call for fashion models. Even if

Barbara had decided to retire, she wouldn't have been much welcomed as a white man's wife in this Republican enclave.

We can't just blame this state; at the time, where interracial marriages were concerned, as Maine went, so did the nation. Killing the relationship probably pleased much of the 1962 theatergoing public.

So give Rodgers and Taylor credit for being too far above the issue of race to discuss it—or say they were too chickenhearted to come to grips with it.

By the way, Carroll in her memoir *The Legs Are the Last to Go* referenced *No Strings* by saying, "I won a Tony Award. My competitors for the prize in 1962 were Anna Maria Alberghetti, Molly Picon, and Elaine Stritch."

Yes, indeed, Carroll did win a Tony as Best Actress in a Musical—but so did Alberghetti, for they had tied. Note the careful way Carroll and/or co-author Bob Morris chose certain words: "I won *a* Tony Award," not *the* Tony Award; "my competitors" versus "the women I beat."

Sneaky.

No Strings didn't have much influence on the black-white relationship in *Golden Boy* (1964–1965).

It had three white writers: librettist William Gibson, composer Charles Strouse, and lyricist Lee Adams. Gibson had taken over after his mentor Clifford Odets, adapting his own 1937 play, had died. In the afterword to his published script, Gibson gave credit to *Golden Boy*'s star Sammy Davis, Jr., for bits and pieces of dialogue, and revealed something telling: "He said one night, 'I leave you with two words' . . . 'Write colored.' I was much encouraged by his conviction that if I only tried hard enough, I could become one of the country's leading colored writers."

Why wasn't a black playwright offered the job? Granted, Lorraine Hansberry was too ill, but both James Baldwin and Richard Wright had written for the theater. And while neither had penned a Broadway musical, Gibson hadn't, either. (However, to be fair, Gibson had had two smash hits in as many tries: *Two for the Seesaw* and *The Miracle Worker*.)

Golden Boy's play had told of Joe Bonaparte, a young Italian American violinist who wanted fast money to help his family and became a boxer. Joe's father preferred that his son have a musical instrument under his chin instead of a fist. If Joe broke his hands, he'd have no chance of making music his livelihood.

Joe fell in love with Lorna, the mistress of his manager Tom. But producer Hillard Elkins had had a brainstorm that would make Odets's original play seem tame: Davis would play Joe, which would up the ante on the romance (and create box office excitement).

Because piano was an instrument that Davis could play—and one more associated with blacks than the violin—Joe was transformed into a budding pianist. After arduous tryouts in Philadelphia, Boston, and Detroit, he simply became a young black man with no particular direction, making him desperate to find his place in the world. As he sang in one of Adams's most pungent lyrics, "Who do you fight when you want to break out but your skin is your cage?"

And yet, the idea of five foot five Davis as a potential boxing champ seemed unlikely unless he were fighting in the flyweight division.

Perhaps that's why Joe's father—simply identified as "Wellington"—feared for his son's life. Truly, though, he wanted his son to be more than "just another colored fighter. Be respectable," he advised.

Joe interpreted that as "live like a dead man." 1964 was still a time when a black man could look to little else but sports or entertainment as routes out of the ghetto.

Boxing wasn't a panacea for those who managed fighters, either. Sang Joe's manager, "Here I am, Thomas J. Moody. Three-year-old suit from Robert J. Hall. Jesus H. Christ!" Lorna's problem was *Mrs.* Thomas J. Moody, who denied her husband a divorce. The frustration may have been one reason why Lorna switched her attention to Joe.

Lorna was, however, a realist about the relationship: "A walk hand-in-hand down the street with half the world biting me at every step." Her ambivalence was a factor in Joe's leaving Tom for the more powerful and flashy Eddie Satin.

Golden Boy made its other daring move here: it established that Eddie was gay—granted, not until act two, scene seven. What's more, it was mentioned only once. Still, it opened up audiences to the possibility that someone associated with sports might be homosexual. (Don't laugh: at the time, many audiences would have rejected the idea as impossible if not ludicrous.)

Satin gave Joe a Ferrari, which resulted in the all-too-obvious foreshadowing from one of Joe's promoters: "He could kill himself in a car like that."

Indeed he did, after Lorna had finally and irrevocably spurned him.

She had two reasons: "Tom picked me out of my filth after a lot of men went through me like traffic in a tunnel" and "I haven't got the guts to make a life with you." So Joe took out his hostility in the ring, murdered his opponent, and then tried to forget by driving his Ferrari too fast and recklessly. His killing himself conveniently took care of the interracial romance.

In Odets's original play, Joe was killed in a car accident—but Lorna was with him and died, too. Here the black man died and the white woman lived. Suddenly, complaining about the ending to *No Strings* seemed trivial.

Most critics said that *Golden Boy* had as many liabilities as assets, but most approved of Strouse and Adams's score, starting with "Night Song," Joe's aria of dissatisfaction. "Colorful" had Joe vigorously celebrate being black, over the times when he was naïvely "green," unhappily "blue," or even "good as gold." Strouse put plenty of blue notes in his jazzy score and was able to, if we may update Davis's advice to Gibson, "write black." That was especially true of "No More," in which Joe built his feelings to a fury prior to his final fight.

The show "danced black," too, for *Golden Boy* had hired a black choreographer: Donald McKayle, who did especially fine work when Joe's family and friends urged him to remember his humble roots in the showstopping "Don't Forget 127th Street." ("The neighborhood is classy; we have rats as big as Lassie.")

Golden Boy had a more interesting character: Joe's strapping big brother Frank. "Ever think of fighting?" Joe's trainer asked him. Frank's answer was "I fight."

Indeed he did: for black civil rights. That was a substantially nobler cause than knocking someone down in hopes that he wouldn't be able to get up again.

Frank was about to go down south where, he observed, "It's very hot in Alabama." He wasn't talking about matters Fahrenheit. Later, when he entered with a bandaged head, audiences knew what had brought on the injury.

But Frank spent most of his time offstage, for Broadway wasn't yet ready for a musical about him. Of course, even if *Golden Boy* had concentrated on Frank rather than Joe, it still wouldn't have beaten *Fiddler on the Roof* as Best Musical. What it would have been, however, was a more fascinating show.

* * *

Patrick Dennis had an inspired notion: ghostwrite an autobiography ostensibly written by a fictitious, faded, B-minus movie "star." In her nod to false modesty, it was called *Little Me: The Intimate Memoirs of That Great Star of Stage, Screen and Television, Belle Poitrine.*

In French, these last two words mean what Dorothy Fields called in *A Tree Grows in Brooklyn* a woman's "points of interest."

Even prepuberty, Poitrine, née Belle Schlumpfert, lived up to the surname that she'd acquire through one of her many marriages. If only her brain were as large! When one of her many husbands called her "nafkeh," she assumed it was a term of endearment, and never learned that it was Yiddish for "streetwalker."

Belle established in chapter one that she'd been born in 1900—but called her last chapter, which took place in 1960, "Frankly Forty." She truly believed that readers wouldn't notice.

What else could a well-developed but empty-headed female become but an actress? The word, however, must be used as loosely as the loose woman Belle was. When a reviewer called one of her pictures "soporific," Belle automatically assumed that this word combined "superb" and "terrific." She told of a film in which she played Marc Antony's unhappy wife, but because "they are both of the Roman faith, divorce is out of the question."

So here was a complete hoot. Producers Cy Feuer and Ernest Martin entrusted their musical *Little Me* (1962–1963) to three writers who had each had one show on Broadway. Composer Cy Coleman and lyricist Carolyn Leigh's *Wildcat* was a flop but not because of their excellent score. N. Richard Nash's wan book and the frequent absences of star Lucille Ball were to blame.

Of Broadway's composers, Coleman was the greatest equal opportunity collaborator. Seven out of his twelve musicals had female lyricists, who gave him larger-than-life female characters: Wildcat Jackson, Sweet Charity, Gittel Mosca, Lily Garland, and, yes, even Belle Poitrine were all women who wanted to better themselves and, more often than not, had the courage to follow their dreams.

This would be his last collaboration with Leigh, however. She *could* be difficult, as was proved in that famous incident during *Little Me*'s Philadelphia tryout; she brought in a street cop to arrest co-producer-director Feuer for changing her work.

Did the contentiousness involve a lyric in "Deep Down Inside"? Belle hailed from Drifter's Row, where the town's most uneducated people lived, so when she sang, "No man is a true pariah deep down inside," one's eyebrows had to rise. They went higher still when she added, "No man is a true Uriah Heep down inside." No, Belle had never read *David Copperfield* and didn't know one of its minor characters. (And *Little Me* took place long before the rock group Uriah Heep was founded.) For that matter, Belle wouldn't know the two dollar word "pariah."

Leigh was guilty of showing off and not writing for the characters. But considering how brilliant the rhyme was, one can understand why she couldn't bear to discard it.

At least during the rest of the show, she provided many gems that sounded right for Belle ("The irregardless truth . . . You're damn well right, the truth.") By the time Belle reached maturity and duetted with her younger self, we could believe that they'd learned enough French to sing, "When it comes to parlez-vous, who could parlez-vous a few?"

Leigh certainly could. The words she wrote for *Wildcat* in "What Takes My Fancy" best express who the woman was: "Them's what treats me girly has to find out early in my mama's litter, I'm the independent critter." Yes, and three Broadway musicals were the richer for it.

For *Little Me*, Feuer and Martin also signed Neil Simon as their book writer. Before he'd had his first Broadway comedy hit with *Come Blow Your Horn* in 1961, he was one of Sid Caesar's writers on the star's three TV series.

If Simon hadn't been so employed, he might have written a better musical.

After Simon read Dennis's novel, he decided to concentrate on the men in Belle's life and have his old boss play all of them. All Caesar would be divided into seven parts: Noble Eggleston, the town's sought-after dashing young man; Mr. Pinchley, a latter-day Ebenezer Scrooge; Val du Val, a Maurice Chevalier–like haw-haw-haw French entertainer; Fred Poitrine, the nearsighted doughboy whom Belle married before he headed off to war; Otto Schnitzler, a German film director; Prince Cherney, a big monarch of a small country; and Noble Eggleston, Jr.—needless to say, a dead ringer for his father.

As a result, Simon gave most of the funny lines to Caesar's characters and had Belle feed him the setups. The gags and quips were superb, but making a tour de force for Caesar ultimately made the show a tour de fuss.

Little Me was as farcical as the musical to which it lost—*A Funny Thing Happened on the Way to the Forum.* But *Forum*'s audiences were rooting for Pseudolus to win his freedom, while the crowds at *Little Me* were thinking, "Gee, what crazy character will Sid Caesar be next?"

If Simon had kept the spotlight on the egocentric, blissfully unaware Belle that Dennis had created, he would have brought to the stage an absurd, hilarious, and sui generis creature. Too bad that Paul Rudnick and Charles Busch were respectively four and eight years old when *Little Me* opened. One licks his lips when thinking of what their takes on Belle Poitrine would have been.

In 1963–1964, *Funny Girl*—the victim of *Hello, Dolly!*—didn't get a single Tony out of its eight nominations. It was a new record of frustration, tied with that season's *High Spirits.* Not even Barbra Streisand could beat Carol Channing.

(Eventually the Tonys were embarrassed by this slight. The 1969–1970 Tony nominating committee gave Streisand a special "Star of the Decade" Award. If it hadn't, Streisand would have never had a Tony, because she certainly wouldn't deign to return to Broadway. Wonder if she knows where her statuette is today?)

Funny Girl would later endure another dubious distinction as the first Best Musical Tony loser to surpass a thousand performances: 1,348, in fact. Although Mimi Hines played about half those performances, Streisand jump-started this imperfect musical to success. If Streisand hadn't succeeded, few today would have ever heard of or remembered *Ziegfeld Follies* and radio star Fanny Brice (1891–1951).

As is almost always the case with a not-so-hot musical, the problem rested with (shall we all say it in unison?) the book. Isobel Lennart showed early on that she knew that the rise-to-stardom story was a most trite one—even for an unlikely star such as the homely Brice. Audiences had for decades seen endless backstage Hollywood "biographies" of one star or another, so what else could they expect but early struggles, big breaks, and eventual success?

Lennart even wittily commented on that cliché: after big-time producer Florenz Ziegfeld summoned a just-starting-out Fanny to his office, she said, "It's coming too easy, that's what's got me scared. Where's all the suffering you're supposed to do before you click? The hard knocks, the setbacks you're supposed to learn from?"

All that was left was the star's personal life. Even here, Lennart couldn't make the story sound fresh: ugly Fanny fell for handsome gambler Nick Arnstein, who eventually agreed to marry her; Fanny's career continued to skyrocket while Nick's "career" didn't. She tried to help him; he lost her money and refused to take any more. So he committed a crime and went to jail. Once he finished his sentence, he told her that the marriage was finished, too. End of story.

End of soap opera, really. It might have been a stronger musical if the truth had been revealed. Said Margaret Styne, who was married to the show's composer Jule Styne, "Fanny's daughter Frances was the wife of producer, Ray Stark. She didn't want the show to say that Fanny was already married when she'd met Nick Arnstein, who'd already been to jail. Fanny always knew that he was a crook and even used to shill for him."

Lennart did what she could with Frances Arnstein Stark's restraints. She endeared us to Fanny right from the opening line, when the star looked in the mirror and immediately addressed the homeliness issue that was on everyone's mind: "Hello, gorgeous."

The world has had more than a half century to accustom itself to Barbra Streisand's looks, but there was a time when she was considered—well, as Pete Hamill said in his 1963 *Saturday Evening Post* profile of her, "What there is would hardly launch a thousand ships." Her most prominent feature was her quite long nose. In one of her subsequent TV specials, she and an anteater were seen in profile, as she sang, "We have so much in common, it's a phenomenon."

A flashback then took audiences from the late twenties to 1910, where Fanny's mother's Rose was entertaining neighborhood friends who tried to discourage Fanny from trying show business. "If a girl isn't pretty like a Miss Atlantic City," they cautioned.

Fanny was indomitable. "You think beautiful girls are going to stay in style forever?"

She certainly didn't look beautiful when she first met Arnstein. She was clowning around backstage on her hands and knees and was soon pretending to be a dog. No wonder that after he left, she expected, "Nicky Arnstein: I'll never see him again."

In matters of romance, Fanny had none of the confidence she had as a performer—even when battling Ziegfeld. When he wanted her to play a beautiful bride (and *why* would he choose this *meeskite* for this role?) she took issue; he reminded her, "This is my theater." Fanny's answer, "And nobody argues with the landlord?"

But Lennart added a too familiar subplot: the loyal friend, Eddie Ryan, who loved Fanny from afar and who would always be sentenced to friendship. At least Lennart made a solid point: Eddie simply wasn't attractive enough for Fanny. Her feeling ugly made her need someone as handsome as Nick. His love made her beautiful.

This spread to Fanny's worrying about her baby daughter's looks. When Eddie said "She's the cutest little thing I ever saw" that wasn't good enough for Fanny, who demanded "But she's *pretty*, isn't she?"

Eventually we returned to 1927, when Nick was released from prison and said that he didn't want to resume the marriage. Fanny lied and said she didn't, either. After he left, we heard a familiar refrain: "Nicky Arnstein: I'll never see him again."

That's when Styne and lyricist Bob Merrill provided a dramatic ending, reprising one of the score's stellar moments: "Don't Rain on My Parade."

It capped a marvelous score. Indeed, next to *Gypsy, Funny Girl* had Styne's best music: "I'm the Greatest Star," "Cornet Man," and "Don't Rain on My Parade" all had drive and power. Although his songs for Rose Hovick will be far more remembered than the ones he wrote for Rose Brice, he did give her a share of a razzmatazzer in "Who Taught Her Everything (She Knows)?" and a nice Bowery waltz in "Find Yourself a Man."

Conventional wisdom says that a Broadway musical had best not give audiences two ballads in a row, for that brings on boredom. When the songs are as stellar as "Who Are You Now?" and "The Music That Makes Me Dance," an exception can be made. And speaking of ballads, "People," people?

Merrill's lyrics weren't afraid to stress Brice's unattractiveness. Neighbor Mrs. Strakosh drolly noted, "When a girl's incidentals are no bigger than two lentils, then to me that doesn't spell success."

But some lyrics said as much about Streisand as Brice: "a nose with deviation . . . who's an American beauty rose with an American beauty nose . . . stiff upper nose, Brice." All the while, Merrill was careful to stress the resolute Fanny: "Looking down, you'll never see me. Try the sky—'cause that'll be me." As Jack Kroll wrote in *Newsweek*, "It's a stony theatergoer who won't agree."

That *Funny Girl* has never been revived on Broadway is not simply because Streisand is no long age-appropriate or available. "And to think," said Mrs. Styne, with a decisive finger point, "when Barbra was first mentioned for the role, Fran said, 'That girl play my mother? I wouldn't hire her as my maid!' She never liked her, even after the success."

Forty seasons later, the male equivalent of *Funny Girl* opened: *The Boy from Oz* (2003–2004).

The similarities: both were about entertainers (here, Peter Allen) who had rocky and ultimately failed marriages (Allen's with Liza Minnelli).

The difference was that Allen found romantic happiness with Greg Connell, at least until he contracted AIDS and died.

The biggest similarity was a head-turning star performance from Hugh Jackman, an easy Best Actor in a Musical Tony winner.

The biggest difference was that Streisand had an understudy in Lainie Kazan who did go on once. Jackman had two standbys—Michael Halling and Kevin Spirtas—but they must have been somewhat ashamed to take the money. Even on the two occasions that Jackman took a week's vacation, they weren't pressed into service. Only if something had happened to Jackman midperformance would one have played the role.

And when Jackman was finished with the show, the show was finished.

Half a Sixpence (1964–1965) was a rags-to-riches-to-rags-to-riches tale. Arthur Kipps, a draper's apprentice, was ostensibly in love with Ann Pornick, a maid. He proposed in scene one and then audiences didn't see her again until scene ten. In between, Kipps learned that he'd come into a fortune. And he didn't tell his fiancée?

No, because Kipps had become involved with Helen Walsingham, a debutante whom he realized was "too far above me" but one he nevertheless wanted. Truth to tell, Helen's family needed Kipps's money more than he needed their upper-crust class.

Despite their poverty, they believed they had the right to change his manners and his speech, which had him dropping "h's" everywhere. Of course, Kipps eventually rebelled and returned to his true love even before he learned that Helen's brother had stolen his money. Luckily, Kipps had invested in a play that turned out to be a smash hit. Even more luckily, he did it in an era where returns on hits were substantially more lucrative than they are now.

Does this seem to be the work of the man who wrote *The Invisible Man* and *The War of the Worlds*? But it was: *Kipps*, H. G. Wells's 1905 novel, was written years after those classics. Similarly, who'd expect the screenwriter of *Jason and the Argonauts*, one Beverley Cross, to provide the book for such a sunny show? David Heneker, who'd done some work on *Irma La Douce* and cowrote the score to a British musical with the unlikely name of *Expresso Bongo*, came up with one terrific tune after another.

The slight show wouldn't have lasted 511 performances had it not been for Tommy Steele's Kipps. He was a marvel, singing enthusiastically, dancing up a hurricane, making us care about the fate of the character no matter what mistakes he made—*and* he played a banjo.

There was even a performance where a chorus boy lost his boater hat during a production number, and Steele in mid-dance was able to pick it up and Frisbee it over to him.

Actually, there were 511 performances in which that carefully planned "accident" happened.

That incident turned out to be telling. Later, when Steele performed in the films of *Half a Sixpence*, *Finian's Rainbow*, and *The Happiest Million-aire*, audiences came to see that every performance offered the same small bag of tricks. There were the raised eyebrows, the arms almost akimbo while he strutted, the eyes he rolled heavenward when he found a certain lyric particularly delicious, and the head he tossed back and forth just a little when he got to the meat of the lyric.

And yet, when Steele was in a situation where he tried to convince someone that all was well—only to find that his optimism was not working—his wide-open eyes turned to slits and his smile went slack. He became tired and quietly exasperated when the other party wouldn't co-operate and capitulate. It all felt phony.

Steele has never again come to Broadway. Perhaps deep down inside he knew he had nothing more to offer us.

Illya Darling (1967–1968) was the musical version of *Never on Sunday*, a popular 1960 film about Ilya (yes, one "l" fewer), a Greek prostitute who was enjoying her life, liberty, and pursuit of happiness—and money. Then Homer Thrace, an American scholar innocent in matters of love, came to Greece, met her, and tried to reform her.

Both felt an attraction, but if Oscar couldn't forgive Sweet Charity for simply sleeping around, how could Homer forgive Illya, who was truly in it for the money?

Manos Hadjidakis's Oscar-winning title song "Never on Sunday" was interpolated into this show, which was a regrettable first. Allowing a movie song into a new score lowered the musical theater bar, for it encouraged future film-to-stage musical properties to include *their* movie songs, too. Even *The Sound of Music* and *Grease* would eventually include their movie songs when they were revived on Broadway.

Hadjidakis added sixteen more songs. Although he was born in Xanthi, Greece, why was it that his score somehow sounded less authentically Greek than the one non-Greek John Kander wrote for *Zorba*?

Purlie (1969–1970) referred to Purlie Victorious Judson, a forward-looking preacher in the long-ago South. In a black church, a coffin was wrapped in a Confederate flag. The deceased was no less than Ol' Cap'n Stonewall Jackson Cotchipee, who'd ruled his South Georgia plantation and terrorized everyone on it.

Said Purlie (Cleavon Little), who was literally preaching to the choir while presiding over the funeral, "He did us a service—dying . . . it would not be Christian for us not to pray for what we know is impossible: his redemption."

One wondered why a white man who was important in his community would have a funeral with dozens of blacks and only one white man in attendance. The answer was to start the show with "Walk Him up the Stairs," a rousing black gospel number that, yes, was written by white composer Gary Geld and white lyricist Peter Udell. The latter was one of three collaborators on the book, which had odd billing: literally "Davis-Rose-Udell" with no first names. (Ossie Davis, author of the original play *Purlie Victorious*, and Philip Rose, the director, were the others.)

Then came a flashback in which Purlie brought home Lutiebelle Gussie Mae Jenkins (Melba Moore)—a name that Purlie said was "an assault to the Negro people." Lutiebelle thought that Purlie's home was "nice," but he felt it never would be "until I own it."

Here was a preacher who was less interested in "that glorious life on the great other side." When Purlie mentioned a rich white woman's car in contrast to "all the transportation I got in the world is tied up in secondhand shoe leather," the primarily black audiences often grunted in recognition.

Purlie had brought Lutiebelle to South Georgia in hopes that she'd pass for a distant dead relative, Beatrice Johnson, who'd been entitled to five hundred dollars from Ol' Cap'n. That would go a long way in helping his cause—and his need for revenge.

Ol' Cap'n had bullwhipped Purlie when he was teenager. Purlie never forgot it and never would. "Something about Purlie always did irritate the white folks," said his sister Missy—probably because "he's got one of the best secondhand educations in this country. Used to read everything he could get his hands on." And while Missy and Lutiebelle were dubious that the scam could work, Purlie believed that "Some of the best pretending in the world is done in front of white folks."

If Ol' Cap'n weren't challenge enough, the three weren't sure if they could trust Missy's husband Gitlow. Ol' Cap'n had put him in charge of the other blacks, and that paycheck and status made him "deputy to the colored" as well as disloyal to his own people. In a world of Uncle Toms, Gitlow was a Great-Uncle Tom.

But Gitlow was a husband, too. Like many married men, he had to cater to his wife, who wanted to try extricating the inheritance. Gitlow's wavering provided some tension.

Ol' Cap'n turned out to be worse than Purlie and Missy had described. The only way in which Ol' Cap'n wasn't intolerant was lactose. His heart was as black as Elizabeth Taylor's eyes in *Who's Afraid of Virginia Woolf?* How else to describe a man who said "Feed the Nigras first—after the horses and cattle." Told by his own son Charlie that "The flour is spoiled, the beans are rotten, the meat is tainted and a little wormy," Ol' Cap's response was "Sell it to the Nigras."

That made Charlie one of Ol' Cap'n's biggest adversaries. The young man came to appreciate blacks at any early age, because he was raised by his father's maid Idella. Charlie didn't dare to say much when his father offered the blacks shoddy merchandise, but when Ol' Cap'n complained of people who believed that "white children and darky children ought to go to the same schoolhouse," Charlie displayed his backbone: "It's the law of the land and I intend to obey it."

Alas, when Lutiebelle was to sign the legal documents, she wrote her own name instead of Beatrice Johnson's. She and Purlie avoided prosecution because Idella told Ol' Cap'n she'd quit if he didn't stop litigation. Here's where we learned how much Ol' Cap'n needed her (not that he ever would have admitted it).

The brush with disaster made Missy urge Lutiebelle to get Purlie to "settle down," in both the marital and political sense. Missy believed that "Being colored can be a lot of fun when nobody's lookin'." Lutiebelle also asserted that "Life is good to us sometimes"—meaning "picnics, fish fries, corn-shuckings, love-feasts and gospel singing, picking huckleber-ries, quilting-bee parties and barbecues."

Purlie, however, remained as steadfast as a character we'd meet later that year: Mayer Rothschild, who wanted money and land not only for himself, but also to liberate his people.

However, when Ol' Cap'n sexually harassed Lutiebelle, Purlie vaulted into action, and not simply out of righteousness. He learned that he cared for this young woman more than he'd thought. Soon he returned, and startled both Missy and Lutiebelle by toting Ol' Cap'n's bullwhip and five hundred dollars. Purlie implied that he killed Ol' Cap'n, but we soon saw that he hadn't. Charlie had given him the whip and the money—and when Ol' Capn' learned that, *that* killed him.

By now, the liberal theatergoing audience had come to feel that the Black Power movement had legitimate complaints. Fewer than two months before *Purlie*'s opening, Leonard Bernstein had held a party and fund-raiser for the Black Panthers in his swank digs at the Dakota on Central Park West. Radical chic was in.

Moore made "I Got Love" one of the decade's most exciting solo per-formances. But *Purlie*'s book relied on that condescending plot twist of having Lutiebelle stupidly sign her own name. Giving Ol' Cap'n a heart attack after he's been betrayed didn't seem in keeping with the tough old bird we'd seen all night long.

Purlie's Best Musical Tony nomination came because of the show's parts, and not its totality. Nevertheless, whatever its faults and flaws, *Purlie* was, at 688 performances, Broadway's longest-running black-themed musical—introducing many black audiences to Broadway.

Coco (1969–1970) lost to *Applause*, which was quite a good musical—until one remembered that its source material was *All About Eve*.

Even such Broadway royalty as Betty Comden and Adolph Green, lyricist Lee Adams, and composer Charles Strouse weren't able to im-prove the story about Margo Channing and Eve Harrington (or Ger-trude Slescynski, if you will).

Bettering a film whose fourteen Oscar nominations still haven't been surpassed wasn't an easy task. But writing a musical about Gabrielle "Coco" Chanel had to be more of a challenge to book writer/lyricist Alan Jay Lerner and composer André Previn. The eighty-six-year-old fashion pioneer could ostensibly look over their shoulders and force constraints à la Frances Arnstein Stark.

Lerner wrote about a retired Coco who'd decided to make a comeback after fifteen years. Solid enough. But as Coco herself said in her eleven o'clock number, "Who the devil cares what a woman wears?"

This was the line on which star Katharine Hepburn most embarrassed herself—acting as if she had a voice. Although Lauren Bacall, *Applause*'s leading lady, couldn't sing, Hepburn *really* couldn't. And yet, after Bacall left *Applause*, it ran ten more months, achieving almost 40 percent of its 900-performance run without her. After Hepburn departed *Coco*, it ran thirty-four days.

Many people said, "Kate's the whole show"—which had to rankle Lerner and Previn, who actually wrote a lovely score. It just didn't sound lovely when Hepburn croaked it.

What's more, whenever young lovers Noelle and George took the stage, or when flashbacks of Coco's life were shown on film, *Coco* bored. Then it was overly flamboyant whenever Sebastian Baye (René Auberjonois) appeared. He, initially hired to help Coco, was described as "almost male, almost female, almost human." Thus, Auberjonois had to play him as an out-of-control, way-over-the-top, vicious queen who wanted to see Coco fail. (The show's most-quoted line, Coco's "There's no bitch like a man," was not, however, aimed at Sebastian, but at a newspaper columnist who'd doubted that Coco could return to greatness.)

Coco opened the second act by saying "Shit!"—which is how audiences learned that the press had panned her new collection. But her flop was celebrated by Baye in the deliriously evil "Fiasco!"

Because *Coco* opened fewer than six months after Stonewall, many theatergoers still hadn't had their consciousness raised and enjoyed Auberjonois's Tony-winning performance. Today many would be offended or repulsed by it.

Meanwhile, over at *Applause*, Lee Roy Reams was playing Duane, a homosexual who was a grounded individual, a self-actualized man who was a good, solid employee, and a friend to Margo Channing. Reams not only didn't win the Tony, but he was also denied a nomination. Subtlety isn't always prized.

If Hepburn was "the whole show," that was almost wholly because Lerner gave her a multitude of impressive lines. ("A sinner can reform, but stupid is forever.") His lyrics were equally tart, although few could tell how good they were because Hepburn's "singing" made them hard to understand.

Reading them, however, displays that they had style, specificity, and wit. Coco rued in her first song, "Time silences the phone, empties every vase, leaving you alone." Thus her great return: "You want the world?" she rhetorically asked young people. "You'll have to fight!" So she challenged, "Peck away, sweet birds of youth!" She'd return, although she'd occasionally "have the type of backache that hypochondriacs can only dream about."

Coco was still financially secure, so she knew that critics and cynics would wonder "why a woman who has money would want to work." But she also knew that "a queen with a lot of jack is a king" and, by doing things her way, she'd be "free to parade up the Rue de la paid up."

One of her lines—"People without standards have nothing to compromise"—often received, to cite that other musical, applause. So did another line in which Coco commented on the decisions made by male designers: "Men are making fun of women."

Coco knew, however, that she'd run the risk of being "the mademoiselle, a sadder moiselle," because she'd have to play the usual games that one must do to stay in business. "Than do all that for bed and board I'd rather be in bed and bored," she opined.

Although she was forward-thinking, Coco did occasionally look back. At one point, she remembered how she'd changed the fashion world after a trip to Italy: "My shoe ensnared my gown and I went down—and 'down' in Venice means really under." Did Lerner write this to transport theatergoers back to Hepburn's 1955 film *Summertime* when her character indeed fell into a Venetian canal? Whatever the case, it "made me wet and made me wonder: would this have happened if by some chance instead of a gown I wore men's pants?"

A film flashback showed that Coco's maverick nature had its genesis in childhood, when she'd asked her father for a red communion dress. Her greater request, however, was that he attend the ceremony. Father said he'd be there when it happened in seven weeks; she corrected him, "Six." That one word showed how much the event meant to her and how it wasn't at the front of his mind.

In fact, Coco eventually remarked that he not only missed the event, but also that she never saw him again. She thus learned to count on no one. Even the song list in the program indicated that she was extraspecial. while many a female character in a musical has had a title song, this one essentially had two, done in succession: "Gabrielle," sung by her father, and "Coco," sung by the lady herself.

The childless Coco found a surrogate daughter in Noelle, an assistant who gave the grande dame a good dollop of hero worship. "God knows you could have had all the husbands you wanted," Noelle cooed. "God knows I did," Coco answered in a definitive and lusty voice. The line deliciously and enigmatically suggested that Coco had either had all the married men she'd ever wanted—or that she'd never wanted any. Lerner's character was well aware that no one would dare pry by asking additional questions.

And, like so many parents and surrogate parents, Coco had to come to terms with some inevitable facts about Noelle: "I find myself thinking of her as my daughter," she said, before becoming realistic: "knowing the way she is, wishing she were a little different, disappointed that she's not perfect."

Neither was Coco, who wasn't above criticizing Noelle's reporter-boyfriend Georges: "I hope when his newspaper goes to press tonight he sends along that suit," she said icily. Although Coco insisted that "Men and women deserve something better than each other" (a line with which many *Coco* attendees agreed), Noelle had to flatly tell her, "I'm just not all I need."

That, of course, disappointed Coco, who roared, "I can see a future for you that you couldn't dream of with opium." But Coco had met her match. Said Noelle, "I don't want to be made into someone no man can satisfy."

Coco's response was a curt "Get out of here!"—and might well have been the component that kept the musical from being an unqualified success. If Coco had given her blessing, the show might have better satisfied the female theatergoers, who were, to be sure, *Coco*'s target audience. Many 1969 wives had already made the choice that Noelle was planning; even those who had wound up in failed marriages still wanted to believe that love was indeed the answer.

In *Applause*, the heroine made the opposite choice. Margo Channing eventually abandoned her glamorous career because "Love Comes First," as she sang in the Philadelphia and Baltimore tryouts. By New York, that song had been replaced with one that made a more potent statement: love was "Something Greater" than a career.

These issues would come up again in Bacall's next and final musical: *Woman of the Year* (1980–1981), adapted from the 1942 movie of the same name. (Poorly.) In the film, *New York Chronicle* columnist Tess Harding appeared on a radio quiz show on which she was asked a question about baseball. Tess couldn't answer and offhandedly mentioned that she had no interest in the subject.

Sam Craig, a sportswriter for the same newspaper, happened to hear her and wrote a column refuting her indifference. Then Tess and Sam met for the first time—and found that each was intrigued with the other's looks.

In the musical, Sam was a comic strip artist who'd created a cat called Katz. Sam's description of him: "Like all New Yorkers, nothing surprises him." Thus, every fourth panel had Katz drone, "So what else is new?"

Tess (Lauren Bacall) was a TV commentator who did an editorial on how she was "sick and tired of the funnies"—which made Sam retaliate by having Katz criticize a TV anchorwoman named Tessie Cat as a purveyor of "lowbrow pursuits" on "stupid shows." Given that 25 percent of every strip had Katz say the same line, Tess may have had a point when she said that the funnies weren't what they used to be.

The difference between the two properties was palpable. The movie's Tess had made a chance remark when asked a question she hadn't anticipated; the musical's Tess engineered a premotivated attack.

The musical's Sam met Tess's mean-spiritedness with more mean-spiritedness before he made an appointment to meet her. When he arrived, Tess kept him waiting and defended herself to her secretary Gerald: "When You're Right, You're Right."

And then the moment she laid eyes on Sam, she immediately sang, "I was wrong."

A show that was supposedly celebrating women was insulting them, however obliquely. Love at first sight is fine for high school and younger, but Tess had already been through one marriage and presumably enough romantic experience to have learned that one favorable first impression wasn't proof of anything.

At the beginning of scene four, Sam was telling off Tess; at the beginning of scene six, they were already married. Granted, things should happen quickly in musicals, but not at the expense of the plot. Tess in the film had expressed doubts before she married; Tess in the musical plowed ahead. Both she and Sam should have known that you don't marry first and ask questions later.

Only now did Sam see what a workaholic Tess was and how impossible her schedule was. In the forties, a man hadn't had enough experience with career women to understand the ramifications of marrying one; by the eighties, Sam would have seen many Tess Hardings and wouldn't have been surprised by her schedule.

So "It Isn't Working," as Sam's friends and Tess's staff gleefully sang six months after the wedding. Why should such schadenfreude amuse audiences? "Marry in haste, repent at leisure" is not a concept that innately gets laughs. What's worse, when the marriage looked doomed, Tess's employees sang, "I Told You So."

It was John Kander and Fred Ebb's least pleasant score, which was especially evident when Tess sang "Shut Up, Gerald." When she was named "Woman of the Year" in the midst of her darkest days with Sam, she sang, "Go shove it and scram, 'cause goddamn it, I am the Woman of the Year." Ever the lady . . .

Then there was the subplot. In the musical, Tess's big subject for a story was Alexi Petrikov, a dancer who was a Soviet defector. In the film, he was Dr. Lubbeck, a Yugoslavian statesman who had escaped from a concentration camp. We all acknowledge the importance of the arts, but compared to a freedom-fighter, the problems of one Russian dancer didn't amount to a hill of beans in this crazy world.

So Peter Stone's book seemed retro, even though he had the good sense to drop such lines as "Women should be clean and illiterate—like canaries." But Stone apparently thought that having Tess incessantly forget the name of her ex-husband's new wife Jan (Marilyn Cooper) and have her say "Jane" instead would be funny.

That Kander and Ebb gave Cooper and Bacall "The Grass Is Always Greener," in which they compared lives, was one reason for their Best Score Tony. The *other* reason was that the other nominees—*Charley and Algernon*, *Copperfield*, and *Shakespeare's Cabaret*—had run a *total* of eighty-four performances and were long gone by Tony time. Never before or since have three Best Score losers amassed so few performances.

Woman was also the only 1980–1981 Best Musical nominee to have an original score. *Sophisticated Ladies*, *Tintypes*, and *42nd Street* had songs that had been written dozens of years to decades earlier.

While *42nd Street*'s secondhand score wasn't eligible, its book by Michael Stewart and Mark Bramble was. Originally producer David Merrick castrated their credit from "book by" to "lead-ins and crossovers by."

If the producer didn't even consider their book a book, why should anyone vote for it?

So Stone's second-rate work won. Audiences were asked to conclude that Tess and Sam had worked out their differences at show's end; they'd be fine from now on. Not a chance.

That the show made such period references as Bjorn Borg, Art Buchwald, G. Gordon Liddy, Tip O'Neill, Phyllis Schlafly, Pia Zadora, Jilly's, and Maxwell's Plum isn't the reason why *Woman of the Year* isn't often revived. Its characters' attitudes made it a dinosaur in 1981.

Finally, if anyone needs any proof that *Woman of the Year* has quickly dated, he need only check this stage direction: "He pulls out a paging device, the sort doctors use."

So what else is new?

Over Here! (1973–1974) did offer truth-in-advertising. Indeed, "The Andrews Sisters" were onstage, even if they were only two-thirds of what they'd been. Patty and Maxene lost LaVerne when she died of cancer in 1967.

There's a funny story about the four Marx Brothers. After they'd finished *Duck Soup*—and Zeppo left the act—someone asked Groucho, Chico, and Harpo if they'd take a proportionately smaller salary. The brothers' response? "We're twice as good without Zeppo." (Which nobody can deny.)

But two Andrews Sisters weren't quite as good as three, for the distinctive triple blend of voices wasn't there.

An aside: *Over Here!* coproducer Kenneth Waissman has said that the sisters had something else in common with the Marx Brothers: "They were nicknamed Nympho, Dyke-o, and Lusho for their habits," he said, before refusing to divulge which nickname was the appropriate one for each sister.

Here, Patty portrayed Paulette while Maxene played Pauline. These DePaul Sisters were two USO entertainers during World War II—a time where trios reigned. Thus, Will Holt's book concentrated on their finding a third voice just as the Andrews Sisters did after LaVerne's death.

They did, via Mitzi (Janie Sell). By the end of the first act, that famous three-part harmony that had sold more than thirty million records was almost identically back in place.

In act two, however, Sam, a black railroad porter, made a plea for racial equality. If that were an impossible dream, Sam would settle for whites admitting to prejudice instead of denying it. "Don't Shoot the Hooey to Me, Louie," he demanded in song.

Suddenly, a musical that had been amiably and nostalgically rolling along made a social statement. Many aging theatergoers didn't welcome it. The irony is that the very next song—"Where Did the Good Times Go?"—had many attendees wondering the same thing during Sam's song.

Holt tried to restore levity with out-and-out nostalgia. Cast members were made to resemble Nelson Eddy, Jeanette MacDonald, Sonja Henie, Joe Louis, Esther Williams, James Cagney, and, last but hardly least, Betty Grable in her famous bathing suit pose. That killed ten minutes.

Then the book collapsed when Holt unmasked Mitzi as a German spy. Audiences had come to like her; to learn that she was a traitor ended the enjoyment.

The Sherman Brothers, most famous for such Disney films as *Mary Poppins*, couldn't be faulted for their score. The pair, who'd enjoyed using such nonwords as "chu-chi," "chitty," "gratifaction," "freebootin'," and, needless to say, "supercalifragilisticexpialodocious," took a more straight-forward approach with *Over Here!* Because the forties were a time when pop songs had overly romantic lyrics, the Shermans were within their rights to write such sentiments as "Until my arms enfold you again, I'll live with that beautiful dream in my heart."

Who knew, however, that they could write on-the-money Andrews Sisters parodies? Or perhaps they couldn't. Three of the five songs that Patty and Maxene sang together carried the disclaimer, "Messrs. Sherman and (vocal arranger Louis) St. Louis wish to acknowledge the creative contribution of Walter Weschler on these numbers." Or perhaps Patty Andrews requested credit for Weschler, who was also known as Mr. Patty Andrews?

If so, it wouldn't be the only demand that Ms. Andrews would make. Although both sisters sang, "Together—working as a team together" in their opening number, Patty demanded to be paid more than Maxene. Coproducer Kenneth Waissman said that made for some unpleasant al-most daily phone calls.

The show greatly benefitted from its young cast, some of whom went on to notable careers. So although theatergoers went in to see the An-drews Sisters, many came out talking about Treat Williams, Samuel E. Wright, Marilu Henner, Ann Reinking, and, last but hardly least, John Travolta.

Over Here!'s director Tom Moore had staged *Grease*, too, and had chosen Travolta as a replacement Danny Zuko. Now he cast him as an incompetent soldier known as Misfit. Interesting, isn't it, that Broadway saw Travolta in goony roles while Hollywood would soon cast him as a hunk?

Shenandoah (1974–1975) had a different kind of hero: a pacifist. And while this issue was a hot topic at a time when the Vietnam War was still waging, the musical instead dealt with the Civil War.

Charlie Anderson, a Virginia farmer, had six sons and one daughter living at home. Even James, now married to Anne, still resided there. The other five sons ranged from twelve to twenty-eight, with Jenny an in-between nineteen. Charlie had to do all the parenting and wisdom-dispensing, because his wife Martha had died during her last childbirth; he spent a good deal of time at her grave talking to her.

Confederate soldiers came by the farm to entice the eldest Anderson sons to enlist. Charlie wouldn't allow it—and they all too conveniently went away.

Shenandoah was never more specific than "time: the Civil War," but history states that the Confederate draft began in May 1863. And while we could infer that *Shenandoah* took place earlier, after Jenny married Sam, he immediately went to war. Whether he enlisted or was drafted was not made clear by book writers Jamie Lee Barrett, Peter Udell (who wrote the lyrics), and Philip Rose (who produced).

If Sam had enlisted, the authors should have given him a scene or a song in which he discussed his plans with his fiancée. If he'd been drafted, they should have told us about the change in Confederate policy. That would have led to further ramifications from Charlie and his sons; some could have worried while others could have rejoiced.

Actually, the sons did rejoice in one song, "Next to Lovin' (I Like Fightin')." This, however, was not about fighting for a great cause but about roughhousing. "Next to poetry and prose," sang the lads, "I like punchin' me a nose." Frankly, nothing in the script ever suggested that the young men cared a whit for poetry or prose. But the latter word did, after all, rhyme with "nose."

Shenandoah also settled for scenes that simply passed time, including Sam and Jenny's wedding. Audiences had barely come to know the couple, had little invested in their love, and weren't all that interested in seeing the ceremony. Most musicals reserved weddings for their final scenes and showed only a few seconds of them. And while some of the theater-going population enjoys seeing an onstage wedding, many find such scenes nondramatic (as they indeed are).

If watching a wedding is boring, observing a bride-to-be and her sister-in-law prepare for it is even more tedious. However, the book writers didn't think so.

At least after the nuptials, they returned to the drama. Charlie boldly confronted a sergeant who wanted to confiscate his horses for the Confederate cause. After he learned that the Union soldiers had captured his youngest son, Charlie was ready to kill—and went out to do just that.

He and his sons did manage to liberate Sam from a POW train. But a Confederate mistakenly mistook Jacob for a Union soldier and shot him dead. The killer was distraught and apologized, but Charlie was barely listening when he instinctively murdered him.

One son, Nathan, was appalled. "He said he was sorry," he reminded his father. Charlie snarled, "Sorry doesn't help Jacob." Jenny then pointed out that "killing him hasn't helped Jacob."

These lines resonated in a country that had been arguing about war for literally fifteen years. The sentiments represented one reason why *Shenandoah* was able to run 1,050 performances; a low payroll and skimpy production was another.

The Andersons would find tragedy in store when they arrived home and learned that James and Anne had been killed, too. But Barrett, Udell, and Rose didn't show us that scene. They instead flash-forwarded to a few days later after the family had had some time to adjust to the news. Not letting us witness their reactions wasn't dramatic enough.

Then while the family was in church for Sunday services the youngest son walked in just before the final curtain. That yielded sighs from some and guffaws from others.

The youngest son was named Robert, but everyone simply called him "The Boy." Always. Even Gabriel, a young black slave whom he'd befriended, called him "Boy."

And yet when the two had an introspective (if up-tempo) musical moment called "Why Am I Me?" Gabriel sang "Why am I Gabriel?" prior to Robert (or The Boy) asking the same question. But actor Joseph Shapiro couldn't sing "Why am I Robert?" or "Why am I The Boy?" in the name of musical symmetry, because each of those names only contained two syllables, and "Gabriel" had three. So Udell "solved" the problem by choosing "Why am I Anderson?" This was the one and only time in the entire musical that he or anyone else referred to him by that last name.

Udell didn't mind matching singular words with plural ones—"Union boys are hard as nails. Johnny Rebel is a cotton tail"—or "m's" with "n's": "I laughed last night 'til I had pain. Johnny Rebel can't write his name."

Who'd have such a strong reaction when encountering an illiterate? A chuckle, maybe. A belly laugh from the more insensitive, perhaps. But laugh until pain invaded one's body? No. Udell seemed to have approached lyric writing as if he were completing a homework assignment. Get it done just to have something to pass in.

Such violations abounded in Charles Small's score for *The Wiz*, too. And yet, this was the same season that Jerry Herman was denied his Best Score nomination for *Mack & Mabel* at the expense of these two nominees.

The curtain rose on the climactic scene in a Joan of Arc drama. Just as the Maid of Orleans was to be set afire, a stage manager crisply came on stage. That made us assume that we'd been watching a rehearsal.

No, this had been a performance. The stage manager had interrupted it because "The last one left in the audience just walked out."

That has to be the writer's ultimate nightmare. Betty Comden and Adolph Green had probably felt as if it happened to them when their *Bonanza Bound* was dying in Philadelphia in 1947. But otherwise, the two book writer/lyricists had had fourteen solid Broadway shows under their belts before they opened *On the Twentieth Century* (1977–1978).

The musical version of the 1932 play and the 1934 screen classic *Twentieth Century* had music by Cy Coleman. The approach they took was opéra comique—a lofty style that hasn't been since tried by any Broadway writer.

It was *The Twentieth Century, Ltd.* until coproducer Mary Lea Johnson (of Johnson & Johnson fame) went to a numerologist. There she was told that her show would be a hit if it had twenty-one letters in its title. (Here's more proof that in show business, everybody listens to everybody.)

Whatever the title, it would be a lighter *Mack & Mabel*: the story of the mercurial—nay, volatile—relationship between twenties theatrical impresario Oscar Jaffee (John Cullum) and Lily Garland. He had transformed her from bland nobody Mildred Plotka into a stage star, his lover; she in turn, turned him into her ex-employer and ex-lover.

And yet, she couldn't completely dump the person who'd made her a star.

Comden and Green made a significant change and a vast improvement from both play and film. Here, Mildred didn't audition for Oscar; she was a pianist who'd been hired by the self-important Imelda Thornton to accompany *her* audition.

The diva, however, wasn't up to the rigorous "The Indian Maiden's Lament," as Mildred was the first to tell her. Imelda was livid that a mere accompanist should turn critic, and refused to pay her.

Hell hath no fury like a pianist threatened with nonpayment. The fire that Mildred had in her belly and everywhere else convinced Oscar that she had the passion to become a great actress.

This wise change increased Lily's indebtedness to Oscar and gave her even more reason to become his lover. In the play and film, Lily was grateful for her career-making break, but also conveyed that she would have been successful even without Oscar. But because Mildred had never given a thought to performing until Oscar discovered what was buried deep within her, she couldn't deny his great role in changing her life.

By 1932, however, with *The French Girl*, his Joan of Arc biodrama closing in Chicago, Oscar was dead broke. Meanwhile, the Mildred in scene four who'd barely been a person was by scene six already referring to herself in the third person. Lily Garland had gone Hollywood and had become a beautiful, glamorous, radiant, ravishing movie star.

Once Oscar had learned that she was taking the *Twentieth Century*, America's most luxurious train, to New York with her new beau Bruce Granit (Kevin Kline), he ordered his henchmen Owen and Oliver to somehow get tickets for Drawing Room A—because he'd overheard that she'd be in Drawing Room B. He'd then entice her to do a play with him.

When Owen and Oliver tried to make Oscar face reality, he was quick to fire them and "close the iron door." Indeed, Oscar "closed the iron door" more often than theatergoers walked out of *Legs Diamond*. And while he'd often slammed it on Lily during their tempestuous personal and professional relationship, he'd now reopen it and welcome her with open arms.

Although Owen and Oliver got Drawing Room A, propinquity was of no help. Lily didn't want to resume working with her old boss—although both ruminated wistfully on happier times in "Our Private World." Coleman's glorious melody went from a nostalgic 4/4 to a pulse-quickening 12/8 and back again.

Bruce was much threatened by Oscar's return. Lily showed her deep feelings for Oscar by turning on Bruce and threatening to "close the iron door" on him. Imitation may be the sincerest form of flattery, but Oscar had even greater pleasure when hearing Lily use one of his trademark expressions.

In the corridors, some mysterious passenger was placing stickers that said, "Repent for the time is at hand." Letitia Peabody Primrose, the founder and president of Primrose Restoria Pills, was asked if she'd seen the culprit. If someone on the train staff had truly been paying attention, he might have read some meaning into Letitia's response that "It could have come straight from heaven."

Letitia took us into her confidence and urged us to "Repent," as she sang, "In the fiery pits of Hades, it's too late for your laments." And in case we didn't grasp the ramifications, she stressed, "They've a fiery pit for ladies and a fiery pit for gents."

Here was another smart move by Comden and Green. Originally Matthew J. Clark was the religious fanatic. But eccentric women are usually more fun than eccentric men. By changing Clark to Mrs. Primrose, Comden and Green also allowed us to get one last blast of glory from Imogene Coca, a fifties television icon from *Your Show of Shows* who hadn't appeared on Broadway in nearly twenty years.

At least the stickers gave Oscar a good idea: Lily Garland as Mary Magdalene. When Owen and Oliver discovered that Mrs. Primrose would back a religious-themed show, Oscar was able to convince Lily to return to the stage under his direction.

Alas, that's when the men in the white coats came and announced, "Mrs. Primrose climbed the fence this morning from the Benzinger Clinic." That led to "She's a Nut," a five-minute-long musical scene that included a chase from Drawing Room A seemingly to Drawing Room Z. Mrs. Primrose was seen evading escape by standing outside on the train's cowcatcher before repairing to the caboose, where she took the liberty of placing another sticker on the train's exterior. It was the type of number that occasionally got the most delightful kind of applause: it started loud, increased in volume, then naturally abated—until the audience felt as if it hadn't let the cast know how much it appreciated it. So the crowd began applauding louder than it had before.

"She's a Nut," however, was surrounded by a good deal of book that wasn't top-notch Comden and Green. A scene in which Oscar tried to sell

Lily on playing Mary Magdalene moved more slowly. And while Comden and Green retained the happy ending in which Oscar and Lily reunited, we knew they'd be warring again—which brought to mind Amanda and Elyot in *Private Lives*, which made this musical pale in comparison.

Musical theater fans want to know, "So was Madeline Kahn fired as Lily or did she quit?" more than "Who killed JFK?" Whatever the case, the Johnson & Johnson heiress and her coproducers suddenly needed more than a Band-Aid to fix the wound that Kahn inflicted when she left the show nine weeks after opening. But as the title song said, "Life and love and luck may be changed. Hope renewed and fate rearranged."

It came from Kahn's understudy Judy Kaye. While she didn't anticipate ever going on, Kaye, like the best understudies, prepared for the part just in case. "I'd practice the songs in my dressing room or backstage, and some people would say, 'Will you go into the wings and let Madeline see what you're doing so she can do it, too?' And I said, 'No, I don't think she'd appreciate that.'"

Eventually, Kahn decided not to do a performance—and then opted to skip seven more. The powers-that-be decided that eight was enough, and Kaye, to her great delight and even greater astonishment, was the new Lily. Those who doubted her ability to seize her chance and deliver a galvanic performance were convinced by the time she arrived at the end of "Babette," her eleven o'clock number. There she hit notes that Kahn never thought of trying to reach.

Kaye might well have won the Best Actress in a Musical Tony had she been nominated. But Kahn was. If the committee from 1970–1971 had still been in place, Kaye might have been acknowledged; that group had decided that Larry Kert, who had rescued *Company* when leading man Dean Jones abandoned it, should get the nomination—and never mind who opened the show.

But the 1977–1978 committee opted to acknowledge lame duck Kahn. Can we rightfully infer that very few voters chose her?

That cleared the field for Liza Minnelli to win for *The Act*. In many ways, Minnelli deserved the honor; she carried a musical that was a glorified nightclub show by singing twelve of its thirteen songs.

Another statistic, however, was equally as telling: Minnelli also missed more than 10 percent of the show's 233-performance run. Once word got out about her erratic absences, many a potential attendee chose not to buy tickets. After all, *The Act* was asking an all-time and astronomical top ticket price of twenty-five dollars. Why put out all that money in advance only to have the magic night arrive and find that Minnelli wouldn't be at the Majestic?

The voters didn't choose Eartha Kitt, whose stage time in *Timbuktu!* wasn't all that plentiful. Few probably even saw the small-voiced Frances Sternhagen in her five-performance run in *Angel*. So Minnelli might well have emerged victorious by default. Had Kaye been eligible, she might have won because she was the new girl in town, which Broadway always loves to discover.

"Miracles come in threes," Oscar believed. *On the Twentieth Century*'s first one was the then-unknown Kevin Kline stealing the show. When Kline's Bruce Granit saw Lily in a new negligee, he did a double take with his eyes and a triple axel with his body.

And while the second miracle was Kaye's making comparatively few miss Kahn, there was no third miracle for *On the Twentieth Century*. Losing the Tony for Best Musical was fatal, and led to the iron door's closing on the show after 449 performances and a sizable financial loss.

And yet, on the night of the Tony Awards, did Johnson and her coproducers think that they had the big prize after Comden and Green were awarded Best Book and then got their piece of the Best Score prize with Coleman?

Best Book plus Best Score had always equaled Best Musical in the ten years in which all three prizes had been given. (The Book and/or Score categories had occasionally been omitted.) Now, for the first time, those two awards did not result in Best Musical.

A song in Coleman's next musical—*Barnum*, which lost the 1979–1980 Best Musical Tony—insisted that "Bigger Isn't Better." Up until now, the Tony voters had agreed. This year, they voted for a one-set musical with a cast of five.

Great expectations played a part. *On the Twentieth Century* had been anticipated as Broadway's next big smash. Director Harold Prince had won four Best Direction Tonys in this yet-to-be-completed decade. When his show didn't turn out to be completely spectacular, voters took what it had accomplished for granted.

Meanwhile, *Ain't Misbehavin'* had opened quietly at the eight-year-old Manhattan Theatre Company that was located in a quite out-of-the-way dump on East Seventy-third Street. But when a good show opens, no matter where it is, New Yorkers usually find it—and producers are eager to move it.

Why not? A cast of five and a small pit band would make *Ain't Misbe-havin'* a herd of cash cows for various touring companies. And by now, with twelve national broadcasts under their belts, Tony voters were start-ing to think about what shows would survive and thrive on the road.

Henry Krieger of *Dreamgirls* fame wrote for another type of black family in *The Tap Dance Kid* (1983–1984). The Sheridans were almost upper-middle-class residents of Roosevelt Island, the two-mile strip of land that's a tramway ride away from the big city.

Theatergoers saw plenty of "relative humidity" here—meaning that every relative got hot under the collar. William was a lawyer, making enough so his wife Ginnie could stay home and tend to fourteen-year-old corpulent Emma, who wanted to follow in her father's legal footsteps, and ten-year-old Willie, who wanted to put his footsteps on a Broadway stage. Dad was of course dead-set against it, in the time-honored (read, trite) tradition. (*A Day in Hollywood* included a song, "I Love a Film Cli-ché," which listed twenty bromides. Number six was "Gee, why can't I make you see I got music inside of me, Pa?")

Willie had inherited his dancing talent from his mother's side of the family, for Ginnie was once part of an act with her father and brother Dipsey. The paterfamilias had since died, but Dipsey stayed in show busi-ness and was working most weeks of the year.

Needless to say, Dipsey inspired Willie, which was one reason why William didn't want his brother-in-law near the house. In fact, William was so single-minded about this issue that one would think his brain only had one lobe.

He did have only one song. After a night of delivering dialogue, Dad suddenly unleashed a hateful diatribe. He said that Dipsey wasn't a man but acted "like a child" and demeaned Willie's ambitions as "dancing like a monkey through his nose." He reminded his wife, "You've got a maid when you could have been one," and that his job filled "the cabinets with far too much food so Emma can stuff her fat little face." And if that line wasn't unfeeling enough, he added that he also saw dancing as something "colored boys," "darkies," and, yes, "niggers" did for "nickels and dimes."

And after this, Willie gave in and relinquished his role in a great big Broadway show. He'd put his dream on hold.

Given that Krieger, librettist Charles Blackwell, and lyricist Robert Lorick were adapting Louise Fitzhugh's young adult novel *Nobody's Family*

Is Going to Change—in which Willie retained the role—why did they change the ending? Perhaps they felt that they needed a surprise, or at least a different plot twist from the one we'd been expecting all along. However, audiences walked out displeased with both father and son. So were Tony voters.

Her story was much too sad to be told. She was one of another hundred people who'd just got off of the plane from London and found herself in the ultimate City of Strangers. The reason that she came to New York was to work and to play. But she didn't bank on having so many short-term relationships.

Such was the story of the unnamed "Girl" in *Tell Me on a Sunday*, which composer Andrew Lloyd Webber and lyricist Don Black wrote as a song cycle in 1978, put on record in 1979, and on television the following year.

People often say that producers don't have any ideas anymore, but Cameron Mackintosh certainly did. In the early eighties, he remembered the tuneful *Variations* that Lloyd Webber had written for his brother, noted cellist Julian Lloyd Webber.

The composer has often been accused of stealing melodies from Puccini, but Paginini was the master from whom he borrowed here. At least Lloyd Webber acknowledged that *Variations* was a riff on the composer's Caprice No. 24 in A Minor.

Mackintosh suggested that *Tell Me on a Sunday* be a one-woman show in its first act and a dance piece in its second. *Song & Dance* opened in London in 1982 and played two years.

When it came to New York in the 1985–1986 season, after both a tweaking and direction by Richard Maltby, Jr., it ran half as long. It was doing fine as long as Bernadette Peters was portraying Emma, as "Girl" was now called. Once she'd finished her yearlong contract, Betty Buckley took over. The songs and dances ended in a month.

Peters was indeed marvelous and received her first Tony Award after three losses. She was wonderfully innocent and vulnerable as she welcomed her first official romance with Chuck.

He was a drummer; 'nuff said. When he started making excuses for his neglectful behavior, Emma demanded, "Spare me the song and dance," which added a nice layer to the title.

Film producer Sheldon came next. He was willing to keep Emma, which she found stifling and boring. Emma didn't much like L.A., either, reducing it to a place where there was an abundance of "Capped Teeth and Caesar Salad," as she told her mother in one of the many letters audiences heard her write to her. Some letters had a white lie or two, but the lies got progressively darker.

Once Emma returned to New York, she met Joe, who'd also come to the city, albeit from Nebraska, for fame and fortune. Emma thought Joe would be the love of her life, which is why Lloyd Webber saved his most beautiful melody, "Unexpected Song," for this scene.

Ultimately, Joe wasn't able to commit to her, and Emma knew the relationship wasn't going well without having to ask the famous "Where are we going?" question that so many women ask of men.

Emma's confrontation was of a different and more elegant kind. She asked that when he broke up with her that he "Tell Me on a Sunday" in a lovely locale such as a park or a zoo. That would take a bit of the sting off the pain—and would presumably give her a day to recuperate before starting the workweek.

Having her heart broken by Joe resulted in the inevitable affair with a married man. Emma saw Paul for a while, but eventually broke it off, giving *him* a song and dance and denying him the courtesy of telling him on a Sunday. As the curtain fell, Emma then realized how unfeeling she'd been with him, and vowed to become the person she once was.

That the British musical had eclipsed the American musical was one thing; now we had to hear that if a nice English girl came to America, she'd inevitably become corrupted and unfeeling after dealing with American men? Weren't there similar men in Britain? Tony voters could be excused for thinking the theme all too simplistic.

By the time the second act began, we'd forgotten about Joe from Nebraska. He, however, wound up starring in this sequence, and expressing his feelings through dance courtesy of Christopher D'Amboise.

After hearing Emma meticulously describe her feelings in the first act, this suddenly "silent musical" didn't give us a detailed explanation from Joe. If audiences were to get two sides of the story, they should have *heard* both.

By now the public had pigeonholed Lloyd Webber as one who delivered spectacles. After such mammoth events as *Jesus Christ Superstar*, *Joseph*, *Evita*, and *Cats*, this Lloyd Webber show—with a cast of nine in *Dance*—seemed slight.

What's more, as thrilling as Peter Martins's choreography was, theatergoers didn't want to lose Bernadette Peters after one act. The second half inevitably felt anticlimactic without her star presence. Having her walk across the stage in act two only underlined how much she was missed.

The show might have done better as *Dance & Song*. Christopher D'Amboise can open for Bernadette Peters—but Bernadette Peters does *not* open for Christopher D'Amboise.

Book writer/director George C. Wolfe didn't state that *Jelly's Last Jam* (1991–1992) took place on July 9, 1941, but it obviously did. Wolfe said the musical was set on "the eve of the death of Jelly Roll Morton," who died on July 10, 1941.

Many a Broadway musical has had a nightclub setting or two, but *Jelly's* set was a very different one: "The Jungle Inn—a lowdown club somewhere's [sic] 'tween heaven 'n' hell." Wolfe apparently meant hell more than heaven, because he had Jules Fisher create a dim atmosphere that bore no relationship to that famous white light that many who have almost died claim to see. Besides, nary an angel was seen all night, but an emcee called Chimney Man was. His presence suggested a locale where the Fahrenheit level is on the high side.

Chimney Man started by telling us of a people whose "story of their pain was set forth in music." He cited Louis Armstrong, Duke Ellington, Count Basie, Buddy Bolden, and Sidney Bechet by name, but stopped short of naming Morton. That, however, was the man he meant when he stated, "he who drinks from the vine of syncopation but denies the black soil from which this rhythm was born."

Morton (Gregory Hines) arrived, a "slumped figure" who "grew in stature" and by the end of the song that introduced him was "strutting, arrogant, and proud."

Too proud, really. "Mr. Mozart would have tipped his hat" at him, he insisted insufferably. In a flashback, Jelly tried to convince his younger self that he was special. As one of Susan Birkenhead's lyrics went, "You are the one / The sun's gonna rise on / The one the world / Is keepin' its eyes on."

Apparently the plaudits took hold, for the adult Jelly believed he was extraordinary to the nth degree. He started calling himself in the third person as "The Roll," a name that some say had its roots in genitalia, but one Wolfe said came because his music was "as sweet as jelly on a roll."

Pride has never been deemed a mortal sin, but Jelly took it to such an extreme that it could have been considered one.

To be fair, he'd inherited his inclinations. His family had always assumed that it was better than most others because it was "one of the oldest and most genteel Creole families in New Orleans." It admitted to having French, Spanish, and Portuguese ancestry. It staunchly denied having even as much black blood as the drop that Steve Baker had ingested from Julie LaVerne's hand.

While Morton did write some music that had what he proclaimed "the Spanish tinge," he was more proud of inventing jazz, which had a distinctly black feel to it. "No, music is the French Opera House," insisted his grandmother. Jelly's consorting with African Americans, however, bothered her much more. "We are who we are and we are not who we are not," she instructed.

Jelly did try to play so-called lofty music. When he auditioned for ragtime pioneer Buddy Bolden, he offered to play from *Il Trovatore*. Said Bolden, "That ain't no music. The notes is written out."

So Jelly took Bolden's advice and played what was inside him. "Ask any of the fools who came before me 'n they haven't got a clue," he proclaimed. "Ask any of the ones who came after 'n they'll tell you it all started with me." That's been long disputed by some musicologists, but it's believed to be true by many others as well.

Wolfe did make Jelly sound musically educated. "I'd come up with tonal variations, the shifts in syncopation, yet letting the melodic structure fly," Jelly said. The audience had a chance to judge for itself, because Morton's actual music was used, albeit to new lyrics by Birkenhead.

Hearing Jelly say that there was "no coon stock in this Creole" might be pardoned on the grounds that he had to deny his blackness to get ahead in early twentieth century America. But Wolfe also had him call Louis Armstrong "that coon, that baboon." Later, when Jelly had feared that his friend Jack was courting his lover Anita (Tonya Pinkins), he insisted that the man be busted from partner in his nightclub to the doorman. "The only thing a nigga can do for me," Jelly said, "is scrub my steps and shine my shoes."

By the end of the show, many were agreeing with Chimney Man when he said, "Hell's too good for you." Considering how unpleasant the story and the main character were, there's no mystery why *Jelly's Last Jam* has since disappeared after it closed after seventeen months. None of the four major musical theater licensing houses took it on for stock and amateur productions. Its 569-performance run was more attributable to Gregory Hines's dynamic Tony-winning performance, which offered impressive singing and extraordinary tap-dancing.

Any musical that includes the line "There's kikes, niggers, and wops. I leave anybody out?" is going to be left out of the envelope that's opened to reveal the name of the Best Musical Tony winner.

Jane Eyre (2000–2001) had John Caird (*Les Misérables*) Cliffnote the famous tale that Charlotte Bronte wrote in 1847. "Plain Jane" was parentless, mistreated at an orphanage, and eventually had to make her way in the world. In the nineteenth century, that usually meant becoming a governess.

Off she went to tend a child at Thornfield Hall, owned by Edward Rochester. She and he soon fell in love and were to be married. Then, just before the ceremony, Richard Mason entered to say that Rochester was *already* married to his sister Bertha.

Jane had been hearing some strange sounds from the third floor, but didn't expect that Rochester's wife was up there. Rochester had squirreled Bertha there because she was certifiably insane. His wanting to marry again without benefit of divorce was wishful thinking.

Contemporary audiences might well have not understood Rochester's problem. While no one would have condoned his throwing Bertha into the street, most wondered why he didn't divorce Bertha, keep her upstairs, and enjoy a happy life with Jane downstairs.

What should have been made clearer is that British law at the time demanded that *both* parties agree to the divorce. Bertha's not being in her right mind prevented her from being able to agree. Divorce reform was part of Brontë's message, but Caird didn't stress it.

When housekeeper Mrs. Fairfax said to Jane, "What do you think of the hall?" Jane may have been impressed, but audiences weren't. Some had been steeped in the Oliver Smith tradition of sumptuous sets for period shows or in the recent British megamusical era. Thus, they weren't much impressed by the lighting technology that only suggested sets. Atmosphere is important to a Victorian story, and lights projected on a few large pieces of cloth didn't do the job.

Much was made of how expensive this new technology was. Nevertheless, the fire looked pathetically cheap, with the hoary device of having a few pieces of red cloth blow upward from the stage in order to suggest flames.

Once upon a time, there used to be musicals for "the tired businessman"—shows like *Hellzapoppin'* and *Star and Garter*, which promised girls and gags. *Jane Eyre* turned out to be a new kind of musical for the tired businessman: one that allowed him to get some sleep.

The Color Purple (2005–2006) was more retro and sentimental than *Caroline, or Change*, so it ran almost seven times longer. To be fair, librettist Marsha Norman and songwriters Brenda Russell, Stephen Bray, and Allee Wills had one great benefit: great name recognition from Alice Walker's best-selling 1983 Pulitzer Prize–winning novel and the 1985 film version.

Although slavery had officially ended for African Americans in the 1860s, one would never know it from the life young Celie Harris (La Chanze) led in the 1930s. Her stepfather had often raped her, which resulted in her being a mother by the age of fourteen. Then he married her off to Ol' Mister, who often beat her and used her to tend his children. That Celie had been separated from her beloved sister Nettie became just another painful fact of life.

The opening song reminded us that "The Good Lord Works in Mysterious Ways." Celie wasn't convinced. She looked to heaven and wailed, "What kind of God are you?" Whether or not God answered her prayers will remain anybody's guess, but Celie did get many gifts beyond any dream she would have dared to have.

They started with Shug Avery, a self-assured black beauty with whom Ol' Mister was smitten. Shug had learned at an early age that if you insist that people treat you with respect, they will. (Being beautiful helped.) She also taught Celie that sex could be more than just a duty and helped Celie feel good about herself for the first time in her life. That allowed her to take the first steps of a wondrous journey.

Although this was the new millennium, *The Color Purple* offered that secondary comic relief couple. Harpo, Ol' Mister's son, would do anything to please his Big Beautiful Woman Sofia: busty, lusty, defiant, and impossible not to admire. It was the role that propelled Oprah Winfrey to stardom, and Winfrey returned the favor by producing this musical.

But musicalizing a well-known and multi-awarded novel and film suggests that the collaborators will improve it. Norman's book only had enough time to hit the high points of Walker's novel. The score was less effective, being pulsating rather than memorable. *The Color Purple* deserved its 910 performances, but not the Best Musical Tony.

Passing Strange (2007–2008) concerned an adolescent who was trying to find himself—just as Pippin had thirty-five years earlier. But it was much less theatrical and considerably less entertaining. Instead of showing what had happened to its central character, as *Pippin* did, it mostly told the story of a character nonnamed "Youth" by way of narration provided by his alter ego Stew (nee Mark Stewart), who collaborated with his on-again, off-again girlfriend Heidi Rodewald.

Youth railed against his religious mother who wanted him to go to church (although she didn't attend, either). He finally did, however, after he met a pretty girl in the choir. When Youth said, "Oh, God!" audiences heard the hoary device of having her misunderstand his meaning, take him literally, and say, "Exactly!"

Music would become Youth's ultimate religion. Smart move: no matter what music an audience cared about—be it Broadway, bourrée, or boogie-woogie—everyone could relate to all that passion.

Youth made the odyssey into sex, drugs, as well as rock 'n' roll. What a lump of clay Youth was, just waiting to be molded by the next person who came along during his travels in Amsterdam or Berlin. And they said that Bobby in *Company* was passive!

Stew expressed his contempt for traditional Broadway musicals, as was witnessed by his drolly saying, "We were planning a show tune, an upbeat 'gotta-leave-this-town' show tune, but we don't know how to write those kinds of tunes."

Actually, Stew *did* know how to write a show tune, as was proved later on with "The Black One," in which Youth was discussed by Europeans. The rest of the time, the music was acceptable pop-rock, with less-than-successful lyrics. "It's all right" was sung many, many times in a row in the song that sunk the show at the Tonys. If this were the best number, TV watchers thought, I'm buying a ticket to *In the Heights* or even *Cry-Baby*.

Why didn't Youth sing what he'd been feeling instead of having Narrator Stew relate in retrospect what Youth felt? Why didn't we hear what Youth was thinking before, during, and after an event rather than have Narrator Stew tell us? Why, at the end of the show, didn't Youth sing his own retrospective on the matter? We wouldn't have needed Narrator Stew to navigate us through his story if he'd dramatized it the way the best librettists do.

But Stew wanted a big part for himself. He often interrupted the action because he never wanted an audience to forget that he was up there in this ego trip extraordinaire. Has there ever been an artist who had a greater I-don't-give-a-damn-about-you attitude? At show's end, he admitted as much: "I've got a lot of explaining," he said, before hastily adding, "to myself, not to you."

Then go home! Leave us alone! You barraged audiences with your story, and then you insulted them? But that was Stew for you. He needed us to intently listen to him and his story, but didn't mind telling us how unimportant we were to him.

This off-putting attitude may well have distanced Broadway audiences from *Passing Strange*. Considering the very good reviews it received, it should have done business. Audiences rejected Stew's massive megalomania and weren't willing to pay for his onstage therapy. Out of the twenty-two weeks it played, it sold fewer than 50 percent of its tickets in ten of those weeks.

Those who hate even the slightest amount of audience participation weren't thrilled with *Fela!* (2009–2010). Because they were supposed to be at an actual evening in the Shrine—the countercultural Nigerian nightclub owned by Fela Anikulapo-Kuti (1938–1997)—Fela himself came out and asked his audience to yell out, "Yeah, yeah!"

Of course, no matter how loud the audience yelled "Yeah, yeah!" Fela judged its efforts as not loud enough, and commanded the crowd to do it again. Many more times an audience would be asked to "Yeah, yeah!" before the night ended. It was also asked to sing "La / La-la-la-la / La-la-la-la / La-la-la" a number of times in a row as well as to stand and clap hands.

Woe be to the theatergoer who didn't. Cast members came into the aisles to monitor. In other words, there was a good deal of forced theatrical fun here. How interesting that a show that criticized a fascistic government should demand so much obedience and conformity from its audience.

The book was a collaboration between Jim Lewis and Bill T. Jones and the latter directed and choreographed. The score was cobbled from songs that Fela had written. Some of the lyrics were supertitled in case audiences couldn't understand the words. Theatergoers had ample time to read them because these were the type of lyrics that were repeated two or three times in a row.

The sound and lights were set very high. If the Shrine was actually this loud, our hearts would have bled for the people who lived in the neighborhood. The extraordinarily bright lights often were aimed right at a theatergoer's eyes. Sunglasses would not have been unwelcome.

Lewis and Jones had Fela saying such sentiments as "Bad teachers always try to make sense out of things." They never explained why he believed that statement. And, as is often the case in some of the worst musicals, there was a superficial romance primarily based on physical attraction.

The audience didn't get to know much about Fela the man. Instead of having the book tell us, headlines from what seemed to be actual newspapers were used. "Fela enflames students," said one. "Fela arrested for armed robbery," said another. The latter statement is especially strong. Was he guilty, innocent, or framed? Fela should have told us his side of the story, but he never bothered. All that he said by way of rebuttal was that "Innocent people go to jail—myself included." And while that is occasionally true, audiences were well within their rights to want the whole story before they believed him.

At the end of the first act, Fela boldly stated that he should be the country's president. Perhaps he should have, but audiences were entitled to hear his qualifications before it cast their votes. Good dramas convince audiences after showing both sides of the story. Here, the crowd was requested—if not compelled—to take Fela's one-sided word as gospel. Instead of spending time on these important details, Jones and Lewis spent time telling about the days that Fela's was constipated.

More than two hours passed before any genuine drama took place. Projected slides of police mug shots, both profile and full face, were shown. Underneath were descriptions of the atrocities that these people had experienced, while a light shone on each of the actors who represented these tortured people. A more effective solution would have had the actors do the talking, but that would have involved genuine writing.

After more than two hours, Lillias White finally got the chance to sing an eleven o'clock number that did offer its rewards. Never, however, did she convince that she was Fela's mother, for she more resembled a Broadway performer.

The final number had everyone marching around and carrying small coffins on which some slogans are painted. Those who sat too far away might have missed such sentiments as "Organized Religion = Organized Repression."

Fela! was like a night in a noisy nightclub in which no one got the chance to know anyone.

Nunsense, that off-Broadway and regional theater staple, seemed at last to come to Broadway by way of *Sister Act* (2010–2011). Both musicals had old-world, black-and-white garbed nuns acting in silly fashion, letting themselves go in a way that suggested they'd been secretly wanting to cut up all their lives.

In the original 1992 film of *Sister Act*, when the nuns sang the pop songs "I Will Follow Him" and "My Guy" (transformed to "My God"), they never once lost their dignity. The glows on all their faces, from ole Broadway pros Ruth Kobart's to Susan Johnson's, showed that their love for God was actually elevated by this joyous music.

In the musical, the nuns were cheapened by the new musical policy. "Shake it like you're Mary Magdalene," they sang. They shimmied, bumped, and bounced their breasts around. One nun came out with a Yiddishism, while another got a rap song (although the late seventies, in which the musical was set, was too early for rap).

There was, of course, the ancient nun who got so excited that she did a cartwheel, which was suddenly and inevitably followed by her putting a hand on her suddenly thrown-out back. As for the stern Mother Superior here—unlike in the film—she decided in if-you-can't lick-'em-join-'em fashion to boogie and shake her breasts along with everyone else.

Perhaps the devil made book writers Cheri and Bill Steinkellner, composer Alan Menken, and lyricist Glenn Slater do it. *Nunsense*'s Dan Goggin became a multimillionaire by using the same low humor, so why shouldn't *Sister Act* pander to an equally low common denominator, to audiences that think nuns in a kickline are a riot?

The monsignor became a show-biz buffoon, too: "Let's give it up for Pope Paul VI," he said into his hand-mike. The show implied that religious people could easily be seduced into show business and that it would become the most important ingredient in their lives. In the film, show business enhanced what the nuns were doing, but it never became the main event.

What a wonderful musical *Sister Act* could have been with the film's original integrity. There, when Deloris learned that the mink coat that boyfriend Curtis gave her was actually a gift he'd given his wife, she marched into his office to tell him off—but didn't get the chance because he was busy killing an informer. That's when she had to seek help from the police, and when Lieutenant Eddie Souther placed her undercover in a faraway convent where she became Sister Mary Clarence.

In the musical, after Deloris realized that she'd been given a second-hand coat, she tried to shake off the slight by singing. "Fabulous, Baby!" was a pop song, so by its end, she isn't angry anymore but triumphant. That was problematic, for now she had to find that anger for the next book scene.

A better solution would have had Deloris express in song that Curtis has let her down many times before. A hand-me-down mink would now mean that the fur was going to fly.

Once Mother Superior and Deloris met, they should have had a duet that showed they were diametrically opposed. Instead, Mother had a tender song about convent life, and for most of it, Deloris sat and listened. If Deloris had felt the nun's influence, that would have worked, but she didn't; only when the song was almost over did she express her reactions, and then only to audiences. That wasn't as effective as a musical face-off between the two.

Souther was more inept in the musical. "Guns make me nervous" wasn't what one expected to hear from a police lieutenant, but it did allow him to conquer his fear and shoot by show's end. Long before that, however, Eddie sang "I Could Be That Guy" who could love Deloris, and he preened as if he were both hot and cool.

Mother Superior lost the dignity she'd had in the movie; using the expression "curve ball" seemed too colloquial, but not as wrong as her using the term "buns" for buttocks. If the writers were intent on using that brand of humor, they should have done what John Pielmeier was careful to do in *Agnes of God* with his Mother Superior: state that she'd joined the convent late in life after her husband had died.

Menken slavishly followed the pop music template of the seventies, so the songs sounded formulaic. But no one could blame Menken for writing pastiche. Whenever he has used his own voice to write quality theater music—*God Bless You, Mr. Rosewater; The Apprenticeship of Duddy Kravitz; Kicks*—he has made far less money than when he wrote variations on other composer's themes, à la *Little Shop of Horrors*. Even *Beauty and the Beast* and *The Little Mermaid* had melodies reminiscent of others composers' styles. Deep within him, Menken has more than he's been encouraged to show in the twenty-first-century musical theater climate.

Slater had some good ideas. Deloris, in her nightclub act, sang a pop song called "Take Me to Heaven," which was meant to be sung to a man who would stimulate her in many ways; Slater then got an additional layer from the same lyrics when Deloris began to think of a heaven in a higher context. Similarly, when Curtis sang "When I Find My Baby," he wasn't talking about regaining lost love, as has always been the case whenever that expression was used, he was saying he'd kill Deloris when he next encountered her.

After Deloris snuck out of the convent in favor of a neighborhood bar, she saw Curtis and his henchmen there. One of his goons noticed that this nun did bear a startling resemblance to Deloris, but then said "Nah" as he came to the conclusion that Deloris wouldn't be dressed as a nun. Given that he knew that she was hiding out—and that nuns aren't routinely found in bars—he should have put two-and-two together. Better still, the Steinkellners shouldn't have gone for this joke.

The script established that Deloris had attended St. Mary's and had had nuns for teachers. And yet, when the nuns asked her to say grace before a meal, she could only start off correctly—"Bless us, oh, Lord, etcetera"—before forgetting the rest of it. She began misquoting from famous speeches in order to get laughs. The truth is that grace is drummed into heads early and often in Catholic schools, and Deloris would have remembered it.

But if you're going to go for this gag—to be fair, the film did, too—why not make it into a song? True, it wouldn't have advanced the action, but *Sister Act* may well have been the postwar book musical with an original score to have the fewest numbers that did that. Most of the score was one pop pastiche after another.

Later Deloris claimed not to be Catholic at all. Were we to give her the benefit of the doubt that she was a non-Catholic whose parents wanted her to have the discipline of a Catholic school education? (It's happened.) Or did she mean that she was born a Catholic but abandoned the religion some time later? (It's certainly happened.)

Douglas Carter Beane, who came in as a show doctor, apparently Googled and discovered that Saint Clarence was "the patron saint of prisoners."

Nice. Too bad, however, that Beane didn't investigate a marvelous 1940 film called *Brother Orchid*. In it, Edward G. Robinson played a gangster who was severely wounded near a monastery. The brothers took him inside and nursed him back to health. Robinson eventually saw the beauty of the monks' vocation, the pleasure of becoming a good person, and rose to their level. *Sister Act*'s thrust was that Mother Superior and the nuns should have sunk to Deloris's level to show that they were "with it"—for what's more important than that?

The following season, in 2011–2012, Menken had two shows nominated in the same season—a first in Tony history. As we've seen, *Leap of Faith* lost.
So did *Newsies*.

Harvey Fierstein revamped the 1992 Disney disaster film (to use that term in a different context) about the Newsboys Strike of 1899. He kept the main conflict: Joseph Pulitzer had upped the percentage newsboys would have to pay to sell his papers, and the kids decided not to stand for it. They loudly protested, pumped their arms in the air, stamped their feet, and threw chairs around in rally after rally. "There's a change coming once and for all," they promised. "Now is the time to seize the day!" they insisted. "Loud and clear, we is here!"

Menken wrote almost as many anthems as the eight that hockey fans would hear at a four-game series between an American and a Canadian team. The hymns started right from the opening number, where turn-of-the-century newsboy Jack Kelly told his disabled friend "Crutchie" that he yearned to leave New York for Santa Fe. But if Jack were that anxious to leave town, wouldn't he go as soon as trouble hit?

Fierstein occasionally inserted a line that rang of decades later—"he doesn't do happiness," and he had Pulitzer say that Theodore Roosevelt was a "Commie," a term that seemed a little early for 1899. Lyricist Jack Feldman got into the anachronistic swim, too, by having Jack sing, "No way" and "catch a break." There was a penis joke, too, that seemed at least a half century too early. Then there was the nine-year-old who said lines that no one his age would ever say. ("Fame is one intoxicatin' potion.")

So the newsies started their strike, and cub reporter Katherine Plumber publicized their plight. Once Katherine's story broke, the newsies sang in glee—not because they might win the strike, but because they got their names in the paper. Feldman could have written a lyric that stressed the kids' happiness at their achievement and not simply the publicity.

Katherine turned out to be interested in Jack, but not until deep into the second act—a little late for a love story in a musical. And then to find that she was actually Pulitzer's daughter . . .

There was also an irrelevant production number at a burlesque theater. Here the star became angry when two chorus girls didn't leave the stage when she was about to do her solo, and fiercely gestured for them to get off in that tired convention of letting audiences see what a difficult diva the average female entertainer is.

One convention that Fierstein employed endlessly was having the newsies spit on their palms before shaking hands with someone. At the end, when Pulitzer capitulated, he too spit on his palm. A better solution would have been to have Jack drop this childish convention for he had now earned his manhood. Instead, Pulitzer came down to his level and spit on his own palm before shaking.

Disney was rewarded by seeing *Newsies* endorsed by rabidly enthusiastic crowds. Because many Americans in 2012 were frustrated and furious with the way the government and big corporations had been ignoring them, *Newsies* emerged as the perfect musical for these times. Tea Party members who believed that they were "taking back the country" must have loved it.

As soon as Bob Fosse saw Federico Fellini's 1957 film *Nights of Cabiria*, he envisioned it as a musical. For *Sweet Charity* (1965–1966), he decided to make a significant and softening change.

Cabiria had been a prostitute, but Fosse thought he'd better turn her into Fan-Dango Ballroom dance hall hostess Charity Hope Valentine. The show would be, as a state-of-the-art electronic LED sign informed us, "The story of a girl who wanted to be loved."

Then why was the logo a black-and-white photograph of Verdon giving us a look that was haughty, experienced, and not at all vulnerable? She had a pocketbook slung over her left shoulder, a dress with a slit that almost reached her buttocks, and an arm that bore a heart-shaped tattoo. Charity was obviously ahead of her time in patronizing a tattoo parlor, but for sixties audiences, a tattoo, especially on a woman's left upper arm, suggested nothing sweet at all.

Audiences were greeted by an overture that started out harshly. The vamp of "Big Spender"—six severe notes followed by an even more severe blare—was certainly a great one, but given that the show was about a fragile waif about whom we were supposed to greatly care, those seven hard-hitting notes instead suggested a show that would feature one tough cookie.

So Fosse could take the prostitute into the dance hall, but he couldn't take the prostitute out of the girl. When the curtain went up, there, with her back to us, bathed in hot pink colors, was Gwen Verdon in a seductive and confident stance. Although she then went into a winsome dance, the first impression remained that Charity was an all-knowing and street-smart woman.

Actually, she wasn't. In the show's first official scene, Charity was shown to be naïve. She was desperately in love with a man she called Charlie, although Neil Simon's script simply identified him as "Dark Glasses."

That alone suggested that he was sinister. His sleazy look and wordless demeanor while Charity bountifully expressed her love for him made audiences know that he was Mr. Wrong. And while they mightn't have predicted that he'd push her into a lake and steal her pocketbook, they weren't astonished when he did. Why couldn't Charity see, as her dance hall colleague Nickie would soon say, that "He wasn't for you"? This naïveté made us lose respect and some interest in Charity—even with Verdon playing her.

Some could argue that the Best Musical Tony winner that season—*Man of La Mancha*—featured a dim-witted title character in Don Quixote, too. But he had loftier goals: no less than changing mankind to see the world in a better light. Charity was merely husband-hunting, and not doing terribly well at it.

That Charity went home with a man she'd just met didn't seem terrible, for he was Vittorio Vidal, a movie star that she admired. (Many of us would have done the same.) Once she was in his apartment, Charity asked Vittorio for souvenirs to prove to her dance hall coworkers that she'd been with him. That was fine in theory, but clunky in specifics. Wasn't it all too convenient that Vittorio would drag out a hat and cane—the oh-so-logical props for the numba that Verdon would now do?

The arrival of Vittorio's girlfriend did lead to a marvelous sight gag. Vittorio quickly dispatched Charity into the bedroom closet, where she decided to have a cigarette. But what to do about the smoke? Then she noticed a garment bag, which she unzipped and exhaled the fumes into it before zipping it closed. She kept repeating the process and got a laugh each time.

So Charity *did* show some intelligence. Fosse, Simon, and lyricist Dorothy Fields were also careful to make her the least randy of the dance hall hostesses. In "There's Gotta Be Something Better Than This," Nickie yearned to be a receptionist, but wasn't above admitting that she'd bed some of the people who'd come into the office. Helene had a dream of becoming a hatcheck girl, although she conceded that if a man were cute enough, "I'll check you," she sang, "and you check me." Charity was the only one who talked about getting a better job without turning her fantasy sexual.

She decided to improve herself by going to the Ninety-second Street Y and taking a class. Before she could get to the classroom she was trapped in the elevator with a claustrophobic man. Charity tried to calm him. She: What's your name? He (trying to be brave): Oscar Lindquist. She: Where do you live? He (all calmness gone, banging the walls in fury): *In an elevator!*

The elevator was fixed, and Oscar and Charity were soon an item, and then a most serious one. As he told her, "You have a quality in you, Charity, that I've never found in a girl before. . . . In you I have found pure innocence. . . . You're the last of a dying species. A virgin."

A virgin with a heart-shaped tattoo on her arm? If Charity was too simpleminded to engage us, so was Oscar.

He eventually discovered the truth about her, but was willing to marry her anyway. We could be happy for both of them—but not for long. After a night's sleep, however, Oscar changed his mind.

That didn't make for a good ending to a musical comedy, so Simon looked for another, and came up with a strange and inadequate one. He had Charity's Fairy Godmother come out looking much like Glinda.

Or so we were led to believe. Just as Charity was believing that this woman was a gift from heaven, the Fairy Godmother spun around and showed the sandwich sign on her back: "Watch *The Good Fairy* on CBS tonight at 8 P.M." Charity smiled, shrugged, and danced off—and audiences went home feeling unsatisfied. There was no way such a show could emerge a Best Musical Tony winner even in a year when there was no *Man of La Mancha.*

Charity received nine Tony nominations, and captured only one. No, Verdon didn't win; she experienced her first-ever Tony loss to Angela Lansbury in *Mame.* Fosse's choreography was the sole victor, for *Charity* was thrilling when it kicked in. Even "Big Spender" came across as a choreographic triumph even though its "dancers" did virtually no dancing in it. It had nine Fan-Dango girls—none of them Charity—trying to seduce customers into dancing (and more). Perhaps Fosse knew that if he put Charity in the number, she'd come across as hard as Barbra Streisand's nails and personality.

On the other hand, he might have wanted to give his star wife a well-earned rest. "Big Spender" was one of the few times Verdon was ever offstage. After the prologue, she still had five numbers to dance. Of the fourteen songs (with excellent music by Cy Coleman and superb lyrics by Fields), Verdon soloed in five, sang in two others, and had to be on stage for four more. Verdon's exhilaration at being with a movie star ("If My Friends Could See Me Now") and feeling that "I'm a Brass Band" when she felt loved by Oscar were solo triumphs, but she also scored when sharing the stage with Nickie and Helene, her two best friends, in "There's Gotta Be Something Better Than This."

And then there was "Rich Man's Frug," which aped the dances that the trendsetters were then doing in discotheques. Dances with themes were the order of the day—"The Swim" actually had its dancers stretching out their arms and taking broad strokes—so Fosse invented two of his own. First came "The Aloof," which spoofed how standoffish the Beautiful People were at these clubs. "The Heavyweight" homaged boxing matches. "The Big Finish" didn't have a theme, but brought the sequence to a terrific frenzy.

And yet, the most moving part of the musical came in a song in which Charity had no part. "Baby, Dream Your Dream" had Nickie and Helene mercilessly mock her budding romance with Oscar and predicted doom if they married.

Until the song's final moments. Then the spritely tempo slowed, as both thought a moment and admitted, "But come to think of it, how happy I would be if I could find the kind of guy who'd say to me, 'Baby, dream your dream. Dream of three fat kids.' Brother: would I buy it."

The musical show whose heart could thus far only be found on a tattoo had finally acquired a real one.

Now how much did *New Girl in Town* (1957–1958) have to do with Fosse's decision to change Charity's occupation?

He'd choreographed this Best Musical Tony loser about a genuine prostitute: a musical version of Eugene O'Neill's very serious *Anna Christie*, starring his significant other Gwen Verdon.

Aside from playing a potential old maid in the Tony-winning *Redhead*, Verdon always played women with unsavory pasts: Claudine, Lola, Sweet Charity, and Roxie Hart among them. None, however, was an out-and-out prostitute, but that's precisely what Verdon would portray in the musicalization of the 1921 hit that had become a legendary 1930 movie.

It was advertised as the film in which "Garbo Talks!" And how she talked right from her opening line: "Gimme a whiskey, ginger ale on the side . . . and don't be stingy, baby!"

Anna had just walked into a bar where she wanted to find her father, whom she hadn't seen in fifteen years. Chris Christopherson now owned a coal barge on which he lived with his worse-for-wear mistress, Marthy (Thelma Ritter). She wasn't happy to see his grown daughter on the scene.

Chris didn't see Anna for what she was. His idealization made Anna contemptuous of him, but she certainly respected him when he saved Mat, a sailor, from drowning. Mat fell desperately in love with Anna, but she knew that once he knew her past, he wouldn't overlook it.

It's a tough play that should have been a tough musical. Bob Merrill wouldn't seem to have been its logical composer-lyricist. Would-be investors must have said, "This is the same guy who wrote 'If I Knew You Were Comin', I'd've Baked a Cake' and 'How Much Is That Doggie in the Window?' Are you *kidding* me?"

What must have given investors hope, however, was the team surrounding Merrill. Directing and writing the book was George Abbott, who brought the show to the producing triumvirate that had mounted his last two Best Musical Tony-winning hits, *The Pajama Game* (1954–1955) and *Damn Yankees* (1955–1956): Frederick Brisson, Robert E. Griffith, and last but—as events would eventually have it—hardly least was Harold S. Prince. Prince would produce and/or direct many a serious musical play in the years to come, but *New Girl in Town* was the first with which he'd be associated.

Merrill made a strong musical theater debut. He started with a rollicking choral opening ("Roll Your Socks Up") before segueing to the tender "Anna Lilla," in which Chris remembered his daughter as she was. Then came "Sunshine Girl," a catchy tune that was meant to be a popular song of the day. It might well have been had it been written then.

But Anna had to let Chris know that she was no "sunshine girl" thanks to her previous life "On the Farm," where her cousins had lusted after her, caught her, and started her on the road to ruin. Verdon also made the most of two plaintive numbers, "It's Good to Be Alive" and "If That Was Love."

To leaven this, Marthy sang a charming song, "Flings," in which she and pals ruminated on their youthful romances that were "wonderful things." No wonder that Merrill and Abbott didn't want to let Marthy drift off the scene, as O'Neill had. Ritter had to be grateful; she got a Tony as Best Actress in a Musical along with Verdon in the first tie in Tony history. Broadway appreciated her more than Hollywood, which eventually gave her six Oscar nominations but no statuettes.

But these were the only Tonys that the show received. Fosse's choreography lost to Jerome Robbins's work in *West Side Story*. But Fosse felt that he would have had a better chance if Abbott had retained "The Red Light Ballet," a look into the brothel where Anna had worked. Abbott, in his memoir *Mister Abbott*, called the number "just plain dirty" and felt it "was false because it pictured the bordello in glamorous, exciting terms, whereas Anna Christie had nothing but loathing for her past." More to the point, Abbott felt that "the audience hated it" and dropped it from the show.

This was one reason why Fosse was determined to be a director-choreographer from then on, and almost always was. (Many who'd seen the ballet say that much of it wound up in *Pippin*, when the title character had his sexual adventures.)

What did Prince, the lowest producer on the totem pole, think? Of the many serious musicals he'd produce and/or direct, seven would win the Best Musical Tony. What might a musical version of *Anna Christie* have been if Prince had been in full control, not only as the acclaimed producer he came to be, but also as the director? Did he see *New Girl in Town* as a missed opportunity to create a significant musical—and was his wanting to do *West Side Story* next a way of rectifying that?

New Girl in Town ran a bit more than a year, and made a 24 percent profit, but might have been a more significant musical if it hadn't been a true "George Abbott show." Still, the story of the prostitute wouldn't have made a Best Musical Tony loser out of Harold Hill and Marian the Librarian.

* * *

But *New Girl in Town* wasn't the first musical with a prostitute to lose the Best Musical prize.

The first one did.

And would you believe that Richard Rodgers and Oscar Hammerstein II wrote it?

The illustrious composer and book writer/lyricist had to be proud of the many firsts they'd had in their careers, but less happy that they wrote the first official Best Musical Tony loser.

For in 1955–1956, merely two musicals were nominated as Best Musical: *Damn Yankees*, the ultimate winner, and *Pipe Dream*, the sole loser.

And because *Pipe Dream* ran only 246 performances and resulted in a near total loss, it has the dubious distinction of being the first out-and-out financial flop to be nominated as Best Musical, too.

Pipe Dream actually received more Tony nominations—ten—than *Damn Yankees* (nine). However, the latter show won seven awards, including that Best Musical medallion.

(Trophy-sized statuettes wouldn't be given until 1966–1967—the first year the Tonys were broadcast nationally. Someone obviously decided that the prizes needed to be more telegenic.)

If *Pipe Dream* were produced today, its producers would boast of "more Tony nominations than any other show this year!" And then, after it took home only one Tony—for Best Costume Design—the producers would have then and forever advertised itself as "The Tony-winning *Pipe Dream*."

Rodgers and Hammerstein, who functioned as their own producers, would have been too honorable to use such gambits, even if they'd occurred to them.

That integrity may, strangely enough, be one of the reasons that *Pipe Dream* failed. It had to be a raunchy show, for a substantial amount of the plot involved life in a brothel. But by now, the public had become accustomed to thinking of Rodgers and Hammerstein in loftier terms.

Carousel, South Pacific, and certainly *The King and I* had sported children in their casts. And while *Pipe Dream* did, too, it had neighborhood children dance with Fauna, the brothel's madam. That it mercifully happened outside the whorehouse on a sunny day was beside the point. Eisenhower-era theatergoers must have been wondering, "Where are these kids' mothers? And do they know with whom their children are hanging out?"

They might have been less inclined to ask these questions if it hadn't been a Rodgers and Hammerstein show.

Hammerstein borrowed characters that John Steinbeck had first created for his novel *Cannery Row* (or, as it was fancifully called in France, *Rue de la Sardine*) and further explored in *Sweet Thursday*. One was Fauna, the owner of "The Happiest House on the Block."

Here's our next irony: Steinbeck based Fauna on Flora Woods, the real-life madam who was known as, according to Steinbeck scholar Susan Shillinglaw, "the Ethel Merman of Monterey."

So why didn't Rodgers and Hammerstein get Merman as their star? All was satisfactory when they produced her in *Annie Get Your Gun*; she'd stayed for the entire thirty-three-month run. Wouldn't the subsequent star *of Call Me Madam* have made a good madam?

Merman was then living in Colorado with new husband Bob Six of Continental Airlines and claimed that she was retired. But perhaps "the Boys," as they were chummily known, should have tried harder. Fewer than ten months after *Pipe Dream* opened, the Merm was back in town rehearsing *Happy Hunting*, which was no worse a musical than *Pipe Dream*. And whose score would you rather sing: Rodgers and Hammerstein's or Matt Dubey and Harold Karr's?

Perhaps "the Boys," already known for some maverick moves, decided that this time their innovation would be hiring an opera star to elevate mere musical comedy to a higher level. Enter Helen Traubel, famous for Brünnhilde and not *Brigadoon*.

That Traubel's name was a virtual homonym for "trouble" turned out to be our next official irony. Many opera singers who deign to do Broadway or sing its songs in concert feel the need to give arch renditions to make the "pieces" sound more important. This diva too was so intent on showing off her voice that many theatergoers might have preferred to see Traubel in Tahiti rather than on the stage of the Shubert.

Having a highbrow play a lowbrow was damaging. But Rodgers and Hammerstein may have wanted to distance themselves from the sordid reality of Steinbeck's character by not making their Fauna seem to be a *real* madam.

But *Pipe Dream* lost not because it was godless, but because it was god-awful. Of the seven adaptations that Rodgers and Hammerstein wrote for the stage, *Pipe Dream* was the only one to fail.

Directing Traubel was a man who'd staged twenty-one Broadway productions in twenty years. Choosing him might have seemed prudent, but Harold Clurman had never staged a musical. Still, he was theatrical royalty—having directed five Clifford Odets plays, including *Awake and Sing*—so he seemed worthy of a chance.

Pipe Dream started by introducing us to Doc, who was up early working in a biological laboratory in Monterey, California—not the most inherently musical of places.

"Hiya, Hazel, baby," was his first line to a man whose mother, Hazel explained, had had so many children that she'd lost track of names.

(And if you believe that, I have two seats that I'd like to sell you for Saturday night's performance of *Breakfast at Tiffany's*.)

Millicent, Doc's one-night stand, came out of the bedroom and expressed an interest in going for at least two. Doc had to work, but before he did, he introduced her to Hazel.

"Hazel," Millicent said dully. "Maybe that explains the whole thing."

As gay jokes go, it's rather mild—but Hammerstein, famous for being gentlemanly, probably thought it ribald.

Hazel did. He indignantly cried out, "You know what she thinks I am?" Doc answered, "I got an idea." But they dared not speak of the love that dare not speak its name.

Doc was brought a patient: Suzy, an unemployed and penniless waif who'd cut her hand after shoving it through a bakery window trying to steal breakfast. Her husky, plaintive voice indicated exhaustion and despair.

She also had a personality not unlike a previous Rodgers and Hammerstein character: Jud Fry. She was as unapologetically crass and argumentative. And yet, when she asked about "the place across the street where the lights are still on" her attempt at a euphemism sounded false. Considering Suzy's vocabulary, she would have called it a cathouse.

Gentility reigned. One townie sang, "If you work like a horse till the day you're dead, you're a part of a horse—and it ain't the head." Many sang about the "stupid sons of fishes." These men were supposed to be toughs, so they shouldn't have sung that they were "as happy as candles that shine on a cake, as gay as the bells on a sleigh."

So it was no surprise that Fauna eventually decided that Suzy was "a complete bust" at her profession and that Doc should "treat her as a lady" and take her out of the whorehouse. Actually, life there couldn't have been so bad; Hammerstein's stage directions stated that its main parlor was "a pleasant room with bright flower-littered chintz. On the card table is a Parcheesi board."

Rodgers wrote an occasional pretty melody. Tyler had the plaintive

"Everybody's Got a Home but Me" and Doc eventually realized that "All at Once You Love Her." There was "Sweet Thursday," a fetching cakewalk for Fauna. But most of the music sounded like melodies that Rodgers had had while he was dreaming, awoke, excitedly jotted them down, and only the next morning realized that they weren't nearly as good as he thought they were.

Pipe Dream wasn't hard-hitting enough to be a serious, groundbreaking musical. It was apparently more frank when it tried out in New Haven and Boston, but audiences didn't like this darker side of Rodgers and Hammerstein. So the team compromised and pulled punches. When that happens, the result is almost always a lesser achievement. Even thinking that Merman could have made the show into a hit would have been a pipe dream.

The Life (1996–1997) was released as a concept album two years before the musical bowed at the Barrymore. In it, composer Cy Coleman sang his own charming melody to a lyric that he and Ira Gasman wrote, delightfully observing that "It's a Lovely Day to Get Out of Jail." His delivery was so winsome that listeners may have assumed the character was a harmless, penniless bum who'd simply been locked up for vagrancy after a toot on the town.

When they show opened, they saw that it was sung by Sonja (Lillias White) and Queen, two tough prostitutes who'd just been released. That wasn't as palatable.

Queen went home and discovered that Fleetwood, her "man," had spent her savings on new drugs and old drug debts. Her response? "He's No Good," a song that might have been effective, but was ruined by the next line: "but I'm no good without him." Why should Tony voters have been interested in this weak woman who victimized herself and enabled an addict? Only after finding that Fleetwood cheated on her did she move to a new pimp named Memphis (Chuck Cooper). Were we to believe that this was the first time that Fleetwood had cheated on her?

By the time the show ended Tony voters had met a producer of X-rated "adult" films and a seemingly innocent young woman who was actually putting on an act to fleece suckers. Then there were pimps who complained about cops, "Why Don't They Leave Us Alone?"

Why didn't Coleman and colyricist Ira Gasman—as well as their co-book writer David Newman—leave this material alone and work on another musical? *The Life* got off on the wrong foot from its first moment. Sam Harris, playing a hustler named Jojo, started waxing rhapsodic over the way that Forty-second Street used to be before Disney got its hands on it. While Forty-second Street does have a preponderance of franchise operations that keep it from being distinctive let alone unique, is there actually anyone who really thinks it was better before?

Considering the unsavory sexual nature of the characters, *The Life* had little chance with Tony voters, who instead endorsed the more rarefied *Titanic.*

When you're the managing editor of *The New Yorker*, you get invited to a great many parties. Joseph Moncure March, who held the post in 1925, decided to write about the Roaring Twenties parties he'd witnessed. His 1926 poem (yes, *poem*) imagined what *could* have happened if matters had got a bit out-of-hand.

The Wild Party, considered so scandalous that it wasn't published for two years, was still hot stuff when it was musicalized in 1999–2000.

Queenie was a blond vaudeville chorine "who liked her lovers violent and vicious." As she said, "People like us, we don't know where to stop." Later she clarified that position: "Isn't everything just one big song and dance for sex?"

Queenie was romantically involved with Burrs, a minor-league Jolson who performed in blackface and used an exaggerated African American dialect.

These two had a love-hate relationship—with an emphasis on the latter. In fact, Burrs suggested that they hold a party to deflate Queenie's latest bout of anger—especially because he wanted her to put down that knife she'd had in her hand.

They argued about the guest list. Burrs wasn't happy that Queenie had invited Kate, her former chorine colleague, and described her as "a dagger-tongued panther."

"When you two get together," he said, "it's broken glass and dead bodies everywhere."

But everyone wants a celebrity guest at a party, and Queenie's best chance was Kate. They'd been in the chorus together, but now Kate had graduated to a genuine role which could propel her to stardom.

When Kate arrived, she brought with her quite a trophy: Black, a name that indicated his skin color. As one of the guests said to Kate, "You know you [sic] a star when the shoes, the dress and the man all match."

Kate was only half-kidding when she responded, "Now that I'm a star, I can't be seen with just anyone." Make that 10 percent kidding.

Black knew that he was "in a roomful of strangers that call themselves friends." Dolores, a once-reasonably-famous entertainer, was one. She was described as "ageless"—which is why Eartha Kitt played her.

For Burrs, the celebrity guests were Gold and Goldberg, two theatrical producers who reasoned that they'd been on Second Avenue long enough. Now they'd make the move to Broadway. "We'll do what it takes to play canasta with the Shuberts," they sang. Composer-lyricist Michael John LaChiusa had them sing it as "Shuuuuuuuberts," establishing their admiration for the theatrical giants in that long-held note.

Burrs assumed that because Gold and Goldberg were in attendance, they had to be interested in hiring him. Kate wasn't above mixing business with pleasure with them guys, too.

As the evening heated up, so did our hostess: "Queenie wants some newer skin . . . newer sex . . . newer sin." Black would oblige, conveniently forgetting that Kate had been keeping him.

Burrs saw that Black was ready to "throw a torpedo in the SS *Queenie*," but what really set him off was Gold and Goldberg's *not* making him an offer. He pulled out a gun in order to kill Queenie; Black intervened and as they both fought, the gun discharged and Burrs died.

Only one thing missing that LaChiusa and his co–book writer George C. Wolfe might have addressed, although it would have been a big departure from the poem: out of the unlucky thirteen characters, there was no one that Tony voters could like. Queenie seemed unstable, and if we had any sympathy for Burrs, it disappeared when he tried to instigate a fight between Phil and Oscar D'Armano.

These were twins who had been so devoted to each other that they might as well have been the Hilton sisters. Burrs wanted Phil to know that Oscar had had a liaison with Jackie, the self-proclaimed "ambisextrous" man. "Good coons take it in the rear," said Burrs, in one of the last millennium's most unfortunate lines.

Lesbian sex was represented by Madelaine, a stripper, and Sally, a morphine addict. Eddie was a black boxer whose onetime championship was fading from memory at a free-fall rate. His girlfriend Mae was content to be the woman behind the wilting wonder.

The only character about whom we could possibly care was Nadine, Mae's fourteen-year-old sister from Poughkeepsie. That had more to do with our worrying that the kid couldn't see how much over her head she was in this crowd.

Nadine was a minor in another way: a minor character. We couldn't get all that involved with a young miss who was often in the background, had a mere eight lines, and sang only one song that she started three times and finished only once.

LaChiusa's score didn't often rely on full songs; it was a snatch of melody here, a snatch there. That was fitting, for that's what one hears at a party: a hint of a song in the background while you're involved in conversation. LaChiusa did a beautiful job of what could be called musical decoupage.

During the same season, another musical version of the same poem was penned by Andrew Lippa. Its off-Broadway production proved to be the ideal setting for any *Wild Party* musical, which needs an apartment-sized space. On Broadway, LaChiusa's *Wild Party* was in a high-ceilinged, commodious apartment that didn't fill the stage of the Virginia Theatre. The fifteen-member cast had much too much room. A party has a better chance of being wild if it's bursting at its seams.

Chances are the off-Broadway rival didn't hurt. Many Tony voters deign to go off-Broadway at approximately the same rate of the appearances made by the village of Brigadoon.

With the greatest preponderance of unpleasant characters known to any musical, *The Wild Party* wasn't a natural for either Broadway or the road, and that's what most sunk its Best Musical Tony chances. By the time that Dolores said, "No party lasts forever," many in the audience might well have muttered, "Thank God."

Rock of Ages (2008–2009) was the latest in the parade of stupid musicals meant for crowds that think musicals are innately moronic. Such audiences believe that the lowering of the bar is just what a song-and-dance show deserves, because "It's just a muuu-sical" and "People don't sing in real life."

What happened in *Avatar*, *The Avengers*, *The Dark Knight*, *Star Wars*, *E.T.*, *Toy Story*, *Transformers*, and *Harry Potter*—all among Hollywood top grossers—didn't ever occur in real-life, either. And yet, no one makes the same charge against these films.

These audiences weren't around or paying attention during a time when musicals were created by artists who brought their hearts, souls, and minds to a project, and not just their tongues in their cheeks.

Just as in 1972 when *Grease* returned us to the fifties, in 2009, *Rock of Ages* went back to the eighties. *Grease* had its aging audience laugh at itself for having once thought poodle skirts and DA haircuts were the ultimate fashion statements. The attendees at *Rock of Ages* roared with the same weren't-we-silly-then response to seeing couples drink wine coolers. They nostalgically flicked their Bics to indicate approval of ballads and laughed at references to Molly Ringwald and *Tiger Beat*. They also enjoyed a decidedly unattractive girl who'd let herself rock and look silly, just as their parents had with Cha Cha Di Gregorio.

Gypsy Rose Lee said at the end of her Tony-losing musical, "Nobody laughs at me, because I laugh first at me." Book writer Chris D'Arienzo felt the same. He knew he had an asinine story peppered with ridiculous characters that was merely meant to get us to the next song which everyone could nostalgically relive.

Young Hopeful Girl came to L.A., got mugged, and then was rescued by Sensitive Guy. They bonded, not only because they had the same goal to become rock stars, but also because they had so much in common. "I love Slurpees" was met with "So do I!" in one of the show's best-written exchanges.

But Sensitive Guy made the tragic mistake of saying he wanted to be her friend. She interpreted that as nonlover, although that wasn't what he meant at all. But she was pretty innocent, as proved by her not understanding what fellatio was.

Such naïveté leads many a woman to being attracted to the bad guy, which in this case was the successful rock star. Of course he treated her terribly, and of course she was devastated—which caused the audience to give out with a pseudosympathetic "Aww!" It's the only type of response an audience can give when it's offered cartoon characters.

The audience never gave a mocking "Aww" when romances looked doomed for Magnolia and Gaylord Ravenal or Julie and Billy Bigelow. After Maria had decided to return to the Von Trapp manse to proclaim her love for the Captain—only to find that he'd become engaged to the Baroness—audiences didn't "awww." They cared and shared her pain, because only moments earlier she'd made the decision to pursue the man she loved—now learning that she was too late.

But this was the post-9/11, post-*Urinetown* era. Musicals were not meant to be taken seriously.

So Young Hopeful Girl became a stripper. Meanwhile, Sensitive Guy who really loved her was making his own inroads into rock stardom. Alas, that meant being turned into a commodity by a promoter and wearing the de rigueur ridiculous outfits befitting boy bands of the eighties. But our lad had integrity; he gave it all up to be himself.

A subplot involved urban renewal. A rock club was threatened by a villain who spoke with a German accent. There was a happy ending, of course, although a gay man died. We were now in the era when producers would do anything to sell tickets to young male heterosexual nontheatergoers, and nothing does that better than seeing a gay guy die.

But even *Rock of Ages'* fans—and there were hundreds of thousands of them—could tell that the book was an excuse to let them hear the memorable songs from their youth with such lyrics as "I love the way you move and the sparkle in your eyes."

Five Tony nominations, including Best Musical, more than 1,250 performances, and a movie. Only twenty-four other musicals can make that claim. But *Rock of Ages* shares with no show the distinction of selling at the merchandise stand an exact replica of a T-shirt worn in the show. It said "Hooray for Boobies."

Or was *Rock of Ages* saying hooray to all the boobies who gave it its Tony nominations?

American Idiot (2009–2010), based on a 2004 album by punk rock band Green Day, was the story of three motherfuckers. No, they literally did not have carnal knowledge with the women who gave them birth. But many years earlier "motherfucker" had become the au courant synonym for "buddy." ("How ya doin', motherfucker?")

These three all maintained that they "don't want to be an American idiot," but throughout the show, each would become exactly that for at least some period of time.

Audiences laughed at how oblivious the three heroes seemed to be, especially at the lad who looked out front and gave the crowd the finger. Another proudly told how he didn't shower. "There's nothing wrong with me," went a lyric. "This is how I'm supposed to be."

Their education? The line, "At the 7-Eleven where I was taught" told the truth. The bulk of what these kids learned came from the streets and not the classroom.

Their home life? "No one really seems to care," they each said. And so, they decided, "I could really care less." Now what they really meant was "I *couldn't* care less," but perhaps lyricist Billie Joe Armstrong got it right—these kids *did* care, or at least wanted to care. Much of *American Idiot* was a cry for help.

Eventually these lads arrived at the big question about their suburban roots: "Are we going to waste our lives or get the fuck out of here?"

And do what? As the Tony-winning *Avenue Q* stressed, "There is life outside your apartment," but innately happy people tend to be happy wherever they live. They find what's wonderful about their environs, and enjoy whatever the place has to offer.

On the other hand, unhappy people would be unhappy even if they lived in Shangri-la. So while one lad said that he lusted for "a new city, new faces, new voices," the problem is that wherever he planned to go, he'd take his unsatisfied, unmotivated, and unfocused self with him.

Still, two of the kids did leave home and get that rush everyone's felt when he's set out for new frontiers. These kids weren't well prepared, however. Their only luggage was their de rigueur guitar cases. One young man said that in order to finance the trip he held up a convenience store; then he admitted sheepishly that he actually stole the money from his mother's purse—before he conceded even more sheepishly that his mother actually loaned him the cash. These kids were truly paper tigers who needed to posture and show how tough they were when, as Armstrong adeptly showed, they were not. (In *A Bronx Tale*, a father told his son who'd been admiring gangsters, "The workingman is the tough guy." He was right.)

When the lads were together, Green Day's music was loud and raucous. When each character was alone and sang, he almost always crooned a ballad; away from those two other influences, only then did he dare to express his inner emotions that ranged from sensitive to scared.

It was good music. Armstrong, Mike Dirnt, and Tre Cool might have turned out DeSylva, Brown, and Henderson worthy melodies if they'd lived in a less chaotic world. The score even had many a hum-um-um-mum-mum-mum-mum-able melody, right down to a pretty folk song on guitars for the curtain call. (John Gallagher, Jr., Stark Sands, Michael Esper, and the entire supporting cast sang it very well.)

So what was in store for these three kids who hadn't done much planning? One stayed put because he'd became involved with a young woman. What an innocent look of glee he had on his face after their first kiss! Men lust, to be sure, but they need love, too. But sex here resulted in pregnancy, with the girlfriend looking blissfully unaware of what she was in for. Some months later, she was a sadder-and-wiser mother who came in saddled with baby equipment while the new father looked bored and irritated. Life as they both knew it was over.

One of the travelers was impressed every time he opened a magazine and saw a famous athlete who'd joined the army as an officer. So the kid enlisted, too, because he needed to find something, anything, in which he could believe. This would do, or so he'd assumed. He would become an amputee after his time in Iraq.

The third young man did drugs—not just marijuana, but wrap-the-tube-around-your-arm drugs. That compelled his girlfriend to indulge, too. His dealer was a goth guy who had the right side of his head shaved clean. "You talkin' to me?" he indignantly asked. Well, Robert De Niro rose to fame saying it in *Taxi Driver*, so it was obviously the thing to say.

If we didn't have so ugly a society, we wouldn't have shows as ugly as *American Idiot*. In the post-9/11 world, everything seemed to be breaking down—including perfect rhymes in lyrics. The set was adorned with many large TV screens that showed atrocities from the Abu Ghraib torture sessions to George W. Bush. The most clever use of those screens occurred during the army hospital scenes, when they morphed into electrocardiogram and electroencephalogram machines. The electronic waves that went up and down turned into words in the Farsi language.

Yet high above the action, easily lost among the many screens, was that famously inspirational "We Can Do It!" World War II poster—the one that showed a woman who resembled a young Tyne Daly wearing a red, polka-dotted kerchief on her head, dressed in a blue shirt, and flexing the muscle in her right arm. Back in the forties, people did believe "We can do it!" Today, in a world still not over Enron, ridiculous salaries for athletes, and ever-resigning corrupt politicians, kids believe, "We *can't* do it." And who can blame them?

Saddest among all the projections were home movies of an innocent and happy toddler, reminding us what each of these young men once was. Who's responsible for the change? "Mom and Dad are the ones you can blame," we were told. "Nobody cares. Everybody left you. Nobody likes you." *American Idiot* was almost unrelentingly grim because it believed life pretty much is.

That is one way to look at it. Forty-six years previously at this same St. James Theatre, Irene Molloy looked at Mrs. Levi and said, "Oh, Dolly, the world is full of wonderful things!" It still is. The fault, dear idiots, is not in your parents, but in yourselves. Don't want to be an American idiot? Then join the drama club.

Many Broadway producers have taken critics' quotations out of context. Others have added exclamation points to statements that never had them in the original review.

But *Million Dollar Quartet* (2009–2010) went a misstep further. Above the title it advertised not the actual people who performed in the show, but the far more famous characters they were portraying: Johnny Cash (1932–2003), Jerry Lee Lewis (1935–), Carl Perkins (1932–1998), and Elvis Presley (1935–1977).

The management undoubtedly figured that anyone who didn't know that Presley, Perkins, and Cash had already cashed in their chips didn't deserve to be told. No statistics have been kept on how many people demanded their money returned after discovering that not even the seventy-four-year-old Lewis was on hand.

Actually, the producers could have advertised their Jerry Lee Lewis as "Tony-winner Levi Kreis! Best Supporting Actor in a Musical!" But so-called "tribute" shows never do that. (If the powers-that-be who do these shows really wanted to pay "tribute" to these legends, they'd do no show at all.)

To be fair, Kreis's name might not have sold many tickets. By now, Tonys were being won by people who almost certainly had never even watched a minute of a Tony telecast.

Million Dollar Quartet was meant to replicate that now famous night of December 4, 1956, in the Sun Record Studios in Memphis. Perkins was recording and Lewis was backing him up. Cash just happened to be there and Presley dropped in. It led to an impromptu jam session.

The big conflict came when Perkins confronted Presley about covering "Blue Suede Shoes," which he'd previously written and recorded; that Presley got to perform it on *The Ed Sullivan Show* rankled Perkins, too. This could have made for some temperamental fireworks, but instead the men took it outside to either discuss or fight. We'll never know, because we were never shown. Some minutes later, each man returned in a sullen mood, and we were left to infer what had happened because book writers Colin Escott and Floyd Mutrux were too lazy to tell us.

At the end of the night, the famous photo of the four—Presley at the piano with the other three looking over his shoulder—was flown in. One would think that set designer Derek McLane would have replicated the Sun studio that was shown in the photo. Similarly, costume designer Jane Greenwood would have been expected to meticulously match the men's clothes to those they'd actually worn that day.

Not at all. On stage, Cash was seen in his trademark black, which may have helped audiences to initially recognize him. But truth to tell, he wasn't wearing black that day; Perkins was. The photo only reiterated the inattention to detail of which *Million Dollar Quartet* was guilty.

The rehearsal and preview periods had been hellish. Leading lady Jane Krakowski decided to bail. Leading man James Carpinello had the wheels of his roller skates soar out from under him. He was so severely injured that he had to be replaced.

Everyone had expected a disaster, anyway, because *Xanadu* (2007–2008) was based on one of Hollywood's worst movies. The 1980 film was such a turd that it gave birth to the annual Razzie Awards for putrid film-making. In 2005, when the awards were celebrating a silver anniversary, it did not forget its roots and thanked *Xanadu*.

But on stage, *Xanadu* knew exactly what it was. "This," said one character, "is children's theater for forty-year-old gay people."

Audiences laughed in agreement, hooted, cheered, and went "Whoo!" after most every number. The 9/11 terrorists obviously didn't have Broadway on their minds, but they may well have inadvertently affected it. While people once liked to laugh when they went to a show, now they apparently needed to—desperately. Shows that offered feeble music, lyrics, and jokes provided therapeutic value: audiences could feel superior to them. And *Xanadu* wore its moronic silliness as flashily as its sequined T-shirts.

The plot had Clio, the goddess of history, planning to visit Venice, Italy, in 1780. She was no goddess of geography or time, for she miscalculated and landed in Venice, California, in 1980. Some gods must be crazy, but this goddess must have been incompetent.

Clio wouldn't waste her trip. She'd help sidewalk chalk artist Sonny

Malone realize his dream of building a disco roller-skating arena. He'd need it: for Sonny, a double digit IQ would be a dream so impossible that Don Quixote would have mocked it.

In twenty-first century Broadway, what goes around Hollywood and bombs comes around to Broadway and succeeds. *Xanadu* was the latest of the so-bad-it's-good musicals that started with *The Rocky Horror Picture Show* and continued with *Little Shop of Horrors*. Both have since spawned many other horrors.

Xanadu was a member of that growing breed called the Off-Broadway Broadway musical—a show that although small is still too expensive to be in a 299-seat house. However, it didn't deserve artistically or financially to take up a major Broadway theater. So *Xanadu* was perfect for the 590-seat Hayes, Broadway's least impressive playhouse. That it resembles a suburban movie theater made the tacky show seem right at home.

People often exclaim, "That's show business!" when something unfortunate happens. When an unexpectedly good fate happens, "That's show business!" too.

Only not nearly as often.

CHAPTER TEN

✳

What Do I Do Now? The Best Musical Tony Losers That Suffered from Following Their Creators' Smash Hits

Here's the timeline of one of Broadway's comparatively few miracles.

May 13, 1954: *The Pajama Game* opens. Richard Adler and Jerry Ross, who had previously only contributed songs to one Broadway revue, provide the entire score.

March 27, 1955: *The Pajama Game* wins the Best Musical Tony.

May 5, 1955: *Damn Yankees* opens. Richard Adler and Jerry Ross provide their second full score.

April 1, 1956: *Damn Yankees* wins the Best Musical Tony.

In other words, two authors see two smash hits open within 357 days of each other.

One author—Adler—sees two of his smash hits win consecutive Best Musical Tonys within 371 days of each other. The other—Ross—doesn't, because he died on November 11, 1955, at the age of twenty-nine.

It's easily one of Broadway's most tragic losses, for who knows if they would have then had three Tony-winning hits in a row?

The fact is that in the next five decades, composers and/or lyricists never duplicated the feat of seeing two of their shows win consecutive Best Musical Tonys.

The problem with coming up with a musical theater blockbuster is that everyone expects the next one to be better.

We've acknowledged that those connected with *My Fair Lady* had a tough time meeting expectations with *Camelot*. At least the shows that follow here got a Best Musical nomination.

And yet, the creators of these shows didn't win Best Musical, and undoubtedly didn't expect to.

* * *

That Jerry Bock and Sheldon Harnick, who'd last written the score for *Fiddler on the Roof*, were doing a new show was exciting. That Mike Nichols would be directing *The Apple Tree* (1966–1967) made it doubly so. Nichols had recently staged three Broadway comedies: *Barefoot in the Park*, *The Odd Couple*, and *Luv*. The last named had run 901 performances, become the nineteenth-longest-running play in Broadway history, and was Nichols's *least* successful of the three. His first movie, *Who's Afraid of Virginia Woolf?* had opened to raves and would soon win an Oscar.

The show was composed of three one-act musicals. As producer Stuart Ostrow said, "So many musicals had second-act trouble that I thought if we just did one-act musicals, we'd eliminate that problem."

Yes, but once a story has ended and another is to begin, an audience must gear up to learn a whole new cast of characters, find out what they want, come to care for them, and become emotionally invested all over again. Although theatergoers are willing to do that at eight o'clock, they may be a little less eager at nine. By ten, they may be too exhausted to start the process one more time.

Let's literally start at the *very* beginning with *The Diary of Adam and Eve*. Bock and Harnick, with some early help from Jerome Coopersmith, adapted Mark Twain's short story. The world's first man met the world's first woman, but Adam considered her "intrusive" and "a nuisance"— although the songwriters in a B section took pains to slow the melody and have him describe her as "beautiful," too.

Eve (Barbara Harris) was constantly shown to be smarter than Adam, with an appreciation for beauty and culture that he lacked. On the other hand, when Eve took up with the Snake and ate the apple, the authors did have her try to shift the blame to Adam. And wouldn't you know that Adam did wind up apologizing to her?

Then they suddenly had a third creature to contend with. "It's a fish," Adam determined because "it surrounds itself with water almost every chance it gets." Or maybe it wasn't a fish, Adam decided, for "on occasion it says 'Goo.'" What fun Harnick had in letting us catch up with him! And talk about advancing the action? Harnick did it superbly in the song's final line, when he had Adam note, "I'll be damned if she didn't find another." He took us forward nine months in only eleven syllables.

Despite their struggles, Adam and Eve grew accustomed to each other's face. By the end, what had been an amusing show unexpectedly became a quite moving one.

Thus, Bock and Harnick's musicalization of Frank R. Stockton's *The Lady or the Tiger?* had a hard act to follow. Remember it from grammar school? A king believed that if he put an accused man in an arena with two doors, a higher power would have an innocent man choose the door from which a lady would emerge and become his wife while a guilty man would pick the door behind which stood a very hungry tiger. So the accused either got death or, the more cynical of us might argue, a fate worse than death.

Then the king's daughter fell in love with a lowly soldier. The monarch wouldn't have it, so the soldier was sent to the arena. The princess knew which door offered the lady and which the tiger. Would she let her love marry someone else or be devoured?

"And so I leave it with all of you," Stockton wrote, before concluding his story with the line, "Which came out of the opened door: the lady or the tiger?" Bock and Harnick retained the same ending, which was dull.

Passionella was better. It told of Ella (Barbara Harris), a chimney sweep who wanted to be a movie star. As she sang, "I'd be so grateful that after preem-yares, I'd sweep out the theater and fold up the chairs."

Thanks to a fairy godmother, she got her wish, as well as beauty and an enormous bosom substantially larger than was ever shown in press photos or Harris's sequence on the Tonys. It was a veritable shelf on which you could have stored every LP, cassette, CD, DVD, and script ever made of *Show Boat*.

Passionella's window of opportunity was slimmer than Cinderella's: "from *Huntley-Brinkley* to *The Late Late Show*," warned her grandmother. (For young 'uns, that means "from Scott Pelley to Craig Ferguson.") But that isn't what made her unhappy. "What does it all mean, if I don't have love?" she melodramatically asked.

Enter Flip, patterned after Marlon Brando's sneering character in *The Wild Ones*. She was worried how he'd react once *The Late Late Show* ended and she reverted to dishrag Ella. One night, after they'd been love-making on the couch and losing track of time, *both* of them turned into low-rent versions of themselves. Flip had had the same fairy godmother.

Some audiences weren't around to see it after the disappointing act two.

The show wouldn't have beaten the groundbreaking *Cabaret*, but it might have been a bigger hit with one tweak to *The Lady or the Tiger?*

When the princess gestured which door her beloved should choose, he should have opened it and met an enormous and voracious tiger. The princess (Harris, remember) would have then looked at the audience and snarled, "Did you really think . . . ?" She would have got a laugh that would have carried the show to act three—and kept audiences there to see it.

The 1964 movie version of *Zorba the Greek* had a scene in which Zorba entered a den of iniquity called the Kit Kat Klub. That was, of course, the name of the nightspot that had been the setting for *Cabaret.*

When composer John Kander and lyricist Fred Ebb screened *Zorba the Greek* to see if they wanted to musicalize it, they must have gasped when they saw the Kit Kat Klub sign. Wasn't this an omen that the *Cabaret* songwriters should make this their next show?

Chronologically speaking, Kander and Ebb didn't follow *Cabaret* with *Zorba* (1968–1969); *The Happy Time* came in between. But *Zorba* seemed to be their heir apparent to *Cabaret* because it had Harold Prince, the same producer-director, and Ronald Field, the same choreographer.

What's more, Prince was reuniting with book writer Joseph Stein, whose last musical had been *Fiddler on the Roof.* Herschel Bernardi, who'd recently had a great success playing Tevye, and Maria Karnilova, the original Golde, would be teamed to respectively play Zorba, the jack of all trades and master of anyone who hired him, and Madame Hortense, the senior citizen who once was a celebrated courtesan and now hoped that Zorba would see her past glory in her.

Zorba the Greek was destined to become a musical. A man who relishes life and seizes every day is one who knows how to sing. But the opening number was utterly wrong. The Leader—a storyteller, really—sang to the assembled, "Life is what you do while you're waiting to die." It was a very clever line and very much in keeping with the personality of Fred Ebb, who was famously dour.

But Zorba certainly does *not* see life as simply what you do while you're waiting to die. As he sang in his first song, he saw each event in his life as if he were experiencing it for "The First Time." He never lost that same sense of wonder he once had.

The collaborators did go overboard. It was one thing to have Zorba sing that he once met a Turk and because each didn't speak the other's language, they communicated through dance. But to claim that he could tell from a dance that the man had a wife, two children, and had been away for eighteen months was gilding the *kpinos*

Ebb realized his opening song mistake by the time the 1983 revival rolled around. He changed his opening line to "Life is what you do till the moment you die." Well, yes, but isn't that a given? The right opening number might have made *Zorba* a success—although it certainly wouldn't have been strong enough to beat *1776*.

Of course, any musical that Michael Bennett would have attempted after *A Chorus Line* would have paled in comparison. Too bad that *Ballroom* (1978–1979) couldn't have been judged on its own terms.

Widow Bea Asher ran a junk shop but did little else with her life. As her friend Angie said, "You gonna have dinner with Walter Cronkite and hit the sack with Johnny Carson?"

Angie had an alternative: come to the Stardust Ballroom and go dancing with her and her friends. Bea's response: "Grandmothers don't go dancing." Angie's rebuttal: "Who says?"

Angie had a point and Bea knew it. She was also affected by Angie's observation that "It took me six months after my husband died to realize they only buried one of us."

So Bea summoned up all her courage, went to the ballroom, and stood outside for a good long time. Bea's biggest fear was "What if no one asks me to dance?" Then she thought of a situation that would have been worse: "What if *someone* asks me to dance?"

Eventually, Bea looked up at the steps that went to the ballroom: "It isn't the Matterhorn, it's only a flight of stairs," she sang in one of Marilyn and Alan Bergman's best lyrics. And that's when her new and improved life began.

Book writer Jerome Kass had her meet a number of middle-agers and seniors who had got to know, care for, and love each other. One of the first scenes showed one of them, Shirley, welcomed back after a hospital stay. "It's great to be back home," she said with gratitude in her voice.

Soon Bea felt the same way. She was making friends—especially with Al Rossi. He wasn't a flashy guy, but he had a good euphemism that made him seem witty while it also minimized his low-level job: "I'm a mailman. A man of letters."

Alas, when friends and relatives are used to your being home—and suddenly you aren't there anymore—their feelings will run from concerned to suspicious. So it was with Helen, Bea's sister-in-law. When Bea wasn't answering her phone late at night in those pre-answering machine days, Helen came by—and found a just-getting-home, still-on-a-cloud Bea.

"Who would have suspected you were having a good time?" Helen snarled, utterly unaware of how that sounded. Even Bea's rejoinder that "It's easier to think of me dead than dancing, isn't it?" didn't deter her sister-in-law. Helen had a different agenda: she was intent on keeping her brother's memory alive by seeing Bea mourn forever.

Bea didn't move fast. One night, after Al escorted her home, she finally had the nerve to ask, "Would you like a cup of coffee?" to which he drolly answered, "For a month now." Once inside, he told her that "You're the best partner I ever had." For better or worse, that partnership would primarily be on the dance floor, for Al eventually confessed that he was married.

So Bea accepted Al on his part-time terms. Audiences might have, too, if Al had given them convincing reasons why he had to stay married and wouldn't get divorced. If Al's wife had been in the throes of a terminal illness, audiences would have admired him for not leaving her in the lurch. But Kass gave no explanation.

Helen would have plenty to say when she learned of Al's marital status. Even before she had that ammunition, she'd called Bea's grown daughter Diane, ostensibly to have her talk some sense into her mother. Both were waiting for her when Bea arrived home at what they considered a too late hour. When Bea explained that she'd been on a date, Diane was aghast and said, "Another one?" Bea had a good answer: "How many am I allowed?" Now it was Helen who referenced what Bea had said before she'd found the ballroom: "You're a grandmother!"

So if Diane hadn't been able to conceive with her husband, there would have been no problem with Bea's dating?

Though Bea's family wasn't supportive, she found a new one that wanted her to be whatever she wanted to be: the clientele at the Stardust Ballroom. Bea came to love her friends so much that she even cosigned a loan for one.

Now Helen phoned not only Diane, but also Bea's son David, even getting him to fly to New York from his California home. Helen wanted an intervention, and she was going to have it.

"Did you all like it better when I only had these four walls for company?" *Ballroom* showed how much some people feared change. Those who didn't had a better time.

When Angie nominated Bea as the Queen of the Stardust Ballroom, she said what we all came to feel: "We've all watched this lady blossom. She showed us what we're capable of."

However, when a family emergency caused Al to miss a night at the ballroom, Bea's understanding (and rationalizing) feelings weren't as cavalier. Eventually she was able to come to the belief that she'd rather have "Fifty Percent" of him than none of him.

But Vincent Gardenia? How astonishing that Bennett, who was so into appearance—one reason why he'd fired Lainie Kazan from *Seesaw*—would hire short, squat, and craggy-faced Gardenia as Bea's love interest. Perhaps he wanted this additional challenge, figuring that when he made it work, he could say, "And I even made people believe that a woman could have the hots for Vincent Gardenia."

Why didn't Bennett cast Robert Preston, who'd become available just in time; before *Ballroom*'s rehearsals started, Preston had closed in Boston with *The Prince of Grand Street*. Granted, Al wasn't the starring role, and Preston might not have been interested. Then to play Rossi, how about the actor who'd played *Di* Rossi in *Do I Hear a Waltz?*—Sergio Franchi.

It would have made for a better show, although *Ballroom* certainly wouldn't have beaten *Sweeney Todd*. It also lacked an important ingredient that had helped *Chorus Line*—youth appeal. At 116 performances, it had less than 2 percent of its predecessor's run.

And yet, a musical about taking a second chance in life, refusing to grow old, and accepting as much good fortune as one could find made *Ballroom* more intriguing than most romantically inclined musicals. That the leading man was an adulterer wasn't altogether pleasing, but many middle-agers and seniors found themselves rooting for this illicit union—which they might not have expected when they'd walked into the theater.

The score was skimpy—only eleven songs, although composer Billy Goldenberg also wrote three instrumentals. A bigger problem was that more than six of the songs were given to insignificant characters. The script tells us that they were Marlene and Nathan, but no one ever called them by their names. They were the band singers.

So the performance songs didn't particularly offer commentary, as the ones in *Cabaret* or *Follies* did. Bennett may well have felt that if his songwriters did that, he'd be accused of being derivative—a label he couldn't tolerate. The result, however, was a namby-pamby score.

Nevertheless, all Bennett needed from these songs was perfunctory background music for the dazzling dancing he offered. He staged a rhumba, samba, hustle, waltz, cha-cha, and even a Lindy. As a result, Bennett received his fourth straight Tony Award for Best Choreography—the only one of the eight nominations *Ballroom* would win. As marvelous as Dorothy Loudon was, she lost the Tony to Angela Lansbury as Mrs. Lovett in *Sweeney Todd*—whom Loudon would eventually succeed in the role.

After Andrew Lloyd Webber's *The Phantom of the Opera* had recently passed its second anniversary of two straight sellout years at the Majestic, his *Aspects of Love* (1989–1990) opened next door at the Broadhurst.

Less than a year later, while *Phantom* was celebrating more than three straight sellout years, *Aspects* was closing after 377 underachieving performances.

It wouldn't have lasted that long without its Lloyd Webber pedigree.

The show began with thirty-four-year old Alex Dillingham standing on stage singing the not-so-hot "Love Changes Everything." Then came a flashback in which seventeen-year-old Alex remembered being a Stage Door Johnny to actress Rose Vibert. On a whim, he invited her to his villa, and on an equally flighty whim, she accepted. While traveling, each got to sing that "Seeing Is Believing," the second straight second-rate Lloyd Webber melody.

The villa didn't actually belong to Alex; he eventually confessed that his uncle George owned it. "I think I should like your uncle," said Rose, in what could have been construed as foreshadowing.

Alex and Rose were soon going through closets. He told her, "Rose, leave things as they are," but she decided to wear a dress that happened to be the favorite of Uncle George's dead wife Delia. So when George unexpectedly (and all too conveniently) showed up and saw Rose wearing the dress, he came close to fainting. This clunky scene made George look a bit weak, but it at least allowed Rose a rescue fantasy.

Rose roared at Alex, "How could you have let me wear this dress?" But Alex had said, "Rose, leave things as they are," hadn't he?

Soon Rose was saying that her manager Marcel had suddenly called her back to rehearsals. Only later did Alex realize that no one knew where she was, so no one could reach her. (This scene took place in 1947, long before the advent of cell phones.)

Why didn't Rose assume he'd think of that and catch the lie? Her apparent passion for George had her throw caution to the wind, if not in the toilet.

Two years passed. George and Rose had become a couple, and Alex came to visit them. That resulted in a song not unlike Sondheim's "Impossible" in *Forum*, in which Senex and Hero, each interested in the virgin Philia, bragged about their strengths before confessing to having weaknesses. Here, Alex and George reached the opposite conclusion— that each was the more worthy—by the time the turgid melody ended.

Alex apparently hadn't got over being dumped by Rose, because he took out a gun and shot her. He "only" hit her in the arm. How astonishing that a servant attended to Rose, while neither George nor Alex was concerned enough to rush to her side. Were they that inured to shootings?

And yet, George soon after said to Alex, "The two of you belong together." After he'd tried to kill her? Late twentieth-century British musicals were notorious for their lack of humor, but this line brought a guffaw, albeit unwanted. Another came after Rose reappeared with a modest bandage on her arm and said, "My life has been draining away."

Audiences laughed more after Rose met Guilietta, who was once George's mistress. One might expect a catfight; they instead chatted amiably, and then, in the next scene, kissed passionately. There's no people like show people.

As act one ended, Alex learned that George had impregnated Rose. Act two began a dozen years later. Late twentieth-century British musicals didn't allow audiences many chances to applaud, but after George sang a sincere song of paternal love to his young daughter Jennie, crowds made time to clap, for here was a situation to which they could relate.

Tween gave way to teen when young Jenny danced with older Jenny. And just as George was reminded of his first love when he saw Rose, so too was Alex smitten with Jenny, the image of her mother. But Jenny was a mere fifteen. How could audiences root for a man who was thinking of consorting with a minor? That Jenny was the aggressor was a point made only later, but it still didn't excuse Alex for even considering it.

Then Jenny entered wearing Delia's dress—the same one that Rose once wore. This time, George was charmed in a paternal way. Audiences cooed as Dad danced with daughter in "The First Man You Remember," but cooled when Alex cut in and became the second man—and the first Jenny would remember in a different way. George was losing his daughter to the man whose great love he'd taken away.

After Jenny said, "It's not as if I don't know passion from living in our house," and Alex added, "I wish to God we had never met," audiences groaned in agreement. While Alex alluded to statutory rape, audiences returned to guffawing and thinking that Alex should have thought of that much earlier.

As Clive Barnes in *The New York Times* said of Robert Anderson's 1968 play *I Never Sang for My Father*, "A soap opera is a soap opera no matter how you slice the soap." One had to wonder if *Aspects of Love* was saying, "Gather all you can reap," as Giulietta had instructed? Maybe it was what Alex told Jenny, "George said that you can have more than one emotion at one time." Perhaps we Americans were just too inhibited for it. But few on Broadway worried about it.

In 2003–2004, composer and colyricist Marc Shaiman, colyricist Scott Wittman, director Jack O'Brien, associate director Matt Lenz, choreographer Jerry Mitchell, cast members Kerry Butler and Linda Hart, and lead producer Margo Lion had a Tony-winning smash with *Hairspray*. It ran 2,642 performances.

In 2010–2011, they joined forces with book writer Terrence McNally, now a veteran of six Broadway musicals and nine Broadway plays, on *Catch Me If You Can*. It ran 2,476 *fewer* performances.

Hairspray was as much a fairy tale as the show that had played the same Neil Simon Theatre twenty-five years earlier: *Annie*. Heavyset Tracy Turnblad's winding up with knockout Link Larkin was as unlikely as Annie's getting the world's richest man to adopt her. Not every mother who grew to be as ample as Edna Turnblad still had a husband desperately in love with her. But if you can't have fairy tales in musical comedy, where can you have them?

But *Catch Me If You Can* was no fairy tale. It was based on the 1980 memoir and 2002 film about Frank W. Abagnale, Jr., who audaciously flew more than a million miles of unauthorized Pan Am flights while pretending to be a pilot. He later conned a hospital and a family while FBI agent Carl Hanratty (Norbert Leo Butz), his Javert, desperately tried to stop him.

In 1969, after a five-year hunt, Hanratty finally caught Abagnale at an airport and proclaimed, "The show is over."

No, as John Travolta said in the movie of *Grease*, "It's only the beginning."

Just as it's said that some people who are tortured remove themselves from their bodies to escape the pain, Frank suddenly escaped in the only way he could when captured: he saw his life flash before his eyes as a sixties

TV variety show somewhere between *The Smothers Brothers Comedy Hour* and *Hullabaloo*. Audiences, then, were whisked from the airport to a TV studio in far quicker time than a taxi ride from JFK to midtown.

McNally seemed to make a wise decision here. Decades earlier, when Bob Fosse was conceiving *Chicago*, he knew that if he put Roxie Hart in a "realistic" musical, audiences wouldn't be able to get behind it, because, as Billy Flynn unapologetically called her, she was "a common criminal." That's what Abagnale was, too, and musical comedies are better when they treat antiheroes in a fanciful fashion. The realistically drawn heels in *I Can Get It for You Wholesale* and *What Makes Sammy Run?*—each in a pretty good show—lumped together didn't stay on Broadway as long as the appealing J. Pierrepont Finch did in *How to Succeed in Business Without Really Trying*. More statistics, when *Catch Me If You Can* was being readied, *How to Succeed* was preparing its second Broadway revival while each of those two other sixties musicals has never enjoyed any.

Just as the comic book approach had helped *How to Succeed* and the vaudeville had worked for *Chicago*, the TV special conceit seemed a way to make *Catch Me If You Can* prosper. Abagnale was suddenly surrounded by a chorus of young, beautiful, and leggy women in scanty costumes. *Catch Me If You Can* seemed to have both tired businessman and gay businesswoman potential.

No one working in musical theater in the twenty-first century is better than Marc Shaiman at understanding the sounds of the swinging sixties (before they really started swinging by decade's end). He is so adept at pastiche that pistachio must be his favorite ice cream.

Shaiman certainly knew how sixties variety shows sounded. The lyrics he wrote with Wittman had wit and style. Director Jack O'Brien kept it moving, and Jerry Mitchell—intentionally or not—made his choreography look as generic as such numbers used to look on TV.

Variety shows had sketches, too, so McNally included some. In December 1964, the Abagnales were celebrating Christmas with a new (here was a nice detail) artificial tree. Frank, Sr., was telling Frank, Jr., how to get ahead in the world: "The Pinstripes Are All They See," he said, citing how the New York Yankees always win. Actually, Frank, Jr., should have guilelessly mused that the team had just lost two consecutive World Series. His retort would have served to show that his father didn't have all the answers. And indeed, as audiences would witness, Senior didn't.

As in the film, Frank's parents were shown to be dishonest: Dad fiscally, Mom sexually. They had no idea how much their behavior would impact their son.

Frank continued to break rules, which again brought to mind *How to Succeed*. When things started going Frank's way, he even sharply turned his head to us as if to say "Look at that! It always *does* work out!" as Finch did.

But Finch's dishonesty wasn't as severe. He mostly told lies of omission or structured his sentences so that people would infer what he wanted them to infer. When Finch told Mr. Bratt that he "was just talking to Mr. Biggley" and that he "bumped into him," he indeed had just done both—meaning that he'd slammed into him while walking and had made perfunctory chit-chat. If Mr. Bratt assumed something more, well, Finch could reason, that was *his* mistake. Unlike Frank, Finch was not an out-and-out crook.

Granted, Frank started off innocuously. Once he was forced out of private school because his parents could no longer afford to pay his tuition, he nevertheless wore his blazer to public school (which said a good deal about him). The first day, when kids began teasing him and one student mocked, "Are you a substitute teacher?" he seized the notion and impersonated one. It was little more than a harmless prank, but Senior was amused when he heard about it. That was tacit approval for the lad to commit more scams.

Just as some sports figures have said, "It ain't bragging if you can back it up," Frank wanted us to feel "It ain't bad if you're clever enough." Some might not have had much sympathy for the big banks that lost money because of his forged and phony checks; we can't solely blame Frank for Pan Am's going out of business. But when Frank pretended to be a doctor in a hospital, there was a real possibility that he could have genuinely hurt or killed someone.

Actually, McNally made a bad decision in the scene that showed how Frank handled himself in the hospital. In the film, Frank was so upset by the sight of blood that he vomited—once. Here, in front of other people—including Brenda, the nurse he'd come to love and who'd return that love—the sight of blood made him vomit three times. The expression "Fool me once; shame on you; fool me twice; shame on me" applies; only the biggest fools would have still believed that Frank was a doctor after three such reactions at the sight of blood.

On the other hand, McNally improved the Frank-Brenda relationship by having her be "the best nurse on the staff." In the film, she was incompetent; Frank felt bad for her after a doctor yelled at her. In the musical, she saved him by giving him good medical advice, making him respect her expertise. "I love that you're good at your job," he said moonily. Such a component has made many fall in love.

Carl went to a tavern to question Senior about Frank's whereabouts. He simply took out of his hands Frank's most recent letter. A better solution would have had Carl immediately glean that Senior was now an alcoholic; he could have pried him with liquor before he pried the letter out of his hands.

Another lost opportunity involved Frank's first (but not last) capture. The lights came up on Frank in a bedroom. He was hurriedly packing his bags, and when Brenda entered and asked what was wrong, he was evasive without being able to hide that something was radically amiss. Brenda said "Everyone's downstairs," and only then did we learn that it was the night of their engagement party. Frank left, and Carl entered to once again find that he was too late.

This scene was better handled in the film. There the party was going full force—and, projected on the wall, was the unmistakable reflection of the rotating red light that means only one thing: a cop car. Frank saw it, too, and went to the bedroom and then played the scene.

Given that the musical had a chorus that it used quite often, it should have been used here—by having the police break up the party. It would have been almost as powerful as the scene in *Fiddler* when the Cossacks ruined Tzeitel and Motel's wedding.

David Rockwell's unit set, which resembled an airport with an orchestra strangely placed upon it, didn't help. When Carl broke into Frank's hotel room, there were no doors to kick open; he just walked down the steps and he was in.

Shaiman and Wittman made two musical miscalculations. After the G-men accused Carl of "not being cool"—a statement with which Carl greatly agreed and even proclaimed with pride—he sang a song that was musically cool. Either Carl should have told the men he was cooler than they thought (and then let the song prove it) or he should have had a song that was lyrically and musically uptight. Actually, in the interest of a varied score, this latter option would have helped, although it wouldn't have been as audience-pleasing as the one that Carl got: "Don't Break the Rules."

The authors and the show's advertising agency were obsessed with imagery that involved flying. While much of the first act dealt with Frank's

Pan Am misadventures, much of the show did not. Why did they make flying the main event?

The airline imagery was even part of the preshow "turn off your cell phone" spiel, which was done in the style of the speech flight attendants give to passengers before a plane takes off. "Fasten your seat belts," the audience was told. Wouldn't it have been nice if theatergoers had needed them because they were about to be blown away by *Catch Me If You Can*? The best that could be said was that it offered some pleasures and made for an amiable night. And that simply wasn't enough from the team that had delivered the far superior *Hairspray*.

Hairspray also offered some great expectations, too, for *Cry-Baby* (2007–2008). Once again a John Waters film would be adapted by book writers Mark O'Donnell and Thomas Meehan. Alas, the score would not be by *Hairspray*'s Marc Shaiman and Scott Wittman, but by newcomers David Javerbaum and Adam Schlesinger.

Actually, the first three songs of their score do suggest that they were closer to the maverick Waters's sensibility than the *Hairspray* songwriters were. For instead of starting their show with titles akin to "Good Morning, Baltimore," "The Nicest Kids in Town," and "Mama, I'm a Big Girl Now," they opted for "The Anti-Polio Picnic," "Watch Your Ass," and "I'm Infected."

And perhaps that's why it closed after sixty-eight performances.

CHAPTER ELEVEN

*

The Same Old Song: *The Best Musical Tony Losers That Had Recycled Music*

Actually, Broadway never got to hear the song entitled "The Same Old Song." Only Philadelphia and Boston, the two cities in which *Lolita, My Love* played in 1971, did.

Book writer/lyricist Alan Jay Lerner and composer John Barry musicalized Vladimir Nabokov's infamous novel. When precocious little Lolita was giving her mother alibi after alibi for her less-than-ideal behavior, Dorothy Loudon began singing that this was "The Same Old Song" with the same old set of excuses.

At least "The Same Old Song" was a *new* song. By the end of the seventies, what had once been unfathomable had happened: shows that were peppered or filled with old songs were getting Best Musical Tony nominations.

In the first twenty-eight Tony seasons, all Tony-nominated musicals had original scores. That came to an end in 1975–1976, when librettist Loften Mitchell took familiar songs and put them in his new book for *Bubbling Brown Sugar* (1975–1976).

The seventies was the decade in which America realized that many large cities were in terrible economic shape and marked by such urban blight that they might never recover. New York was among the most threatened; bankruptcy was a real possibility. Between the premiere of *Bubbling Brown Sugar* in Washington in the summer of 1975 and its Broadway opening on March 2, 1976, the Big Apple had been treated to the infamous New York *Daily News* headline: FORD TO CITY: DROP DEAD.

Unfortunately, Harlem was one part of the city where many fearful Americans felt that they *would* drop dead after being shot. Rosetta LeNoire (1911–2002), founder of the AMAS Repertory Theatre Company, wanted to dispel this notion. She hired Mitchell to write a musical that would show a positive side of Harlem.

So Mitchell created Jim and Ella, two young African Americans who were visiting Harlem—although they had their doubts about it, too. Then they met Irene, John, and Checkers, who'd entertained in local nightclubs some decades earlier. They told the young couple about the Harlem Renaissance of the twenties and thirties. It had produced some very good music, courtesy of Count Basie, Duke Ellington, and the less loftily named Fats Waller.

Mitchell took their songs as well as others from a half-dozen lyricists and three times as many composers to prove his point that at one time Harlem had first and foremost represented good times.

Bubbling's engagement at the National in Washington was simply a summer attraction, nothing more; it had no Broadway theater booked. If some producers became interested, LeNoire assumed, they'd let her know.

Five did, including director Robert M. Cooper. *Bubbling* moved to Manhattan for 766 performances. It couldn't have won Best Musical in the season of *A Chorus Line*, but it would have had a hard time winning even with less lofty competition. Broadway wasn't ready to reward a musical without an original score.

The 1976–1977 Tony nominating committee was just as desperate. It made an unprecedented and lamentable move in judging *Happy End*, which Kurt Weill, Bertolt Brecht, and Elisabeth Hauptmann wrote in 1929, a "new" musical. The loophole was that it hadn't ever played Broadway.

Note that the nominators endorsed *Happy End* when there was another secondhand musical around, and one not nearly as old: *Godspell*. Stephen Schwartz's first smash had opened off-Broadway on May 17, 1971, and stayed there until June 13, 1976. Four days later it moved to Broadway, so it was in its tenth month when the nominators made their 1976–1977 selections. They gave Schwartz a nomination, but nothing else to *Godspell*.

Did the nominators fear that the TV audience, when hearing a Best Musical slate that included *Godspell*, would say, "Hey, wait! That's not a new show!" Fewer viewers had heard of the much more obscure *Happy End*.

There was more secondhand music among the 1976–1977 Best Musical nominees, courtesy of *Side by Side by Sondheim*. At least the first songwriter anthology to be nominated celebrated the best composer-lyricist of the age.

Fewer narrow escapes would occur as the years went on. In fact, the next year there was no escape from rewarding recycled music. That two of the four 1977–1978 Best Musical nominees had recycled music was a new low.

For in addition to winner *Ain't Misbehavin'* there was *Dancin'* (1977–1978). Director-choreographer Bob Fosse didn't feel the need for a new score.

This was a far cry from what is considered the Golden Age of the American musical (1943–1966). Then, the usual sobriquet found under most every title on most every window card was "a new musical."

So *nu?*

Leader of the Pack (1984–1985) took its title from the 1964 number one hit by the Shangri-Las. The song was the tearstained story of a girl who loved a motorcyclist. Her parents insisted that she break up with him, and once she did, he went off driving much too fast. Whether his death was an accident or a suicide was the listener's guess.

The song was written by either George Morton or the team of Ellie Greenwich and Jeff Barry, depending on what source you care to believe. But in this Greenwich biomusical, she claimed authorship with Barry.

They started out as business partners, then married, and lasted three years—substantially better than the girl and her biker. Of course when we saw them wed, we heard their hit song "Chapel of Love." It was that kind of show. *Leader of the Pack* was about as much fun as the labor an expectant mother experiences on day 273 of her pregnancy.

Because Bob Fosse had had such a success with recycled music in *Dancin'*—at 1,774 performances, it became Broadway's longest-running song-and-dance revue—he'd try his luck with recycled music in a book show.

What confidence to call it *Big Deal* (1985–1986)! Yes, it was based on the 1958 Italian film *Big Deal on Madonna Street*, in which thieves bungled an easy job. And yet, retaining that part of the title invited critics to say that the show was "no big deal."

Indeed, it wasn't. Fosse switched the locale to the South Side of Chicago, a heavily African American part of town. Making blacks his thieves—and incompetent ones at that—wasn't the best message to send.

Avoiding working with a living composer and lyricist was also insulting. By now, Fosse wanted little friction from anyone, and most of the four dozen songwriters he chose to provide his score were long dead.

When dialogue is about to burst into song, there's less excitement when it turns out to be a song we've heard many times before. Book musicals should be more than just greatest hits albums. What a shame that Fosse's last new Broadway show could only run sixty-nine performances and was no big deal.

Then there were the classic movie musicals that became a close-to-carbon-copy Best Musical nominees. The first was *Meet Me in St. Louis* (1989–1990). The small, pre-CinemaScope film was blown up and put into what was then Broadway's biggest theater (the Gershwin). No wonder that the family didn't want to move to New York; they would have had to give up so much room.

Nice Work If You Can Get It (2012–2013) may have been chosen as a title for this "new Gershwin musical" because *Dumb and Dumber* had already been taken.

Book writer Joe DiPietro, according to the credits, was "inspired by material by Guy Bolton and P. G. Wodehouse." He mostly raided their 1926 hit *Oh, Kay!* in which the title character and her brother, both British emigrés, were broke and turned to bootlegging. They stored their liquor in a deserted Long Island manse which, they later learned, belonged to socialite Jimmy Winter. Kay was unaware that he was the man she had saved from drowning the previous year.

It was all silly fluff, as were most twenties musicals, but at least it gave us a solid George and Ira Gershwin score: "Someone to Watch Over Me," "Dear Little Girl," "Maybe," "Clap Yo' Hands, "Do, Do, Do" and "Fidgety Feet."

But not "Nice Work If You Can Get It," a song from the 1937 film *A Damsel in Distress*. Like *Crazy for You*, which had twenty years earlier played with the earlier Gershwin hit *Girl Crazy*, Gershwin songs would be taken from here and there for this new show that would open eighty-six years later at the Imperial Theatre where *Oh, Kay!* had played.

Here, the focus was on Jimmy. Third time wasn't the charm where marriage was concerned: Jimmy was about to wed wife number four. Of his latest fiancée, modern dancer Eileen Evergreen, Jimmy said, "She's so brilliant that when she steps on stage, no one knows what she's doing."

But why was he marrying as often as Alan Jay Lerner? Because Jimmy explained, "Mother will let me take over the family business," if he's married. Billie Bendix, a secret bootlegger, wanted to know what that business was, to which Jimmy said, "Mother won't tell me." Didn't he learn during his other three marriages?

DiPietro would have done better to have made this Jimmy's first engagement. Then audiences could have felt that the devil-may-care playboy had finally decided to please his mother; such a decision would have made him at least slightly altruistic. Besides, after three divorces, Mrs. Winter would have probably decreed, "Three strikes against marriage and you're out."

For Jimmy had been a disappointment at college, too. He established that he'd been thrown out of many. His charm, as he explained it, was that he was "just rich and good-looking."

Matthew Broderick was certainly rich from grossing $100,000 a week from *The Producers* and from marrying Sarah Jessica (aka Carrie Bradshaw) Parker. But by 2012, the suddenly fifty-year-old Broderick appeared bloated and prematurely old.

Of course, one could argue that Jimmy's dissolute life and three failed marriages could take it out of a guy—making Broderick perfect for the part. But DiPietro's character descriptions said that Jimmy should be "dripping with charm." Broderick was so stiff that his shoulders seemed to be in the same position as a butterfly whose wings had been pinned to a dry mount.

No such problem with Kelli O'Hara as Billie. That the logo showed O'Hara literally carrying Broderick in her arms was most apt; she did carry him and the show, too.

Jimmy didn't know that Billie was a bootlegger. He just happened to mention that he has a "huge Long Island house that I never, ever, ever, ever use." (Yes, three "evers" after the "never.") That gave Billie enough time to realize that she'd found the ideal place to store her booze.

Billie and fellow bootleggers Cookie McGee (Michael McGrath) and Duke Mahoney knew that this would please their boss Brownbeard. When audiences hear that "No one's ever met Brownbeard," they know that they'll not only meet him—or her—but also that the character will turn out to be someone who doesn't remotely resemble a man with a brown beard. So was it the case in this musical. Jimmy's mother was Brownbeard.

So *that* was the family business. At least at the end of the show Mother acknowledged the problem of entrusting it to Jimmy. "Do you really think he's capable of running a million-dollar bootlegging operation?" she asked.

Or carrying a Broadway show? When he and O'Hara did a pas de deux in "'S Wonderful," he made it a pas de dull.

To impress Jimmy, Billie claimed that she went to Harvard, which Jimmy had attended. Considering that the musical took place in the twenties, he should have brought up that Harvard didn't accept women. Indeed he did—but not until an act later, when Billie admitted she hadn't matriculated there and he finally said that he'd known that all along because of the no co-ed policy. By that time, we'd spent an hour assuming he was really stupid.

Actually, he was, among other flaws. He slept with a teddy bear—not that the character would actually use one, but director-choreographer Kathleen Marshall hoped to get an easy laugh out of making Jimmy infantile. Ditto when he saw chorus girls undress (in a living room, yet): he patty-caked his hands in glee.

But of course he was an engaged man, and his fiancée was about to enter. He urged the chorines to hide behind the couch. "How will we know when the coast is clear?" one asked. "Come out when you hear me shout the word 'love,'" he instructed.

Of all words! Why that one? Because DiPietro saw a scene in which the suspicious Eileen would show up, Jimmy would work hard to convince her that he was innocent of any infidelity, and just as she was ready to believe him, he'd say, "I love you," and the chorines would pour out to get him in deeper trouble.

Actually, Jimmy was more attracted to Billie. But how much could that mean to audiences when he'd been married three times? We lost respect for Billie for liking him, too, before he confessed that he'd inadvertently become engaged to Eileen before the divorce from wife number three was final. Billie now became genuinely livid that he'd been so irresponsible. Jimmy finally snarled, "We're too different," before launching into the Gershwin song that begins "You say *eee*-ther, and I say *eye*-ther."

No, the altercation had already gone too far for it to devolve into an issue over one's choice of pronunciation. The song "Let's Call the Whole Thing Off" was originally meant to be more playful. DiPietro should have called off this notion.

And why was Billie so incensed that Jimmy was lying to her when she'd been lying to him all along? To paraphrase a line that Billie sang in "But Not for Me," it was all bananas.

The Gershwin songs weren't just shoehorned in, but jackhammered into place. After DiPietro had firmly established Billie's independent nature, he had her sing how she needed "Someone to Watch Over Me." Granted, many self-assured people feel more vulnerable than they let on, but O'Hara's dynamic stage presence thus far had had her display a more-fierce-than-usual independence.

And here was a sign of the times: O'Hara wielded a tommy-gun while singing the song; when Gertrude Lawrence introduced it in *Oh, Kay!* in 1926, she held a doll.

Jimmy wasn't the most dim-witted character. When chorine Jeannie Muldoon asked Cookie, pretending to be a butler, the identity of the man standing nearby, he immediately said "Duke"—and then, because he thought he'd divulged too much about the criminal, he decided to add "of England." Never mind that the way Duke was dressed or that his demeanor hardly suggested regal breeding *and* that he didn't remotely sound English. Jeannie bought it because DiPietro needed to continue his increasingly ridiculous plot.

When Duke finally came clean to Jeannie, only then did she say she'd suspected as much because he didn't have an English accent. Why didn't DiPietro's characters immediately state their suspicions the way real people do?

More idiocies abounded. An offstage cop on a bullhorn was heard to say, "We have the place surrounded except for the back window"—allowing the bootleggers a back-window escape. By 2012, that line would have been more welcome in a theater-of-the-absurd play.

One could argue that DiPietro was taking us back to a sunnier and more innocent era of musical comedy by writing a valentine to shows gone by in their silly, carefree style. If that's the case, why not just revive *Oh, Kay!* with its original Bolton-Wodehouse book?

Oh, wait—David Merrick did, in the 1990–1991 season, first from November to January and then in April, when it closed in previews.

Still, how much worse could the original *Oh, Kay!* be? DiPietro should have benefitted from the nearly century's worth of improvements that previous librettists had given the art form.

DiPietro did catch the style of those twenties shows where a haughty nouveau riche fiancée Eileen Evergreen must be taken down a peg while a good honest girl—Billie—deserved to be deemed her equal.

But Billie wasn't a good honest girl. DiPietro wanted us to forgive her because prohibition was a bad and unpopular law.

There were plenty of situations meant to get easy laughs. Halfway through Eileen's bath, six previously unseen "bubble girls" leapt out of the tub. There was no reason why they were there except to surprise us at any cost. Again, this is a convention from the twenties, but the tone of the new book was more knowing, making this device come out of left field (in a ballpark thousands of miles away).

Eileen caught Jimmy with Billie, so the bootlegger quickly pretended to be a Cockney maid, whom Jimmy identified as Bobbie. When Billie later forgot and referred to herself by her real name, Jimmy was questioned: "You said her name was Bobbie, and she says it's Billie." Jimmy's explanation was "It's Billie Bobbie." Once again, no one suspected anything, because DiPietro gave no one a brain in which suspicions could grow.

Similarly, when the authorities wanted to see if the illegal booze was in the cellar, Jimmy desperately told them not to, "because—'cuz 'cuz 'cuz 'cuz." And no one could see through his stalling that he was lying.

If you're going to have bootleggers, you must have a pro-Prohibition character. She was Countess Estonia Dulworth (Judy Kaye), the founder of The Society of Dry Women, in another wan DiPietro joke. She was drawn in the Margaret Dumont clueless tradition: a high-toned woman whose dearth of street smarts was her fatal flaw. Once Cookie served her liquor and she unknowingly drank it, she quickly (and predictably) developed a taste for the stuff. Not long after, she was swinging on the chandelier. (That is not a colorful way of saying that she was dead drunk; she literally was swinging on the chandelier.)

The final indignity came when Billie was disguised as a servant, although Jimmy had already told a police chief that she was his wife. So when the lawman came in and saw Billie in her outfit, he asked him, "Hey, what's your wife doin' wearing a maid's uniform?" Jimmy, of course, wasn't able to come up with an explanation, but Billie was. "Actually, Officer," she said, "it's a little bedroom fantasy of my husband's." After Jimmy agreed, she bent him over her knee and spanked him. "Bad Jimmy!" she chided, as he gave an enthusiastic "Yes!" after every swat. To this, the chief responded, "Ah, I remember when the ex-missus used to do that to me. Good times, good times."

No. Even today, most people are reluctant to divulge their sexual kinks. And while this era was known as the Roaring Twenties, people living then were much less likely to be this frank.

Such a show always ends in marriage, which represents the ultimate happiness. Even the train on Billie's wedding gown was of an excessively and absurdly long length—as was *Nice Work If You Can Get It*.

CHAPTER TWELVE

*

Not a Loser Anymore, Like the Last Time:
The Best Musical Tony Losers That Turned Out to Be Winners

We don't much hear the term "the Fabulous Invalid" these days. But in the early part of the last century, it was an oft-used term that described the theater as an endangered species that somehow always managed to survive.

If we had to pick one musical to typify "the Fabulous Invalid," wouldn't it be *Candide* (1956–1957), which has endured despite its original seventy-three-performance flop?

The musical version of Voltaire's comic novel had music by Leonard Bernstein and lyrics by (let's see if we can get them all) Bernstein, Lillian Hellman, John Latouche, Dorothy Parker, and Richard Wilbur.

Contrary to popular belief, the reviews of the original 1956 production weren't all bad; John Chapman in the *News* called it "a great contribution to the richness of the American musical comedy stage." Walter Kerr, however, termed it "a really spectacular disaster" in the *Herald Tribune.* Many who saw it claimed it moved about as fast as the line for the ladies' room at an opera house.

Candide did, however, get a 1956–1957 Best Musical Tony nomination. It was the shortest-running show in this category until 1974–1975 when *The Lieutenant* undercut it. But this was still the era when people sauntered into record stores and were interested in finding out what was happening—or had happened—on Broadway. The original cast album of *Candide* was one that made listeners say, "This show has to be terrific."

But as Sondheim has often said, it's not that Lillian Hellman's book was bad; it just wasn't right for Bernstein's soufflé-light score. With such lines as "White slaves are impractical; they show dirt," the Hellman

266

estate's decision to never let her script be revived is all for the best in this best of all possible worlds.

Considering the amount of absurdity Hellman put in her book, she seemed to have been influenced by Eugene Ionesco. After an utterly lost Candide asked a vendor, "Where am I?" he was told, "I don't know where you are. I am in Lisbon." Soon an Arab was informing Candide that an infant fortuneteller [sic] "don't like you. She says you are a force for good." Pangloss, Candide's rosy-glassed teacher, later said, "A few hours after my death, I awoke unharmed." The Old Lady thought nothing of barging into the bedroom of Cunegonde, Candide's intended, and stating, "She's not getting undressed; she's getting dressed." Cunegonde's brother Maximillian said that the Governor was "writing a book on the ugliness of C-flat. Last week he was writing a book on the beauty of C-flat." That Governor also observed while drinking, "It's a modest wine because it has nothing to be immodest about."

He wasn't the only one in power to have skewered views. A Duchess, catching a glance at the Prefect of Police, was surprised he was alive. "Last week he lost his fortune and vowed to kill himself. I went to the funeral." The Duke of Naples dealt with death, too. "My mother died at dinner. Or if she didn't, she will die at breakfast."

What's more, seeing Candide in denial over and over again not only made the show repetitive, but also made him seem simple-minded. A satire on being optimistic didn't need a second act to show more and more calamities befalling its heroes and villains. There was a reason Voltaire told his story in about a hundred pages and exited. *Candide* could have been shorter—but then we wouldn't have had all that music, would we?

No wonder that escape-seeking Broadway audiences of the fifties rejected this theater-of-the-absurd musical. The following season, as we've seen, *The Music Man* beat *West Side Story*. Who would have thought that the first person to lose two successive Best Musical Tony races would be Leonard Bernstein?

Sondheim, who was originally asked to work on *Candide*, finally did, but not until the now-famous 1973–1974 revival. His work, Hugh Wheeler's new book, and Harold Prince's environmental staging rescued the show. The new production ran 10 times longer than the original, and became a staple of musical theater all over the world. Wasn't that fitting for a story about a lad who is told to be optimistic at all costs?

So who knows how many other Best Musical Tony losers will someday get new eyes to look at flaws and know how to fix them? There's the famous story about *A Funny Thing Happened on the Way to the Forum*: it was dying in Washington until Jerome Robbins told Stephen Sondheim he needed an opening number that would tell the audience that it was about to see a "Comedy Tonight." That one number changed the show from a flop to a Best Musical Tony-winning hit.

How many others were only one song away from success?

Maybe one of these days, one of those musicals will get that one song—or scene or performance or directorial vision—that *Candide* got.

Or maybe a show will wildly succeed with no appreciable work done to it at all.

Until the 1975–1976 Tonys, five musicals had tied for the worst record in the Tony races. *Gypsy*, *High Spirits*, *Funny Girl*, *Half a Sixpence*, and *Mack & Mabel* had all been nominated for eight awards and had taken home none.

Now a musical would be shut out despite eleven nominations: *Chicago*, based on Maurine Dallas Watkins's play of the same name.

Watkins had reported on two sensational 1924 trials in which a married woman was accused of killing her lover. On March 11, 1924, Mrs. Belva Gaertner was accused of murdering her lover Walter Law while both were in a car. Only eighty-seven days later, on June 6, she was found not guilty.

If justice seemed swift in that case, it was even speedier for Mrs. Beulah Annan. She was accused of shooting and killing her lover Harry Kalstedt on April 3. Only fifty-two days later, she was acquitted.

Watkins turned Annan into Roxie Hart and morphed Gaertner into Velma, not even bothering to give her a last name.

In the fifties, Bob Fosse was interested in doing a musical version that would star (who else?) Gwen Verdon. The rights took years to secure, but once Fosse had them, he signed John Kander and Fred Ebb to write the score; with the latter, Fosse would also collaborate on the book. Verdon would play Roxie, Chita Rivera the newly surnamed Velma Kelly, and Jerry Orbach Billy Flynn, the lawyer who would wangle an acquittal for both women.

It was to open in 1974–1975, but Fosse's heart attack kept that from happening. (One wonders if Fosse, en route to the hospital, recalled a line from his biggest film success: "Well, that's what comes of too much pills and liquor.")

That *Chicago* didn't open until the 1975–1976 season certainly cost it plenty of Tonys, including Best Musical; it would have easily beaten *The Wiz*. A few wins might have helped it run more than 936 performances, too.

Not that 936 performances wasn't an achievement. But shows were running longer now. Twenty years earlier, 936 would have made *Chicago* the eleventh-longest-running musical. Ten years earlier would have had it in nineteenth place. In 1977, when *Chicago* closed, 936 performances suddenly meant that thirty-one musicals had run longer.

Some complained that the show was cold: four shootings, one hanging, and five staunchly unapologetic murderesses. Billy Flynn openly called manly Mama Morton "Butch." Velma said, "Can you imagine Roxie Hart a mother? That's like making Leopold and Loeb Scout Masters." (Once again, here was proof that comedy is tragedy plus time.)

Others hated that there was no one to root for. Roxie gave herself away in act one, scene one, for after she shot her lover, the first thing that went through her head was "I gotta pee." After Amos, the husband she'd cuckolded, told police that she was indeed the murderer, she meant it when she accused him: "You are a disloyal husband."

Velma wasn't a honeybunch, either. As she told Roxie upon meeting her, "Look, I don't give no advice. I don't get any and I don't give any. You're a perfect stranger to me and let's keep it that way."

Billy Flynn (who coincidentally had the same initials as his director-choreographer) was an utterly corrupt lawyer, simply out for the money. "I didn't ask you was she guilty or innocent," he said to Amos. "I didn't ask was she a drunk or a dope fiend. No foolish questions like that. No. All I said was 'Have you got five thousand dollars?'"

Fosse ameliorated the harshness by making *Chicago* a concept musical with vaudeville as its motif. He put Roxie atop a piano à la Helen Morgan for "Funny Honey" and gave her an Eddie Cantor dance for "Me and My Baby." Amos channeled Bert Williams's "Nobody" in "Mister Cellophane." Mama Morton was Sophie Tuckerish in "When You're Good to Mama." And Mary Sunshine, the "sob sister" newspaper reporter, was as much a female impersonator as Julian Eltinge ever was.

The expression "do a tap dance" had over the years come to mean a situation in which one person tries to con another; Fosse replicated one while Roxie was trying to get Amos's help. Perhaps most brilliantly, at a press conference, Billy provided all of Roxie's words through a ventriloquist's act.

The era had long passed in which a musical could hire twelve people to fill a jury box. Some directors might have ordered cut-out figures to represent the jurors, but Fosse had more imagination. He gave one actor a chair and a good deal of facial putty, and had him create different faces, gestures, and postures to become different members of the jury.

So *Chicago*'s record-setting zero-for-eleven Tony loss was not commensurate with its achievements. It suffered, too, from being the first musical of the seventies to raise its prices. For seven years, musicals had held steady at a fifteen-dollar top—until *Chicago* demanded seventeen fifty. When a show wants nearly 17 percent more, it had better be great and not just good.

In fact, it *was* great. Funny that a show that stressed how fleeting celebrity is—and that the public is ready to lose interest in someone at any given moment—should find its celebrity lost to the upstart *A Chorus Line*.

Chicago has since been redeemed, of course. When its revival opened on November 14, 1996, much was made of its timing. Only thirteen months earlier, the nation had endured a similar circus trial in which a person many had presumed guilty of murder got off as scot-free as Roxie Hart: People of the State of California versus Orenthal James Simpson. The public, it was said, had grown far more cynical in the twenty-one years since *Chicago*'s debut.

But *Chicago*'s original production opened only ten months after a much more dramatic national event. True, its media circus didn't result in a trial—but one would have certainly happened had President Richard M. Nixon not resigned on August 9, 1974. So no one can say that after the Watergate scandal the nation's cynicism wasn't in high gear.

The original *Chicago* couldn't live up to its hype or its competition. But the 1996–1997 revival didn't endure much of a contest from its fellow revivals—*Annie*, *Candide*, and *Once upon a Mattress*, which had all flopped. *Chicago* also opened before any new musical could debut in 1996–1997, and when they did arrive—*Juan Darien*, *Play On! Dream*, *Titanic*, *Steel Pier*, *The Life*, and *Jekyll & Hyde*—each had more critics than admirers.

The 1996–1997 Tonys had to be a bittersweet night for Kander and

Ebb, for they were the songwriting team for *Steel Pier*, which had eleven Tony nominations.

And no awards. In fact, in four categories, *Chicago* had bested *Steel Pier*.

But who knows? On Sunday, April 18, 1976, *A Chorus Line* won in every category in which it was nominated except for costumes (and considering that Theoni V. Aldredge only had to put actors in street clothes, her nomination was probably due to coattails—no pun intended, at least not initially). The staff of *Chicago* probably left the Tony ball quite early, if any of them attended at all.

Too bad that Fosse didn't live to see (and oversee, for that matter) the production that won the 1996–1997 Best Musical Revival Tony. What a shame that neither lead producer Robert Fryer nor star Gwen Verdon lived long enough to witness the film version win the 2002 Best Picture Oscar. (No other property has ever won both of these awards.)

Fred Ebb was gone, too, by 2009 when *Chicago* became the longest-running revival in Broadway history. None of them would ever know—or would have ever dared dream—that the day would come when *Chicago* would surpass *A Chorus Line*'s original stint. But in 2011, it did.

So perhaps there's hope for other Best Musical Tony losers. Many of them may well see the day when they get similar validation—not to mention revenge.

BIBLIOGRAPHY

*

Abbott, George. *Mister Abbott*. Random House, 1963.

Adamson, Joe. *Groucho, Chico, Harpo and Sometimes Zeppo*. Simon & Schuster, 1973.

Barer, Marshall. "300,000 Mattresses." *Dramatics*, October 1984.

Bell, Marty. *Broadway Stories*. Limelight, 1993.

Bloom, Ken. *American Song*. Schirmer, 2001.

Bogar, Thomas A. *American Presidents Attend the Theatre*. McFarland, 2006.

Burrows, Abe. *Honest, Abe*. Little, Brown & Company, 1980.

Carroll, Diahann and Bob Morris. *The Legs Are the Last to Go*. Harper-Collins, 2008.

Chapin, Theodore S. *Everything Was Possible*. Knopf, 2003.

Ebb, Fred, John Kander, and Greg Lawrence. *Colored Lights*. Faber & Faber, 2003.

Ewen, David. *Complete Book of the American Musical Theatre*. Henry Holt and Company, 1959.

Flinn, Denny Martin. *Sugar: The Last Musical*. Unpublished.

"Ford to City: Drop Dead." New York *Daily News*, October 31, 1975.

Fordin, Hugh. *Getting to Know Him*. Random House, 1977.

Fredrik, Nathalie and Ariel Douglas. *History of the Academy Award Winners*. Ace, 1974.

Gilvey, John Anthony. *Before the Parade Passes By*. St. Martin's Press, 2005.

Goldman, James and Stephen Sondheim. *Follies*. Random House, 1971.

Goldman, William. *The Season*. Harcourt Brace, 1969.

Green, Stanley. *The World of Musical Comedy*. Grosset & Dunlap, 1960.

Guernsey, Otis. *Best Plays of 1966–1967.* Dodd, Mead, 1967.

Hamill, Peter. "Goodbye Brooklyn, Hello Fame." *Saturday Evening Post*, July 27, 1963.

Harris, Andrew B. *The Performing Set.* University of North Texas, 2006.

Kasdin, Karin. *Oh Boy Oh Boy Oh Boy!* Sibyl Publications, 1997.

Kirkwood, James. *Diary of a Mad Playwright.* E. P. Dutton, 1989.

Kissel, Howard. *The Abominable Showman.* Applause, 1993.

Lehman, Ernest. *Sweet Smell of Success.* Signet, 1957.

Lennart, Isobel and Bob Merrill. *Funny Girl.* Random House, 1964.

Leonard, William Torbert. *Broadway Bound.* Scarecrow, 1983.

Maas, Jon. *42nd Street* souvenir booklet. 1980.

Mandelbaum, Ken. *"A Chorus Line" and the Musicals of Michael Bennett.* St. Martin's Press, 1989.

Mandelbaum, Ken. *Not Since "Carrie."* St. Martin's Press, 1991.

McKechnie, Donna. *Time Steps.* Simon & Schuster, 2006.

McNally, Terrence. *The Full Monty.* Applause, 2002.

Miletich, Leo N. *Broadway's Prize-Winning Musicals.* Haworth, 1993.

Miller, Scott. *Let the Sunshine In.* Heinemann, 2003.

Mordden, Ethan. *Coming Up Roses.* Oxford University Press, 1998.

———. *The Happiest Corpse I've Ever Seen.* Palgrave Macmillan, 2004.

———. *One More Kiss.* Palgrave Macmillan, 2003.

———. *Open a New Window.* Palgrave, 2001.

Morrow, Lee Alan. *The Tony Award Book.* Abbeville Press, 1988.

Napoleon, Davi. *Chelsea on the Edge.* Iowa State University Press, 1991.

Norton, Elliott. *Broadway Down East.* Boston Public Library Books, 1977.

"On the Rue Streisand." *Time*, April 3, 1964.

Ostrow, Stuart. *Present at the Creation, Leaping in the Dark, and Going against the Grain.* Applause, 2005.

Prince, Harold. *Contradictions.* Dodd, Mead, 1974.

"Producer David Merrick Rules Broadway." *Life*, December 13, 1968.

Reynolds, Regina Benedict. *Paper Mill Playhouse: The Life of a Theatre.* David M. Baldwin, 1999.

Rich, Frank. *Hot Seat.* Random House, 1998.

Rose, Philip. *You Can't Do That on Broadway.* Limelight, 2004.

Russell, Bill. *Side Show.* Samuel French, 1994.

Seff, Richard. *Supporting Player.* Xlibris, 2007.

Shillinglaw, Susan. *A Journey into Steinbeck's California*. Roaring Forties Press, 2006.

Stevens, Gary and George, Alan. *The Longest Line*. Applause, 2000.

Suskin, Steven. *More Opening Nights on Broadway*. Schirmer, 1997.

———. *Opening Nights on Broadway*. Schirmer, 1990.

———. *Second Act Trouble*. Applause, 2006.

———. *The Sound of Broadway Music*. Oxford University Press, 2009.

Swayne, Steve. *How Sondheim Found His Sound*. University of Michigan, 2005.

Taylor, Theodore. *Jule: The Story of Composer Jule Styne*. Random House, 1979.

Turan, Kenneth and Joseph Papp. *Free for All*. Doubleday, 2009.

Uhry, Alfred and Jason Robert Brown. *Parade. Show Music*, Summer 2000.

Viagas, Robert. *The Alchemy of Theatre*. Playbill/Applause, 2006.

Whitburn, Joel. *The Billboard Book of Top 40 Albums*. Billboard Publications, 1987.

Willson, Meredith. *But He Doesn't Know the Territory*. Putnam, 1959.

Zadan, Craig. *Sondheim & Co*. Macmillan, 1974.

Author interviews with Luther Davis; Keith Edwards; Helen Gallagher; Larry Grossman; Sheldon Harnick; Robert Kamlot; John Kander; Judy Kaye; Robert Klein; Bill Liberman; Hugh Martin; Walter Newkirk; Lonny Price; Stephen Sondheim; Peter Stone; and Margaret Styne.

INDEX

*

Italicized titles are to musicals, unless otherwise designated. Boldface page numbers indicate extended discussion of a musical.